The Impact of State Restructuring on Indonesia's Regional Economic Convergence

The **ISEAS – Yusof Ishak Institute** (formerly Institute of Southeast Asian Studies) was established as an autonomous organization in 1968. It is a regional centre dedicated to the study of socio-political, security and economic trends and developments in Southeast Asia and its wider geostrategic and economic environment. The Institute's research programmes are the Regional Economic Studies (RES, including ASEAN and APEC), Regional Strategic and Political Studies (RSPS), and Regional Social and Cultural Studies (RSCS).

ISEAS Publishing, an established academic press, has issued more than 2,000 books and journals. It is the largest scholarly publisher of research about Southeast Asia from within the region. ISEAS Publishing works with many other academic and trade publishers and distributors to disseminate important research and analyses from and about Southeast Asia to the rest of the world.

The Impact of State Restructuring on Indonesia's Regional Economic Convergence

ADIWAN FAHLAN ARITENANG

ISEAS YUSOF ISHAK INSTITUTE

First published in Singapore in 2016 by
ISEAS Publishing
30 Heng Mui Keng Terrace
Singapore 119614

E-mail: publish@iseas.edu.sg
Website: <http://bookshop.iseas.edu.sg>

ISEAS Library Cataloguing-in-Publication Data

Aritenang, Adiwan Fahlan.
The Impact of State Restructuring on Indonesia's Regional Economic Convergence.
1. Structural adjustment (Economic policy)—Indonesia.
2. Economic policy—Indonesia.
3. Decentralization in government—Indonesia.
4. Indonesia—Economic conditions—Regional disparities.
5. Southeast Asia—Economic integration.
6. Indonesia—Economic conditions—1966–1997.
7. Indonesia—Economic conditions—1997–
I. Title.
HC447 A71   2016

ISBN 978-981-4620-37-6 (soft cover)
ISBN 978-981-4620-38-3 (e-book, PDF)

Typeset by Superskill Graphics Pte Ltd
Printed in Singapore by Markono Print Media Pte Ltd

*For Dad and Mom, this book is impossible
without your love, intellectual support and endless prayers.*

CONTENTS

LIST OF TABLES

LIST OF FIGURES

PREFACE

The idea for this research began one morning in 2007 when I was reading an offer for a PhD scholarship in a local newspaper. I immediately informed my father, Dr Wendy Aritenang, the then General Secretary of the Indonesian Transportation Ministry. After an extensive discussion, later that night he encouraged me to study the impact of both decentralization and ASEAN FTA on Indonesian regions as a topic for my PhD research. Despite his civil engineering background, he has a wide and in-depth expertise on decentralization and free trade agreements as a result of more than thirty years of experience in the government. Consequently, the PhD thesis and this book benefit much from short and distance discussions with him in London, Jakarta, Batam, Bandung and Singapore. The thesis and this book are definitely an intellectual production of a father and a son.

This book derives from my PhD thesis at the University College London, United Kingdom. In writing the thesis, I would like to express my sincere and deep gratitude to my supervisor Dr Jung Won Sonn. I appreciate all his knowledgeable contribution, support and critiques at every stage of the writing. His guidance extensively helped me in understanding my thesis and integrate each part to form the thesis. I also owe my gratitude to my thesis co-supervisor Professor Nick Phelps whose ideas and knowledge helped deepen my research. I am fortunate to have Professor Andres Rodriguez-Pose of the London School of Economics and Political Science (LSE) as my thesis external examiner. As a leading scholar in the research topic, his expertise and advice greatly helped with the intellectual amendments. I would also like to express my gratitude to Dr Nikos Karadimitriou as the internal examiner who gave invaluable suggestions for the improvement of the thesis.

I would like to thank the Ministry of Communication and Informatics, Republic of Indonesia for their support in the form of a scholarship for funding this research. Additionally I would also like to thank the Agency for Assessment and Application of Technology (BPPT) that has supported me to pursue this doctorate degree. The intellectual development of the PhD thesis is also a result of formal and informal discussions with friends at UCL Bartlett School of Planning, UCL Enterprise Society 2009, Indonesian Student Society in the United Kingdom and colleagues at the Indonesian Embassy.

Some staff members of the ISEAS – Yusof Ishak Institute contributed towards the completion of this book. It is an honour to have the valuable opportunity to be a Visiting Research Fellow under the postdoctoral fellowship scheme in the institute. The institute provided a fresh and new intellectual environment for me in the area of Southeast Asian Studies. Since the first day of my arrival at the institute, the people have been nothing but welcoming me and ensuring that I settled smoothly. My gratitude goes to ISEAS Director Mr Tan Chin Tiong, Deputy Director Dr Ooi Kee Beng, and Head of Indonesia Study Group Dr Hui Yew-Foong. My sincere thanks to my Indonesia Study Group colleagues for the friendship and mentorship: Dr Aris Ananta, Dr Evi Nurvidya Arifin, Dr Alpha Amirrachman, Dr Ulla Fionna, Dr Alexander Arifianto and Dr Maxensius Sambodo. I would like to express my gratitude to the cooperation and support from the administration office and ISEAS Publishing colleagues: Mrs Y.L. Lee, Mr Ng Kok Kiong, Ms Rahilah Yusuf, Ms Karthi Nair and Ms P.P. Susha. My special thanks to Ms Foo Shu Tieng and Ms Kathleen Azali for proofreading and revising the book manuscript. I am also very grateful for the sincere friendship from other members of ISEAS – Yusof Ishak Institute: Mr Rodolfo C. Severino, Dr Francis Hutchinson, Ms Sanchita Basu Das, Ms Reema Bhaghwan Jagtiani, Dr Rizwana Abdul Azeez.

Additionally, I would like to thank my Indonesian colleagues who have contributed to my intellectual journey across Indonesia, the United Kingdom and Singapore: Mr Fiki Satari and Dr Tita Larasati of BCCF; Dr Tatang A. Taufik of BPPT; Professor M. Rizza Sihbudi of LIPI; Professor Tommy Firman and Dr Delik Hudalah of ITB; Professor Yanuar Nugroho, Dr Saharman Gea, Dr Suyanto Mahdiputra, Mr Vishnu Juwono, and Mrs Dessy Irawati in U.K.; and Mr Adhi Priamarizki, Ms Fitri Bintang Timur and Professor Sulfikar Amir of Nanyang Technological University.

This PhD thesis itself would not have been completed without financial and spiritual supports from my family — Dad, Mom, Dina and Andi. I am very grateful for their prayers, love, and support from Indonesia.

For my mother, Dra. Tjut Wanda Lisa, who had countless times visited us in London and Singapore, it is always refreshing and a blessing for your one to two weeks visits. I am also thankful for my family in Riau, Papa, Mama and Rio, for their prayers and support. I would also like to thank Om Mul's family for their support over the years. My special thanks to my wife, Ayu, who has been very supportive and patient in the four years of my PhD study in London; our daughter, Farah, whose birth became a spirit booster to complete the PhD thesis; and our son, Faris, who was born during my fellowship in ISEAS – Yusof Ishak Institute, as the sunshine in our life who has given new meaning on life and family.

Adiwan Fahlan Aritenang
Jakarta, January 2016

ABBREVIATIONS

AFTA	ASEAN Free Trade Agreement
ASEAN	Association of Southeast Asian Nations
BAKOSURTANAL	Badan Koordinator Survei and Pemetaan National (Coordinating Agency for National Survey and Mapping)
BAPPENAS	Badan Perencanaan Pembangunan Nasional (Agency for National Development Planning)
BATAN	Badan Tenaga Nuklir Nasional (Agency for National Nuclear Energy)
BCCF	Bandung Creative City Forum
BIDA/BIFZA	Batam Industrial Development Authority/Batam Indonesia Free Zone Authority
BII	Batam Intelligent Island
BP	Badan Pengusahaan Batam (Batam Free Trade Zone Agency)
BPPT	Badan Pengkajian and Penerapan Teknologi (Agency for the Assessment and Application of Technology)
BPS	Badan Pusat Statistik (Central Bureau of Statistics)
CBO	community based-organization
CEPT	Common Effective Preferential Tariff
DAK	Dana Alokasi Khusus (Special Allocation Fund)
DAU	Dana Alokasi Umum (General Allocation Fund)
DBH	Dana Bagi Hasil (Profit Sharing Fund)
DPR	Dewan Perwakilan Rakyat (Indonesian Parliament)
DPRD	Dewan Perwakilan Rakyat Daerah (Indonesian Regional Parliament)

DRD	Dewan Riset Daerah (Regional Research Council)
DRN	Dewan Riset National (National Research Council)
FDI	foreign direct investment
FTZ	free trade zone
GDP	gross domestic product
GRDP	gross regional domestic product
IPTN	Industri Pesawat Terbang Nasional (Nusantara Aircraft Industry)
ITB	Institut Teknologi Bandung (Bandung Institute of Technology)
KADIN	Kamar Dagang dan Industri Indonesia (Indonesia Chamber of Commerce)
KAPET	Kawasan Pembangunan Ekonomi Terpadu
KPPOD	Komite Pemantauan Pelaksanaan Otonomi Daerah (Committee Monitoring the Implementation of Regional Autonomy)
LAPAN	Lembaga Penerbangan dan Antariksa Nasional (Institute of National Aeronautics and Space)
LIPI	Lembaga Ilmu Pengetahuan Indonesia (Indonesian Institute of Sciences)
MERCOSUR	Mercado Común del Sur (Southern Common Market)
MNCs	multi-national corporations
MoF	Ministry of Finance
MoHA	Ministry of Home Affairs
MoT	Ministry of Trade
MPKT	Musyawarah Perencanaan Kegiatan Tahunan (Annual Activities Planning Forum)
MPR	Majelis Permusyawaratan Rakyat (People's Consultative Assembly)
MTI	Masyarakat Transportasi Indonesia (Indonesian Transportion Society)
NAFTA	North American Free Trade Agreement
NEG	new economic geography
NIE	newly industrialized economies
NIS	new industrial spaces
NTB	non-tariff barriers
NGO	non-government organization

OSS	One Stop Service
PINDAD	Perusahaan Industri Angkatan Darat (Army Industry Company)
PNPM	Program Nasional Pemberdayaan Masyarakat Mandiri (National Community Development Programme)
RIA	regional integration agreements
RCTI	Rajawali Citra Televisi (Rajawali Citra Television)
SDO	Subsidi Daerah Otonom (Autonomous Region Subsidy)
TIM	territorial innovation model
TPI	Televisi Pendidikan Indonesia (Indonesia Education Television)
TVRI	Televisi Republik Indonesia (Republic of Indonesia Television)

1

INTRODUCTION

This book is an attempt to decipher regional district economic disparities during the state-restructuring events that occurred after the entry into the ASEAN Free Trade Agreement (AFTA) in 1992 and the governmental decentralization policy in 1999. Following the financial crisis in 1997, Indonesia's political arrangement shifted from a centralized regime to a decentralized government system. The new system delegates political, administrative, and fiscal autonomies to provincial and districts level. The decentralization process increased the Indonesian administrative size from 26 provinces with 292 districts in 1997 to 33 provinces with more than 491 districts in 2012.[1]

This book examines the determining factors for Indonesia's development from a centralized government regime to the state-restructuring period. This book has adopted an empirical approach by using growth theory and the historical institutionalism approach in order to examine the impact of state restructuring. However, the impact would be determined by institutional capacities and the governance level of local governments to exploit opportunities from state restructuring processes as it would affect the rate of growth and economic development.

State restructuring refers to the creation of more logical organization where the state operates more efficient and effective (Young 2002). In this sense, the book defines state restructuring as a politico-economy shift of state organization and operation through two events (AFTA and decentralization) that accelerates state management and service delivery through the participation of stakeholders, management of production factors, and state administration to achieve development goals. This study worked with the hypothesis that decentralization and AFTA would provide local district authorities ample opportunities in which to accelerate economic growth through authority over resource allocation and mobility. Furthermore, state restructuring provided opportunities in which to accelerate economic growth through the promotion of property rights and lower transaction cost. The book investigates how the state restructuring policy would affect regional economic convergence and what are the economic growth determinants. The main argument for this book is that state restructuring institutional changes would be able to explain regional economic divergence through path dependence and inherited past institutions within individual regions.

The nature of the research question has meant that the study required the use of a variety of quantitative and qualitative analytical methods. The deductive research questions which are utilized in this study were formulated through a critical review of relevant literature and current conditions in Indonesia. This study examines Indonesian regional district development by using the municipality and regency (*kota* and *kabupaten*, respectively) as the spatial unit of analysis. The dynamics of regional development in Indonesia should be understood and viewed through statistical analysis before one can begin to discuss the variations in state restructuring effects.

The use of both quantitative and qualitative analytical methods enabled a much more comprehensive analysis and enhanced the validity of the research as one method served as a test on the other's accuracy and veracity (Read and Marsh 2002). The quantitative method, which utilizes an econometric analysis of local endowment, explored the determinants of economic growth. This exploration was crucial in understanding the local economic structure and institutional arrangements as the basis of the qualitative study. The qualitative method featured the use of in-depth interviews in order to clarify the role of local endowments and institutional arrangements in terms of economic growth.

RESEARCH BACKGROUND

Since the 1990s, following the decline of oil and gas production, there is a shift of deregulation in the manufacturing sector. At the same time, the emergence of manufacturing sector in the ASEAN region accelerates the ASEAN FTA between the association's member countries. This marks the shift of Indonesia economy towards a non-oil industrialization that lasted until 1997. The Asian Financial Crisis (AFC) that striked Indonesia resulted in the fall of the New Order regime and provided the path of decentralization on politics, economy, and administration. Both events shifted the state management, strengthened regional governments and improved public participation in national development process. At the same time, Indonesia became more involved with the global economy through trade integration and cooperation.

Thus, it is important to conduct economic and political analysis at the district level as it is crucial to our understanding of the impact of trade liberalization and decentralization on economic growth disparities. The implementation of AFTA and decentralization led to a shift in the decision-making process from government-centric to multi-stakeholder governance (Jessop 2002) and also economic growth only in certain regions, which Brenner (1999) called "the spatial selectivity of special regions". Regional disparities are more pronounced in developing countries due to higher political and social issues discontent in these lagging countries (Rodríguez-Pose and Gill 2006).

This is illustrated with persistent economic growth divergence among districts in Indonesia. Despite a decade of decentralization in which the Indonesian central government transferred significant political and administrative authority to the district level, government services and public reform have barely improved (von Luebke 2009). Instead, von Luebke's study demonstrated that there was a continuity of non-transparent and elite-centric agreements on public employment, government contracts, and party list positions despite decentralization efforts.

One reason for this lack of development was the persistent socio-political challenges. In the local jurisdiction, for instance, there has been a significant increase in the number of provinces and districts due to the decentralization process. Supporters of this regional administrative division argue that as the geographical area is too large with poor infrastructure, decentralization as it is has failed to provide access to health and education services for people in remote areas (Fitrani, Hofman and Kaiser 2005). Other reasons for further regional administrative division were made on the basis of religion, ethnicity, and bureaucratic and political rent seeking (Booth 2011; Fitrani, Hofman and Kaiser 2005).

Another issue is how direct elections have been criticized as monopolized by local elites. At the early stages of the government decentralization process, there were a number of former civil servants who successfully won elections at the district levels. Since the decentralization process started in 2001, 70 per cent of the new regional heads were bureaucrats and the general public by 16 per cent. Meanwhile, only 10 per cent of the regional heads secured a second term and only 12 per cent of the regional heads were from the Armed Forces (Malley 2003). These leaders were seen as part of the New Order regime which continued to exploit resources for self-enrichment or wealth accumulation to boost status rather than regional development.

On the other hand, AFTA is expected to accelerate Indonesia's industry and trade competitiveness. However, the literature predicts that trade liberalization would increase imports in lagging countries and thus ineffective industries will struggle to compete with cheaper and higher quality imported products. Furthermore, Rodríguez-Pose and Gill (2006) argued that trade liberalization increased the development gap for regions that were lagging in manufacturing industries as these industries tended to be located near industrial complexes and urban areas.

At the local level, the effect of this trade liberalization becomes more significant when the size of regions is considered. In Indonesia, with more than 400 districts and each with different local economic structure, the effect of trade liberalization will be widely varied (Feridhanusetyawan and Pangestu 2003). Logically, districts with a large economic base and higher trade rates will gain wider market access from trade liberalization, while poorer regions with less efficient products will struggle to penetrate the market and compete with other regions. Thus, poorer regions potentially become market destination for import products. This is similar to Ramasamy's argument (1994) that in the early stages of AFTA, the agreement might increase inter-ASEAN imports to 60 per cent.

REGIONAL DEVELOPMENT: THE THEORETICAL DEBATE

This section frames the theoretical debate in which the empirical studies are presented in this book. To examine the equalization of regional development, we approximate using regional convergence. Regional convergence refers to the declining gap of regional economic growth due

FIGURE 1.1
Map of Indonesia

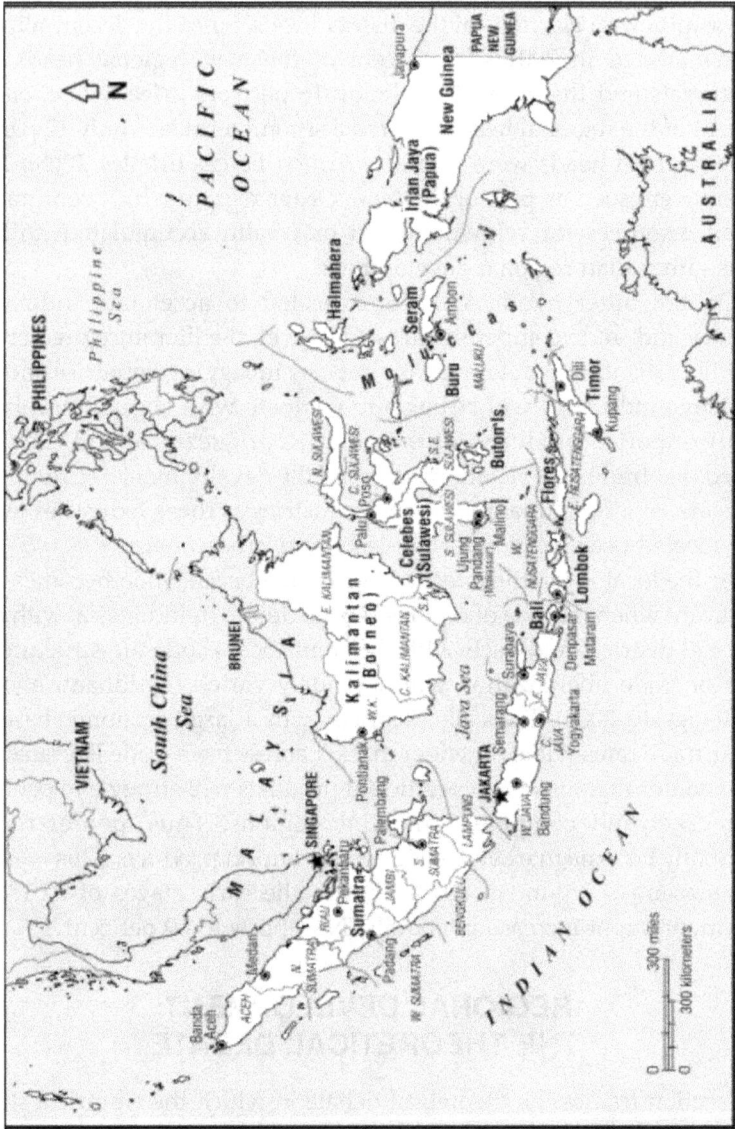

Source: Bertrand (2004). Reproduced with kind permission of Cambridge University Press.

to advance regions having lower growth rate compared with lagging regions. Thus, in the long run, there is a converging economic growth between these regions. The discourse in economic convergence is rooted in neoclassical economic perspectives where development is encouraged by open market and free trade, thus allowing the factors of production, such as labour and capital, to mobilize in locations where they are most efficient (Williamson 1965). More recently, the convergence analysis has dominated econometrics modelling approach as it acknowledges the features of neoclassical analysis (labour–capital), whilst adopting the new growth theory by allowing the possibility of increasing returns as a result of technology (Barro 1991, 2000).

On the other hand, persistent uneven development in Indonesia suggests the failure of neoclassical economy to explain this economic disparity leads us to revisit the literature on economic divergence perspective such as location theories (von Thünen 1966; Weber 1929; Hoover 1948; Losch 1954), the cumulative causation, and growth centre theories (Myrdal 1957; Hirschman 1958; Perroux 1950). Since the 1990s, divergence theories expanded rapidly by elements of trade, cultural, knowledge spillovers and local innovations including the New Trade Theory and New Economic Geography by Krugman (2003), dynamic models by Quah (1993, 1996), and Institutional Economic Geography (Scott and Storper 1987; Cooke and Morgan 1998). While the notion of innovation models emerged from the industrial clustering and agglomeration phenomenon that emphasizes on the institutional arrangements and actor networks including Collective Learning (Capello 1999), New Industrial Spaces (NIS) (Storper and Scott 1988), Industrial Districts (Lagendijk 2006), and Flexible Production System (Piore and Sabel 1986). These literature later led to the emergence of studies on how to create innovative cities via learning regions (Pike, Rodríguez-Pose and Tomaney 2006) and creative cities, based on the works of Scott (2011), Pratt (2009) and Peck (2005).

Recently, there is a growing study on the importance of local socio-culture institutions to support local economic growth, particularly through the studies on community (Rodríguez-Pose and Storper 2006), property development and housing (Doak and Karadimitriou 2007) and technological innovation (Taylor 2009). Turning to comparative politic literature, the historical institutionalism approach emphasizes the importance of past knowledge and culturally bounded institutional shifts on local responses and adjustments (Thelen 1999, 2004). Institutional analysis highlights how previous institutions determined the local level governance and the creation of a new development path. This study also examines the networks of relationships among the local government, NGOs, and academics to illustrate how such factors influenced the shift in economic mode. By acknowledging path dependence and historical differences, this study sought to argue that local policies are bound by antecedent institutions and past knowledge. This approach enabled the elucidation of the economic policies and growth divergence amongst districts.

As these studies abandon the assumption of diminishing returns in neoclassical economic literature, the studies provide evidence that regions are uneven and that the determinants of economic growth range from land, interregional economy, and other institutional factors.

RESEARCH LOCATION: INDONESIA, BATAM AND BANDUNG

Indonesia was chosen as a case study in the current research because of its rich district-level statistical datasets. Available data include socio-economic statistics covering gross regional domestic product (GRDP), population, levels of education, road accessibility, and fiscal data. Furthermore, detailed data on plant-level manufacturing and complete AFTA tariff data for the periods under observation were available from the Central Bureau of Statistics (Badan Pusat Statistik). The development of the manufacturing industry in Indonesian regions varied widely depending on the type of industry.

The dynamics of the Indonesian economy was useful to study the effect of state restructuring prompted by trade liberalization and decentralization on regional development. In order to establish the argument for this book, statistical analysis was first employed to provide evidence of divergence in regional development. Thereafter, this study examines the extent of the effect of trade liberalization and decentralization on regional divergence across the periods under observation. Finally, the study explores the role of institutions, along with state restructuring, in determining the pathways for regional development. In the latter, particular focus is directed towards embedded institutional capacities that influenced the effect of state restructuring on local regional development. The current study explains the effect of state restructuring induced by trade liberalization and decentralization based on the variations in the development of regional districts.

The variation of economic dynamic should be viewed as a continual and evolving process that progresses along development paths. However, this process might be intervened by the presence of politico-economic events such as AFTA and decentralization as a disturbance. Thus, these events serve as an opportunity for a new development path.

In order to explore the impact of the institutional arrangements on regional development during the state restructuring period, specific regions were used as case studies. As Indonesia is a culturally and economically diverse country, two districts — the cities of Batam and Bandung — were selected as case studies as both cities have large and significant manufacturing industries that were established prior to the decentralization process. (See Figure 1.2 for their location within Indonesia.) Batam received official support from the central government in 1978 following the creation of a manufacturing bonded zone by the central government (Keppres No. 41/1978; Phelps 2004). Meanwhile, the Bandung manufacturing industries were accelerated by the Paket Oktober (Pakto) 1992, a policy from the central government which provided funding and land for manufacturing activities in the city (Fromhold-Eisebith and Eisebith 2002). Both policies were successful in initiating manufacturing development and economic growth in respective cities.

Furthermore, both cities are adjacent to major metropolitan centres for market and infrastructure access. Batam was seen to be geographically close to Singapore and was expected to receive a portion of Singapore's manufacturing plants following the Singaporean government's decision to have a more service-oriented economy in order to position itself as Southeast Asia's financial hub (Kumar and Siddique 2013). On the other hand, Bandung is located just over 2-hour drive (122 km away) from Jakarta and it is also the capital of West Java Province. In addition, the city of Bandung was part of the Bandung regency before decentralization.

Batam was the only city with a special economic zone in Indonesia for more than three decades, and its development was heavily dependent on state policy. The city also symbolized the location where trade liberalization encountered regional autonomy in the post-decentralization period. In addition to exploring the relationship between actors and institutions on the process of policymaking and development plans over the study periods, this research also analysed how historical institutions and path

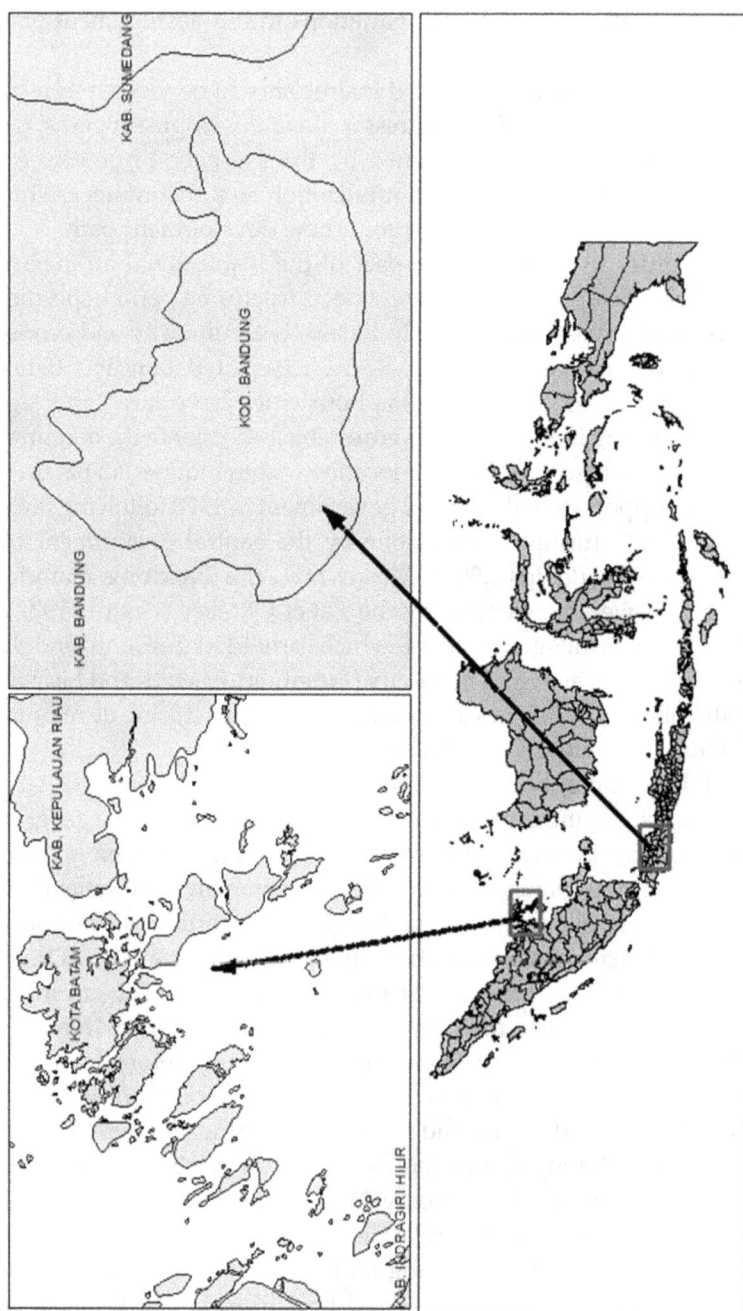

FIGURE 1.2
Map of Batam and Bandung

dependence determined the city's current policies and future paths. On the other hand, the Bandung industrial region gradually developed into a service-oriented and creative city through education, business and concentration of creative projects. The presence of universities and proximity with Jakarta leads to the emergence of highly skilled young professionals who live in Bandung and market their products in Jakarta. As Bandung and Batam were similar in terms of economic structures, their relationship with the central government, and in terms of market access, the working hypothesis for the study — where institutional arrangement of each city might influence the impact of state restructuring — becomes more feasible to study.

THE STRUCTURE OF THE BOOK

This book is divided into three main parts: the first part introduces background research and methodologies as part of the research design. As the empirical studies were based on distinct methodologies and research aims, the specificities of the methodology are explained in each of the chapters presenting the methods used. The literature review chapter revisits the discourse on economic convergence and the impact of state restructuring in order to contextualize the research question of this book.

The first part of the book also explores the impact of state restructuring literature. The main argument for decentralization is the development in the regions, including efficiency in the allocation of resources, income distribution, and macroeconomic stability (Musgrave 1959). Furthermore, to understand the significant institutional changes of decentralization, the study should also consider the supply side of decentralization such as the local government capacity (Prud'homme 1995) and the economic dividends that are the result of decentralization processes (Rodríguez-Pose and Bwire 2004).

Trade liberalization influenced trade structures such as the agricultural commodities and the manufacturing sector; they also influenced economic convergence (Rodríguez-Pose 2005). Furthermore, Sjöberg and Sjöholm (2004) pointed out that trade liberalization affected economic growth through economy agglomeration of spatial concentration, market scale and supplier access. Furthermore, institutional arrangements of international multilateral trade agreements also determine the trade effect on member countries through trade creation and diversion. Studies show that regions with abundant infrastructure and especially in border regions will have higher economic growth (Juan-Ramón and Rivera-Batiz 1996; Paelinck and Polèse 2000; Elliott and Ikemoto 2004).

The second part of the book described the theoretical framework and empirical context of the research. Furthermore, it discusses a wide range of classical and contemporary literature on regional convergence as the foundation for this study. Chapter 3 illustrates the political and institutional shift at the districts in the state-restructuring period, which was stimulated by the supranational agreement in AFTA and policymaking and public services in decentralization. This chapter presents the challenges faced by national and local actors in responding to these state restructuring.

The final part consists of analysis based on data gathered as part of this study. Chapter 4 explores the dynamics of Indonesia's regional convergence through economic, geographical, and sectoral analysis and answers the first research question as to whether the state restructuring affected regional disparities. The chapter found persistent economic disparities among regions and the uneven geographical location of manufacturing industries. Specifically, the result reveals that disparities are more pronounced at the district level than at provinces. This suggests that the decentralization of policymaking and governance process have higher effect at the local level.

Chapter 5 elaborates on the effect of AFTA and decentralization on regional district convergence by using a large set of statistical data and econometric analysis. The research shows a mixed effect on regional economic growth — decentralization reduces regional economic growth, and AFTA has an insignificant effect. One possible explanation is the reluctance of the central government to devolve a larger tax base to bolster its own source revenue (OSR) and the limited balancing power of intergovernmental transfers (IGT), including the unattractiveness of the AFTA CEPT tariff and poor AFTA institutional capacities.

Chapter 6 studies the effect of past institutions and institutional changes on state-restructuring on the regional disparities. The differences in regional growth are explained through the remaining importance of past institutions to influence local development path trajectories. However, institutional learning is possible through the mobilization of actor networks that shaped local policies and resources allocation. The last chapter summarizes the research findings and policy implication of the effects of AFTA and decentralization on Indonesian regions.

The following chapter discusses relevant literature and contextualizes the research into the present discourse.

Note

1.   BPS website, <www.bps.go.id>.

2

STATE RESTRUCTURING AND REGIONAL CONVERGENCE
A Review of Theories and Debates

This chapter examines the theoretical understanding and discourses regarding the impact of institutional changes. However, current regional development and economic literature neglected to provide an explanation on the divergence of economic performance at the district level. This chapter attempts to provide an exploration of contemporary development theories and debates on the politico-economy, governance, and institutionalism as a way to explain such dynamics in Indonesia. A research framework was then put into place in order to study local development processes.

I first revisited theoretical perspectives on neoclassic theories and followed by the divergence theories section. Then the role of institutionalism in economic geography and the construction of an empirical research framework was discussed. The final section addressed research summaries and emphasizes the importance of place-specific policies to enhance local economic performance.

REGIONAL DEVELOPMENT DEBATE: CONVERGENCE OR DIVERGENCE?

The theories on development convergence were premised on the neoclassical perspectives that economic development is accelerated by an open market and free trade. By allowing labour and capital — the factors of production — to be mobilized to the locations where they can be most efficient, these events would lead to the new spatial and international divisions of labour (Perrons 2004, p. 134).

The neoclassical approach posited the traditional convergence of local economic development (Williamson 1965) (Figure 2.1). In this literature, economic growth was the core subject of economics and focused on the long-term decrease of disparities in income per capita (Pike, Rodríguez-Pose and Tomaney 2006). Economic growth theory postulated diminishing returns condition suggesting that world economy will be convergent as poor regions grow at a higher rate than the developed economies.

The basic idea of neoclassical theory was one of diminishing returns. Early nineteenth century economists, including Thomas Malthus and David Ricardo, introduced the concept of diminishing returns with regards to the process of economic growth. This concept simply explains that economic growth must be quantified in real terms of per capita income to represent real purchasing power per capita. Suppose output Y, is a function of labour L, with land N; therefore the production function can be stated in the general form as follows:

$$Y = F(L, N)$$

By assuming that (1) land N, was a fixed supply, and (2) there was an absence of technology, the only way to improve output would be to increase labour L. However, with a fixed amount of land, labour would be subject to diminishing returns as there would be a point at which adding more labourers would not improve production due to the lack of optimum production space. Hence, as more labour is added to the production process, output would rise with decreasing increments. At the district level, this limitation to growth would lead to regional convergence as resources and production in advance regions would decline and in parallel lagging regions would develop at a higher growth rate.

Neoclassical theory measured economic growth as the increase of production or income and described the capacity of the region as one

FIGURE 2.1
Neoclassical Output Growth

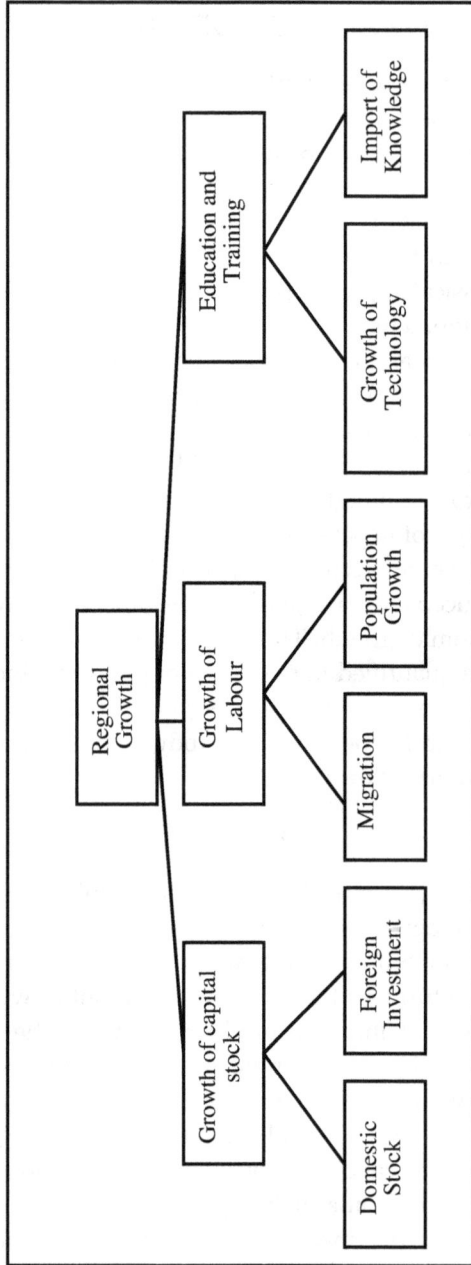

Source: Aritenang (2012). Adapted from Pike, Rodríguez-Pose and Tomaney (2006), p. 63.

that was able to generate and accumulate resources and capital (Pike, Rodríguez-Pose and Tomaney 2006). The basic neoclassic approach assumed technological changes and other determinants (savings, population growth, and human capital) as exogenous; that is, independent of capital and labour input. This assumption had two main impacts on growth analysis (this is otherwise known as the exogenous growth theory); firstly, as the supply of capital increased, economic growth would decline to a halt, which would lead to convergence among regions following diminishing returns to investment in richer regions. Furthermore, poorer regions would have their resources exploited. The second impact on growth analysis is that as regional growth is determined by the rate of technological progress and the relation between labour and capital, productivity per worker will only increase if the capital increases. This is known as diminishing marginal returns (Clark, Gertler and Whiteman 1986) and is defined as when the marginal output of the product per unit decreases beyond a specific level of input. When equilibrium is achieved, the marginal output reaches zero and there would be no incentive to increase the capital per labour ratio.

By neglecting increasing returns in production function and assuming that labour flow to higher wage regions, the NC theory argues convergence development and neglects economic agglomeration (Richardson 1979).

However, the economic growth in the 1950s introduced regional disparities, and regional economist began to study the factors that led to these uneven development. In his seminal book on modernization theory, Perroux (1955) argued that undeveloped countries ought to mobilize natural, social, and economic resources, and that the governments ought to focus the resources on selected industries (growth poles) in certain regions (growth centres). This argument countered Schumpeter's (1951) in the sense that Perroux claimed that inter-regional transfer would equalize production and capital overtime.

The growth pole concept referred to mobilizing natural, social, and economic resources to a particular industry that becomes the propulsive industry.[1] The growth pole concept is also based on potential linkages between propulsive industries and local industries through forward and backward linkages on the supply chain[2] (Hirschmann 1958; Perroux 1950). The geographically concentrated growth poles would become the growth centres on the basis of a national policy on regional planning that allocates resources to a few selected industries in a select number of regions that promotes the trickle-down growth effect to surrounding regions. This concept has been the cornerstone of regional policymaking for developing countries with limited development budgets as the policies aim to establish regions that would grow rapidly and have a multiplier effect (Armstrong and Taylor 2000).

Furthermore, Myrdal (1957) argues that the effects between factors of production and growth in developed regions impacted peripheral regions as the development of the prosperous regions would benefit other regions through labour and resource linkages, known as the "spread effect". This theory is known as "trickle-down effect" (Hirschman 1958) that explains the cumulative effect would lead to economic growth and development through technological diffusion and market channels. The opposite of this concept would be the absorption of resources by rich regions, known as the "backwash effect", where richer regions exploits the resources in poorer regions.

However, Myrdal also acknowledged that as the economy is mechanized in a circular and cumulative way, growth would bring unevenness and polarization of development among regions. It is through the increasing returns of the accumulation of external economics and the historical path of localities. As a result, regional transfers seldom occur and capital tends to concentrate on the growth centres following and economic agglomeration. In addition, as the backwash effect is embedded within the nature of liberalization (Hirschman 1958), the effect also applies during the economic crisis in which shocks to the advance regions would also suffers lagging regions. As a result, the lack of intervention and soft state lead to increasing polarization among regions (Myrdal 1957).

The Endogenous Growth Model

The revival of growth theories since the 1980s led to the emergence of endogenous growth theory that sought to incorporate local endowments and institutions into the neoclassical growth theory (population growth, saving rates, human capital, and technological change). Hence, this theory attempted to introduce increasing returns to neoclassical theory by specifying the relationship between technological change and innovation to the process of economic growth. As technological innovation is embedded within the region, technology is endogenous to growth process (Pike, Rodríguez-Pose and Tomaney 2006, p. 104). Technological change can be explained through the number of workers in the knowledge-producing industry and the process of transfer technology.

This theory critiqued and rejected the neoclassical economic assumption that human capital and technology were exogenous factors of economic growth and argues that economic growth as the results of actions by these economic agents. With this basic argument, the endogenous growth theory allows for the analysis of regional economic divergence in the long run. This model regarded the sub-national entity of the "region" as the geographical focus and introduced the mechanism of increasing returns into the neoclassical production function in order to determine the growth rate within the model. As a result, the model may be able to explain the geographically uneven rates of regional convergence and the clustering between the different rates of regional development. The idea of increasing returns implies that there are two characteristics of regional development: agglomeration and geographical spillovers. These characteristics will be explained in the following section.

Agglomeration can be seen as the result of knowledge accumulation and distance proximity. The endogenous growth model explicitly specified the relationship between technological change and innovation to economic growth. As economic agents see the benefits of incentivizing the production of new ideas and knowledge for profit, technological progress can be internalized in the production function. The production function can be determined by the number of workers in the knowledge-producing industries, the existing stock of knowledge and the rate of technological transfer (Romer 1990). Exogenously produced technology is embodied in capital goods determines regional technology progress through stock capital, and vice-versa, an opposite condition causes lack of regional capital stock which variation of innovative environment among regions (Pike, Rodríguez-Pose and Tomaney 2006, p. 104).

Besides being locally produced, knowledge can also be obtained or transferred via a spillover effect through geographic distance. However, as knowledge is embedded locally, the marginal product of knowledge is subject to diminishing returns. The endogenous growth model follows the Neo-Schumpterian approach in arguing that spillovers are non-rivalry and semi non-excludable, particularly as technological and knowledge mobility decreases as geographic distance increases (Romer 1990). As a result, geographical spillovers can occur in locally bounded knowledge exchange locations and thus, geographical spillovers are crucial in accelerating technological mobility. Another factor is that geographical proximity compensates the cost of transportation. Transportation cost that influenced the process of agglomeration in a complex and non-linear way (Krugman 1991), where if transportation cost is too low, there would be no incentive for concentrating in the urban areas, although manufacturing and trade volume increases (Rodríguez-Pose and Gill 2006, p. 1205). Furthermore, the geographical spillovers are bounded by the institutions and policies, as well as prospective investments. In this sense, fiscal policies and public infrastructure would determine the mobilization of resources as indigenous potential at the local and regional levels.

Thus far, the discussion has revisited the regional development debates and the importance of endogenous factors on regional economic convergence. The following section discusses the potential effect of decentralization and trade liberalization as state restructuring on regional economic convergence. Consequently, the section introduces the role of institutions and political influences on local economic development.

STATE RESTRUCTURING IMPACT

Administration Autonomy

Past studies have looked at the importance of regional development with variation perspectives. The impact of devolution on convergence and its results in consequence are seen as quite varied. Musgrave's (1959) theory of public sectors stated that there were three main objectives for public administration: efficiency in allocation of resources, income distribution, and macroeconomic stability. Canaleta, Arzoz and Garate (2004) argued that the first objective could be met through devolution, while the latter two could only be performed by a central government. The decentralization proponent's main argument is that decentralization promotes economic efficiency (Calamai 2009). The effect of devolution has been discussed widely in the literature (Figure 2.2).

The first potential problem of decentralization is the lack of expertise and human capital which might hinder the benefits of decentralization. These factors are crucial to support government's institutional capacities to deliver better policies and strategies (Rodríguez-Pose and Ezcurra 2010, p. 622). Past studies on decentralization have mainly focused on the actors' demands and have neglected the supply side. The supply side concerns

FIGURE 2.2
Framework of Decentralization Impact on Regional Disparities

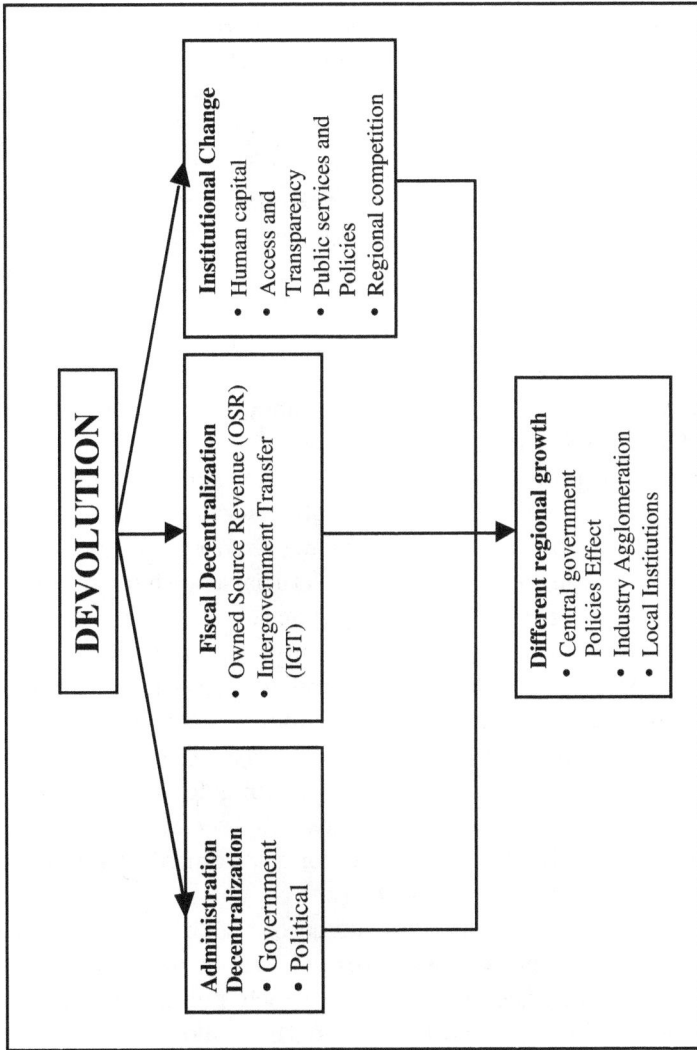

Source: Author's interpretation.

the quality and skills of local government officers with limited skill and managerial ability (Prud'homme 1995). In the centralized regime, the central government has better institutional capacities with higher salaries, experience and more efficient administration, which is in contrast with regional capacities. Furthermore, central government officers have higher human capital through better education level and on-job-training compared the local officers. In decentralization, the institutional capacities influence the development mechanism that increases regional disparities (Rodríguez-Pose and Gill 2005). On the other hand, in decentralized regimes, regional development tends to be overseen by local officers with low education levels and inadequate national policy knowledge, which hinders the delivery of optimum public services at the local level. As a result, competition among local administrations leads to the emergence of new ideas and innovative policies (Rodríguez-Pose and Gill 2005), which suggests that institutional capacities hinders local economic growth.

Another impact is the significant variations on administration effectiveness that would lead to different public service capacities. This may undermine the potential benefits in generating and implementing policies that match the regions' need and public service (Rodríguez-Pose and Ezcurra 2010, p. 623; Rodríguez-Pose and Ezcurra 2011, p. 622). Regional capacities become more important and crucial as each region has different needs and preferences in terms of public services. For instance, citizens have the choice to increase their welfare by relocating to the preferred combination of taxes and services (Armstrong and Taylor 2000).

Thirdly, citizens also have the freedom to support politics by voting based on their preferred taxes and public services. Transparent and good governance can then be established, leading to better public service. Decentralization also encourage effective civil society that, in turn, would be the most effective monitoring tool for government performance, based on society and the people themselves.

Fourthly, decentralization would encourage inefficient development, such as two or more neighbouring regions developing the same infrastructure, or residents would lose their public services to another region (Islam 2003). Thus, further differences would become more apparent with these varieties of public services. However, as the government becomes more accessible to its citizens, the emergence of governments with particular vested interests might occur; these interests can lead to business relationships and the corruption of public servants. The government may also be captured by elites that are rent seeking and engage in collusion. This would hinder the government's policymaking, particularly when deciding on effective regulations. This may instead introduce regulations which would harm economic development such as levies and other apportionments to raise revenues (Rodríguez-Pose and Ezcurra 2010, p. 625).

The following section discusses the effect of fiscal decentralization. The section highlights the complicated and various regulations of decentralized fiscal arrangements.

Fiscal Decentralization Arrangements

Fiscal devolution has two impacts on regional disparities, financial and non-financial. In terms of financial impact, the difference in tax policies and welfare regulations will differ with the region's economic performance. The autonomy that regions gain allows regions to customize taxes and welfare policies based on its development objectives, such as tax holidays, tax targets, and other financial policies. Different region sizes and regulations result in revenue variations due to the various types of economic activities and taxed workers.

While fiscal devolution seems to have positive outcomes, there are several implication of fiscal decentralization on regional development. First, decentralization potentially causes regional disparity as regions may lack the necessary size to deliver public service efficiently (Rodríguez-Pose and Ezcurra 2011, p. 622). Economies of scale are required to provide public services that are capital-intensive and involve large fixed facilities (Prud'homme 1995; Rodríguez-Pose, Tijmstra and Bwire 2009, p. 2044). As smaller regions have smaller population sizes, it is less cost-effective to deliver public goods and services, and the local district governments would have less capacity to maintain efficient public policies. The limited capabilities to guide and oversee the process to deliver efficient public policy may potentially raise the development gap among regions. There are abundant studies linking intergovernmental transfers with regional economic growth. For instance, a study by Kessler and Lessmann (2010) showed that fiscal decentralization in the OECD countries had a positive and significant impact. Using cross-section and panel analysis, the study found that countries with higher levels of intergovernmental transfers and grants had higher inter-regional disparities than countries with lower transfers. Thus, fiscal decentralization per se has the capacity to increase economic gap among regions.

Fiscal decentralization also influences the region's capacity to generate its own source revenue (OSR), especially in terms of taxes. In the short run, the transfer of power to tax residents will benefit regions with more developed economies through the larger tax base (Rodríguez-Pose and Ezcurra 2010). Thus, there is an incentive for regions to compete and deliver higher economic growth. These incentives are greater for less developed regions as they have more need for development by fiscal competition and flexible labour markets than the more developed regions. These competing objectives requires a strong system of redistribution in terms of intergovernmental transfer fund as well as strong regulatory systems as absence of these two requirements would only lead to increased disparities and growth divergence.

It has been long acknowledged that good OSR is crucial to vertical assignment in order to ensure that local taxes do not distort the movement of economic goods and activities and that there are incentives to provide the right sorts of cost signals to the community in terms of fiscal decisions (Oates 1993). Local revenue is important for two reasons; first, the provision of funds from the central government tends to come with strings attached which will in turn influence the development of local programmes. If local programmes depend heavily on central transfers, they will be the result of negotiations between central and local authorities. Secondly, heavy reliance on central government fund transfers will discourage local governments from delivering high impact development programmes. Thus, OSR is considered a crucial tool to look at the local programmes' margins of success during the fiscal decentralization process (Oates 1993, p. 241).

The failure to generate OSR and limited intergovernmental transfer that cause inadequate or unfunded mandates are common in the process of decentralization (Rodríguez-Pose, Tijmstra and Bwire 2009, p. 2044; Rodríguez-Pose and Ezcurra 2011). This reduces the degree of control regional governments have in adjusting their spending on local preferences and would compromise policies and services. In this sense, regions would have to find their own revenue sources through taxes, decrease spending per capita, or increase efficiency (Rodríguez-Pose and Gill 2005, p. 414). They would have to rely on more levies and compulsory appropriation to fund their limited economic growth potential (Rodríguez-Pose and

Ezcurra 2010, p. 625). This is important as it concerns how poorer regions will challenge richer regions in terms of attracting investments with a lack of infrastructure endowments and inadequate institutions for revenue management (Rodríguez-Pose, Tijmstra and Bwire 2009; Oates 1993).

The above factor leads to the next impact, which is zero-sum competition, between local governments to attract labour and capital. This competition will occur between fiscal devolution efforts and the efforts to maintain strong forms of national co-ordination (Tewdwr-Jones and Phelps 2000). Rich and advanced economic regions have better capacities in which to extract and mobilize resources through tax collection, foreign direct investments (FDIs) and economic policies.

Furthermore, these regions also have political advantages in dealing with the central government by contributing significantly towards the national revenue (Rodríguez-Pose and Gill 2005). This situation represents a factual divergence where rich regions have more voice and influence in central government policies. In the long run, this distribution of financial influences over central policy-making is likely to cause an asymmetry of power between regions (Rodríguez-Pose and Gill 2005, p. 412). In this circumstance, the central government offers preferential treatment for regions based on its importance in terms of political and economic issues. The central government is likely to pacify regional governments with threats as well as opportunities that bolsters its own legitimacy. Poorer and less influential regions will be less protected by the centre, while richer and more powerful regions would benefit the most from the decentralization. Meanwhile, the unequal contribution to the national budget leads to richer regions having greater political capital in influencing the central government's decision than any kind of predetermined formula. With poorer infrastructure, tax base, and less influence over the discretion aspects of central government finances, the less developed regions often lack resources and power necessary to address local problems (Rodríguez-Pose, Tijmstra and Bwire 2009, p. 2044). As a result of weaker institutions and lower public spending, the influence that lagging regions have over the political process and territorial development is much less, and this would include the access to distribution of funds that are limited (Rodríguez-Pose and Ezcurra 2010, p. 625).

In order to fully understand state restructuring effects, one should also examine the effect of trade liberalization on local economic development.

In addition, the following discussion also explores the effect local economic structure that determines local gain from trade liberalization.

Trade Liberalization Effects on Economic Growth

The first impact of trade liberalization is the economic impact that depends on the size of trade creation and trade diversion[3] (Schiff and Winters 2003). There are three economic impacts: Firstly, the external economic shocks, following the systematic effects of the global economy on the world market (ibid., p. 104). The global economy's condition can influence economic growth fluctuation and changes through commodity price and cycles in international finance. In addition, the efficiency external shock is linked with the trade composition rather than trade per se by both New Economic Geography (NEG) and Heckscher-Ohlin (H-O) model (Rodríguez-Pose and Gill 2006, p. 1205). The paper found evidence that higher manufacturing ratio to agricultural on trade composition is proportionately associated with higher economic disparities.

Secondly, the type of industrial sector that dominates a region also influences the region's economic performance. The reason is that manufacturing industries tend to agglomerate and be located adjacent to urban areas, which leads to a concentration of activities and labour. On the other hand, agriculture tends to spread activities and labour can be reallocated following new agriculture lands (Rodríguez-Pose and Gill 2006). This is more profound in the service sector as it requires location-specific factors to develop, such as institutions, socio-economic interaction among agents, and highly specialized labour within the locations. In addition, Sjöberg and Sjöholm (2004) pointed out that trade liberalization may have affected convergence through the high concentration of activities it creates, although they realized that the effect may differ across countries and regions. However, even if trade liberalization does not have spatial consequences per se, the sectoral impacts lead to spatial impacts because each district has a different composition of industrial sectors. The level of the sector's development and the degree of the sector's composition in a district determines the district's economic development. Thus, developing countries, with greater disparities dimension and larger reliance on primary sector, trade and protection market globally, faced further regional disparities (Rodríguez-Pose and Gill 2006, p. 1217). The type of exported manufacturing products also determines economic growth. To achieve this, the manufacturing goods and services should have high technology contents. In their paper, Haussmann, Hwang and Rodrik (2005) argued that the quality of exports was important and reflected the region's technological content which determines their economic growth. Another study by Ocampo and Parra (2007, p. 117) provided evidence that during the period of 1962–2000, per capita growth in developing countries was negatively correlated with continuity on the export of primary goods and natural resources. In contrast, countries that have higher economic growth are linked with exports on high and medium technology manufacturing. This confirms that the labour-intensive exports or stage in the process of high-technology production chain diminishes the growth potential of these exports. The study shows that the highest growth concerning GDP per capita shifted from the exploitation of natural resources to the manufacturing exporters. In the case of countries, like Indonesia and Malaysia, despite a reliance on natural resources exports, they also diversified to low and medium technological manufacturing (Rodriguez 2007a, p. 129).

Thirdly, the scope of sectoral trade also plays an important role as only selected sectors are included in trade liberalization. Regions that have small proportions or lack of such sectors will have lower penetration rates in terms of trade liberalization. These regions will have smaller market access in which to promote their products as trade liberalization provides larger market access for the selected sectors product. Thus, larger and more diverse economic regions have higher gains from trade liberalization as compared to poorer regions. As a result, these regions' economy is less dynamic and has lower incentives to develop, which exacerbates disparities among regions. If one follows the endogenous growth model, higher market access would imply higher product demands and revenues that finance research and grants (Lucas 1990, p. 73).

Empirical studies have shown that trade liberalization has had a small impact on economic disparities but it promoted specialization in manufacturing industry as trade liberalization relied on FDI, which was expected to be more targeted than domestic investment (Sjöberg and Sjöholm 2004). The opposite is true with domestic firms that are based on home localities before expanding and considering bigger cities. The research also emphasized the lack of international hub ports for industry and investment in the regions. The study by Sanchez-Reaza and Rodríguez-Pose (2002) introduced the idea of bordering states and found that oil and bordering states increased divergence among regions. However, by using absolute models, this study neglects variation in the economic structure of economies. Using a similar method, Fujita and Hu (2001) compared policies by looking at open-door policy bias and coastal infrastructure of special economic zones in China. Interestingly, studies confirmed the accumulation causation phenomenon where larger regions attracted more suppliers and products, which in turn increased production and FDI, and in turn, the FDI sought higher returns for their investments. This highlights the importance of technology transfers with the establishment of joint ventures in high technology industries between foreign and domestic firms. Rodríguez-Pose and Gill (2006) confirmed the importance of technology transfers and found divergence or discontinuance of convergence in cross-country cases in European countries. When one uses the ratio of agriculture and manufacturing to approximate trade reform, the study has several implications. Firstly, provinces with higher manufacturing output tended to have higher growth than provinces that are largely subsistence-oriented. Secondly, as manufacturing and FDI favour large and concentrated urban areas, this led to further economic disparity among districts.

There is also evidence that trade reforms have little impact on wealth distribution with regard to industrial sectors at provincial level (Aswicahyono, Bird and Hill 1996). Despite the changes, it did not differ significantly from the previous decentralization period. Rivas (2007) studied the impact of trade liberalization that the North American Free Trade Agreement (NAFTA) had on Mexican regions using econometric analysis and found that trade liberalization is likely to benefit states with higher incomes and infrastructure. The study approximated trade liberalization as the ratio of trade activities with gross regional domestic product (GRDP). The paper found that trade liberalization promoted convergence but trade liberalization increased disparities if interacted with other variables such as infrastructure and per worker income. It should be noted that this measure neglected to consider sectoral contributions and that of state policies, thus it fails to acknowledge variation of level trade penetration among districts. Using similar econometric analysis, Madariaga, Montout and Ollivaud (2004) illustrated Mexico states' economic growth and convergence during MERCOSUR (Mercado Común del Sur/Southern America Common Market) during the macroeconomic stabilization period from 1994 to 2002. However, when one compares its economic performance during NAFTA, there seems to be less convergence between Mexico and the United States. This comparison between MERCOSUR and NAFTA suggests that country partners and trade integration level determine trade effects.

Second, trade liberalization affects regional development. Social factors such as institutions, human capital and the availability of infrastructure plays a passive role as "framing conditions", rather than direct determinants of regional economic growth (Ocampo and Parra, 2007, pp. 100–101). The trade liberalization effect on economic growth depends on structural or institutional conditions (Rodriguez 2007b, p. 200). Thus, regional disparities in developing countries are also exacerbated by political and social discontent (Rodríguez-Pose and Gill 2006).

Another impact is specialization of regions that influence the production economies of scale and market access. This capacity is realized by factors such as the capacity to enter markets, economies of scale, and transformations of the structures of production (Ocampo and Parra 2007, p. 101). In this sense, Schumpeter (1961) highlights the introduction of new goods and services, marketing strategies, and new market accessibility. Globally, the level of exposure to international trade have increased economic growth from 2.9 percentage in 1970s to 5 percentage in 1980s (Dollar and Kay 2002; Rodriguez 2007b, p. 184). In addition, it should be noted that different character of technological change occurs between advance and lagging regions. For example, in developed countries innovation are related to technological improvements; in developing countries these technological innovations are linked with current emerging industry sector and depend on technology developed in the advance countries (Ocampo and Parra 2007, p. 113). Thus, trade directly shapes and influences the level of regional economic performance.

Furthermore, regions with abundant local endowments and infrastructure accessibility have higher capacity to attract investment and economic activities. A similar process occurs in regions that have more developed infrastructures. The opposite event occurs in poorer regions with economic activities and wages becoming stagnant or declining. There have been studies which showed that rich provinces and border provinces with geographical proximity to advanced countries gained the most from free trade agreements (Juan-Ramón and Rivera-Batiz 1996; Logan 2008; Rodríguez-Pose and Sanchez-Reaza 2005). Trade will increase population and economic specializations following a process cycle where urban areas with extensive infrastructure and facilities would attract rural people to work there. Economic growth would lead to industry agglomeration and talent reallocation from the border provinces. This, in turn, would have further repercussions for economic development (Armstrong and Taylor 2000; Florida 2008). Logan (2008) confirmed the cause for agglomeration and cumulative causation as he found that trade increased employment rate and labour concentrations. This leads to divergence among regions, but there is an assumption based on neoclassical economics where the economy will eventually find its equilibrium. This equilibrium would be the result of a balanced economy where the poorer regions would experience further economic development as the richer regions become too expensive for production (Baldwin and Wyplost 2006).

Another impact is on the border provinces as it is adjacent to neighbouring countries. The border provinces with a burgeoning economic sector and local endowments could be more engaged in the trade liberalization process. Past studies (Logan 2008; Rodríguez-Pose and Sanchez-Reaza 2005) have argued that as trade integration increases, bordering provinces become the gate and hub to inland provinces. However, those studies have shown that trade liberalization impact on bordering regions is insignificant and largely depends on the level of trade integration. For instance, border regions in Mexico had higher economic growth during the GATT period as in the NAFTA regime. However, the economic growth rate remained lower than during the substitution era (Rodríguez-Pose and Sanchez-Reaza 2005). The study also showed that higher economic growth in the bordering regions compared to inland regions increased the level of regional disparities.

The following section introduces the notion of institutional change as a result of state restructuring. The following case study, which uses two types of local district economies, the manufacturing and creative city, allows for an analysis which can combine the institutional economics and comparative political science's historical institutionalism approach.

THE INSTITUTIONAL SHIFT EFFECT: THE CASE OF CREATIVE AND MANUFACTURING DISTRICTS

North (1994a, 2005) characterized institutions that determine economic performance. He emphasized the role of property rights and the transaction cost effect on economic performance. Property rights fit in the neoclassical and endogenous growth theories as property rights act as a determinant in explaining how investment and ideas affect economic growth. Property rights refer to the rights to use and optimize the property or investment that a person has for their own benefit. This is the right of the individual over their own labour and the goods and services they possess (North 1990, p. 33). At the state level, property rights can be defined as rules or regulations that guarantee individual or group asset and investment. Countries with poor regulation enforcement and policy inconsistency would be less likely to attract investments or in other words, "the more likely a sovereign alter property rights for his or her own benefit, the lower the expected returns from investment and the lower in turn the incentive to invest" (North and Weingast 1989, p. 803). This explains how countries with poor institution and weak law enforcement have low economic performance.

Property rights provide incentives and disincentives for individual actions through extending formal rights granted by the government (Hodgson 2007, p. 152). Human's interest in property rights is the function of legal rules, organizational forms, and enforcements and norms of behaviour, as defined by the institutional framework. Some valued attributes are in the public domain and individuals have to pay to capture these resources, which is a transaction cost. As a transaction cost changes radically between periods and regimes, the mix between the formal protection of rights and individual attempts to capture rights or devote resources varies significantly (North 1990, p. 33).

Institutions provide the structure for exchange and determine the cost of transacting and the cost of transformation. Institutions required to accomplish economic exchange vary on the level of complexity, motivation of the players, and the ability of the players to measure and enforce the environment (North 1990, p. 34). Furthermore, the literature differentiates institutions that are necessary, based on the level of economic exchange. A small-scale production and local trade exchange require repeat actions, cultural homogeneity and self-enforcement. The transformation cost is high as specialization and division of labour is basic. As the size and scope increase, economic exchange requires impersonal exchange, trust, bonding, and a merchant code of conduct. Following the increase in complexity level, the increasing role of the state becomes apparent to protect merchants and the revenue of potential economic activities. However, the state becomes the source of insecurity and a higher transaction cost. Finally, the presence of third-party enforcement is critical to successful modern economies and economic growth. Effective third-party enforcement is maintained through a set of rules that then create effective informal constraints (North 1990, p. 35).

This institutional shift is closely related with the emergence of the new production system under the post-Fordism discourse. The shift in industrial organizations to support rapid technological development in order to differentiate production often leads to new social institutional arrangements. The internalization of social institutions into production systems magnifies if transaction cost is minimized and frequent. The regional innovation literatures including territorial innovation model (TIM), the regulationist approach, cultural and cognitive turns, and creative regions (Moulaert and Sekia 1999; Lagendjik 2006; Krätke 1999, Storper and Salais 1997; Scott 2000; Storper and Venables 2004, Moulaert and Sekia 1999; Barnes 2001, and Florida 2008) argues that divergent development occurs as a result of the differences in structural organizations, socio-economy and policies, and cultural traditions at the level of the local firms and district levels. Thus, this book is interested in understanding the effect of state restructuring on district development, it is important to examine institutional shift of production system at the district level.

Districts should be considered to be more than merely an accumulation of capital and labour; rather it should be seen as the host for social, cultural, and political spaces (Scott 2006). With this in mind, there is a continuity of interactions and a complexity in creative and socio-economic change that have led to the agglomeration and specialization of cities. The former refers to the question on how and why activities exist, and the latter is interested in how division of labour emerges. Using manufacturing and creative city comparison, the following discussion attempted to illustrate the effect of institutional shift on the post-Fordism production system, industry interdependencies and agglomeration, and local economic path dependence.

First, the study of innovation on individual firms concerns the impact of Fordism and post-Fordism on industrial development. The difference of institutional arrangements between these periods lies in the production system and "nodes of social regulation". The Fordism theory on spaces of production emphasizes the "physical form" of mass production in the twentieth century.[4] On the contrary, the post-Fordism period provides a "window of locational opportunity" that leads to labour market flexibility and the emergence of entrepreneurship. Specifically, the emergence of creative city is regarded as a representation of post-Fordism economy that rearranges the labour production and transforms local social and physical fabric.[5]

Second, post-Fordism period also introduces the territorially based agglomeration, innovation and business interconnected in sectors on neo-artisans, high-technology content, financial service, and specialized products. These industries are identified as a spatial system of proximity of agents, action, interaction, communication, and adaptability. The agglomeration of firms and workers with daily interactions forms common socialization and cultural sense. This became the input for trust and networks of agent and production system causing the economy externalities of traded and untraded interdependencies.[6] Considering the flexibility of production and knowledge spillover effects, post-Fordism period industries should develop tacit knowledge[7] that stays within a specific location and is accessed only through social and cultural interactions, while codified knowledge ought to be transferrable, mobile, and non-location specific (Coe, Kelly and Yeung 2007, p. 136).

Third, post-Fordism industries are also subject to path dependency as it emphasizes on inherited of culture and institutions. As these factors are geographically bounded, post-Fordism industries requires policy intervention to unlock the skills and local labour market Thus, policy intervention often accelerates the economy through transaction interdependencies enhancements (Scott 2006). For instance, the creative city policy transfer illustrates the thick network of agents consisting of specialized consultants, intermediaries, research centres, and by agent-sponsored exchange and interpersonal networks. This policy intervention leads to a complex matrix of production, work and social life in a specific urban context" (Scott 2006) which simply rejects the "Xerox-policies", where policies are copied with little or no variation between places (Pratt 2009, p. 7). Furthermore, Scott (2006) argues that clusters and concentration of firms do not guarantee innovation and networks. He claims that Silicon Valley provides an example where institutional building leads to information flows and functional clusters for collective action. The location is open to external influence and interchange, and this provides opportunities to adapt, survive and innovate.

The above discussion illustrates the complexity by which one needs to take into account in order to examine the local economic and policy effect of institutional change at the state level. The following section takes a look at the regional performance model as an analytical framework which differs from the theories above, particularly in the way they define the actors and property rights. The district performance model has been adjusted in accordance with this study's objective.

DISTRICT PERFORMANCE MODEL: AN ANALYTICAL FRAMEWORK

Historical institutionalism approach refers to the study of how social and political institution structure interactions influence distinctive national trajectories (Hall and Taylor 1996). The distinctive trajectories lie in the political theories, where institutions of polity and economic structure conflict and cause unevenness in the structuralism that saw policies and economics as the principal factor of collective action for generating different outcomes. This study employed historical institutionalism in order to overview the variety of ways in which pre-existing institutions, at both the local and national levels, determined the degree to which local governments had the capacity to establish institutions and policies necessary for economic development.

The following discussion explains the role of historical institutionalism in identifying regional economic divergence from the economic performance perspective (Figure 2.3). The belief system determines the property rights and transactional costs. The degree to which property rights are exploited by agents is bound by transactional cost. The belief system consists of the institutional development path that binds the path chosen at a critical juncture; the rate of institutional reinforcement and reproduction determines learning capabilities. This belief system also determines local growth trajectory and institutional adaptability.

This research studied the two characters of historical institutional approach, which are the critical juncture and feedback effects (Thelen 1999, p. 394), in understanding the persistence of Indonesian regional economic divergence. Path dependence can be viewed as a path that certain institutions choose regardless of previous knowledge and restrictions. Another definition is the inability to break free from its own history or

FIGURE 2.3
Models of Historical Institutional Analysis and Economic Performance

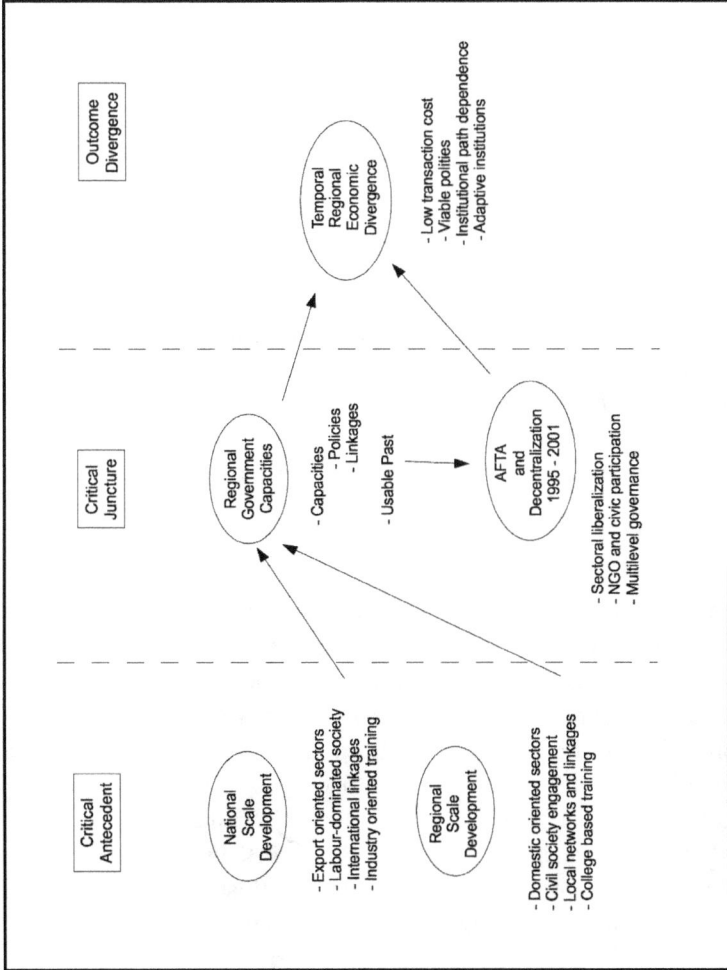

Source: Aritenang (2012).

whose outcome evolves as a consequence from its history (Martin and Sunley 2006). The feedback effect suggests that, with past trajectories, institutions will continue to evolve and respond to changing political conditions and thus, reinforce distinctive patterns (Thelen 1999).

Another factor is the presence of interventions which would greatly influence the progress of regional institutions. There are two sources of such interventions: the legacies of previous institutions, and the result of institutional learning and adaptation. The historical institutionalism perspective argues that regional development is a result of cumulative causation through path dependence. Regional development and change are bound by past knowledge and behaviour that allows only certain changes on existing institutions. The historical institutionalist approach features four types of institutional change, namely, displacement, layering, drift, and conversion (Mahoney and Thelen 2010). When one considers how this approach might be used for the Indonesian context, the institutional transformation of learning and adaptation is of particular interest as they are channelled through institutional conversion. This can occur with the presence of new actors who find opportunities in the system due to institutional changes; institutional layering, where the modification of systems are incorporated into existing structures, is also of interest (Thelen 2004).

Finally, in order to understand how institutional change determines local economic divergence, it is important to observe the institutional adjustments through developmental processes which follow political and economic shocks (North 1994a, 2005; Rodríguez-Pose and Storper 2006). This segment examines the effect of this institutional change on governments and political institutions, and how it influenced regional economic divergence. This research also observed the capacity of an institution to adapt at the local level whilst being bound by the decentralized regime.

The historical institutionalism framework (Figure 2.4) is primarily used in this study in order to identify independent institutional variables as critical antecedent factors in the preceding conditions. All components in the graph operate under a belief system that varied between vertical dotted lines, indicating variations in institutional arrangements over time. The first dotted part shows the pre-existing institutions which are identified as determinants and are studied for their effects by comparing them to a precursor period (labelled in the diagram as "critical antecedent"). The second dotted part represents a combination of causal effect factors, such as the pre-existing

FIGURE 2.4
Institutional Research Methodology

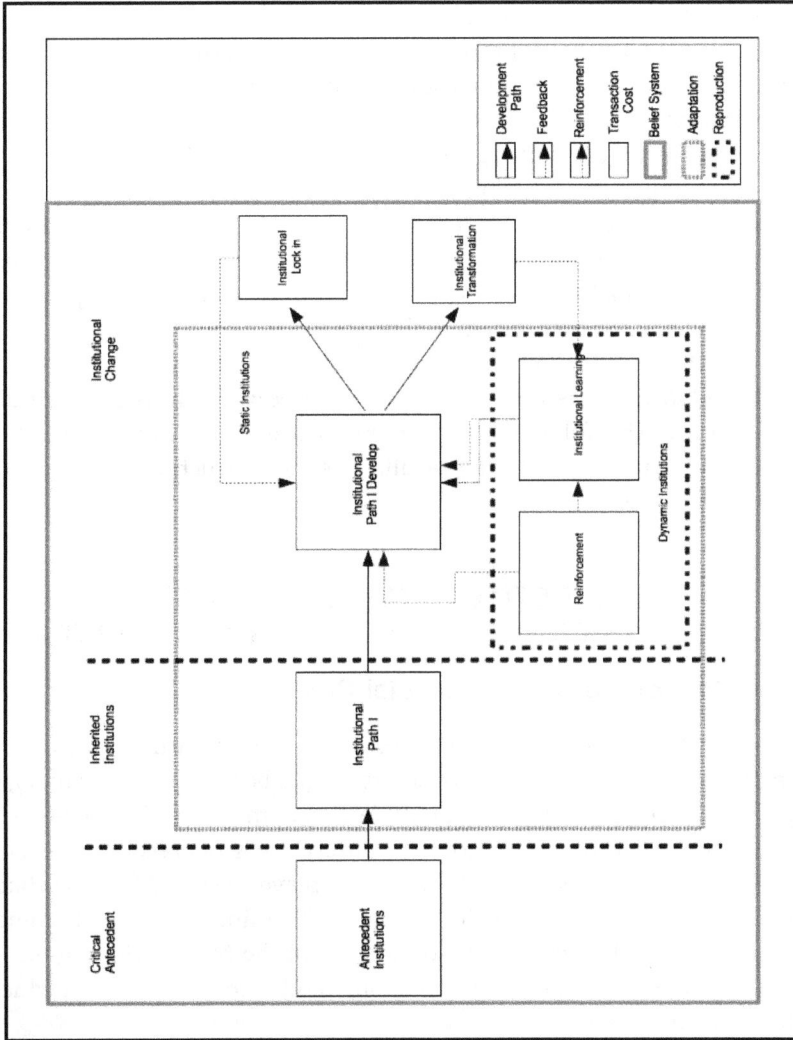

Source: Aritenang (2012).

institutional capacities and the critical juncture, in order to produce a long-term divergence estimate. During critical junctures, local governments faced various choices of institutional arrangements and capacities gained from the past. AFTA and decentralization acted as an external shock that generated further a variety of regional development paths.

The third dotted part shows that pre-existing government experiences influenced the divergence in institutional capacities that shaped economic performance. At this stage, variation in institutional arrangements influenced economic divergence through feedback effects that either differentiated the policymaking process or increased the possibilities of a particular policy chosen. The historical-comparative aspect of the study follows previous empirical analysis by other researchers (Eaton 2004; Sinha 2004, Skocpol 1979; Sorensen 2010; Zukowski 2004) in order to identify common causal factors and to explain common phenomena between regions.

The theoretical framework above has highlighted the importance of inherited institutions, critical juncture and feedback effects on institutional trajectories. The following section introduces the institutional shift in Indonesia with regard to the results of state restructuring as a result of decentralization and AFTA.

THE INSTITUTIONAL SHIFT IN STATE RESTRUCTURING: THE CASE OF INDONESIA

The Role of the Asian Financial Crisis

In order to examine the political-economic situation that leads to state restructuring in Indonesia, two factors should be reviewed. The first factor is the financial crisis that hit Indonesian economy which led to the second factor, the latent social and economic unrest. The global economic situation that struck Indonesia and East Asia in 1997 played a crucial factor in shaping the politico-economic shift in Indonesia. The financial crisis became an external shock that shook the foundation of the New Order regime. The financial crisis destabilized the economy and increased inflation which in turn led to the contraction of the national economy.

The financial crisis was an exogenous factor that triggered shifts at the domestic level at both the economic and political levels. At the economic level, the result of the ongoing deregulation and trade liberalization were the new actors (business actors and conglomerates) that protested their objection to the financial situation that hampered their business and wealth. On the other hand, as the pressures of the financial crisis deepened, political and social unrest emerged. Meanwhile, politically the crisis awakened latent dissatisfied local elites who demanded a more balanced development and greater local authority (World Bank 2000). The regime's strong centralized and patron-client relationship were replaced by demands to manage natural resources and taxes revenues at a more local level. The unequal revenue-sharing proportions and top-down governance with low political participation limited the regions from their own development plans. Following the fall of New Order regime, new ideas and discourses emerged to shift political and administration responsibilities, especially the intensification of decentralization discourse across Indonesia. Along with this, the political bureaucrats' and technocrats' prominent role ended, marked by President B.J. Habibie's defeat in the 1999 elections.

During the transition period, the Habibie administration attempted to accelerate the regional decentralization with the legislation of two decentralization laws: No. 22 for political and administrative devolution, and No. 25 in 1999 for fiscal devolution. Decentralization began in 2001 despite doubts over the provinces' administrative preparedness and human capital capacities. Despite the official explanation regarding the level of autonomy that was to be had at the district level, which was meant to bring the government to greater levels of accessibility, the informal reason of decentralization was to avoid the secession of provinces from the republic at large (Seymour and Turner 2002).

The implementation of the decentralization law is reflected in several administrative and fiscal transfers. First, local offices (*kantor wilayah*) of state ministries were converted into provincial agencies, which implied that the developments were funded by the central government and operated by regional governments, rather than by the central government as in the centralized regime. Second, the legislation of laws and regulations differed substantially in terms of quality. Each region has individual developmental objectives and interests that are channelled through the creation of these policies. However, these administrative and political autonomy appeared to harm the economic growth climate. For example, more than 4,000 out of 13,000 local regulations had been cancelled by the central government because it threatened the investment climate.[8] These regulations are allegedly asking for more levies and additional taxes or rent seeking.

There are two reasons that unpinned local development during the centralized regime. First, the head of provinces (Governors, Mayors and Regents) were appointed by the central government without a direct and transparent election process. This led to the absence of local political and economic accountability to develop the regions. Second, following their limited authority, there was a lack of control and power to establish viable policies in order to mobilize local resources for economic development.

Decentralization and Government Administration Shift

Following the financial crisis and political changes, Indonesia entered its decentralization era. The implementation of Laws (Undang-undang) 22/1999 and 25/1999 marked a new administration and fiscal decentralization era in Indonesia. Decentralization was conducted at the local level for political and governmental reasons. It was a political reason as the provincial level might lead to independent conflicts, while the governmental and efficiency proponents claimed that local governments are closer to understanding the needs of local citizens. This law marked the abolition of a hierarchical relationship between the central, provincial and district governments. Meanwhile, Law 25 regulated the financial relationship between the regional and central governments (Booth 2003). Undang-undang 22/1999 had several points which reduced the central government's power and increased the power of the DPRD/local parliament.

According to the decentralization law 22/1999, decentralization at the provincial level was of the deconcentration and devolution variety. On the other hand, the devolution was introduced at the districts (municipalities and regencies) and villages. The law further states that the district governments are responsible for transportation, health, local economics, and other local region-specific sectors. Meanwhile, nationally sensitive sectors such as foreign policies, national security and defence, national finance, law, religion, macro-economy policies and macro-political policy remain under the purview of the central government (Chandra 2008). The law enables regions to form cooperation with other organizations in a foreign country, both public and private owned. These opportunities should be an opportunity for the regional governments to expand local development through domestic and international cooperation agreements.

The district governments were responsible for making political decisions such as government acts and regulations. They were also held accountable for implementating the decisions. The local government agencies (*dinas*) are autonomous and falls under the municipal/regency government. Meanwhile the provincial government, in addition to administrating its own provincial government offices, also coordinates the central government's provincial agencies, such as the field administration offices in education, religion and port administration. The decentralization law granted higher authority and responsibility for the local parliaments (DPRD). At both the province and municipality/regency levels, the members of parliaments were elected through direct political election. The local parliament was responsible for representing the people and observing the government administration. Together with the government, it was charged with administering and making acts and regulations.

Law 25/1999 has several points which revolve around fiscal laws that relate to shared revenues for local governments. The fiscal decentralization law also provides local governments with the ability to borrow domestic and foreign funds for provincial governments. The law, however, does not specify whether the regional government means provincial or district governments. Furthermore, the law does not specify how much funds the regional governments are allowed to borrow. When one follows the available literature on decentralization (Rodríguez-Pose and Bwire 2004; Rodríguez-Pose and Gill 2005; Seymour and Turner 2002), the fiscal decentralization in Indonesia has five main stated goals. The first goal is to decrease fiscal imbalances between the national and regional government (vertical imbalances) and between regions (horizontal imbalances); the second goal is to improve public services; the third goal is to enhance the efficiency of national resources exploitation; the fourth goal is to improve governance, transparency and accountability in fiscal transfers to regions; and the fifth, to support fiscal in macroeconomic policies. Furthermore, fiscal decentralization increases the local governments' ability to raise local taxes and promote local finance management accountability at the regional level.

After almost a decade of decentralization, there were numerous cases that hindered regional growth. This included local regulations that harmed investments, natural resources related social and political conflicts, and overlapping administration and responsibilities. These problems and its impact on regional development will be discussed in the following empirical chapters. The following section introduces the ASEAN Free Trade Area and Indonesia's political and economic progress for trade integration.

The ASEAN Free Trade Area in Indonesia

The ASEAN Free Trade Area (AFTA) was established at the ASEAN summit in 1992. Its council supervises, coordinates and reviews the implementation of the Common Effective Preferential Tariff (CEPT) scheme for ASEAN FTA. The main objective of this agreement was to increase the international competitiveness of ASEAN industries and the region as an investment destination. This goal was pursued by minimizing the costs of investing and business to attract more FDI and intra-regional investment and trade activities. AFTA has four key measurement goals for trade liberalization: (1) the reduction of tariff rates under CEPT-AFTA; (2) the elimination of non-tariff barriers (NTB); (3) the prohibition of quantitative restrictions; and (4) the enhancement of trade facilitations (this includes harmonization of standards and the testing and certification of products) (Thangavelu and Chongvilaivan 2009).

The main tool for the ASEAN free trade area tariff elimination is the CEPT (ASEAN Secretariat 2008). The aim of the CEPT was to gradually lower and abolish intra-ASEAN trade tariffs based on industrial sectors rather than on a product-by-product basis. This approach was more reliable and easier to implement (Elliot and Ikemoto 2004). The ASEAN FTA (AFTA) CEPT consisted of four main product categories: the inclusion list (IL), the temporary exclusion list (TEL), the sensitive list (SL), and the general exclusion list (GEL), all included either in the Fast Track Programme or the Normal Track Programme (Chandra 2008). The IL category was composed of products under immediate CEPT liberalization and should be included in the Fast Track Programme tariff-reduction measure. The TEL consisted of products that were protected for a certain period of time and should be transferred into the IL by January 1996. The SL specifically consisted of agricultural products as well as other non-tariff barriers. The SL appeared because several member countries were agricultural producers and consumers. Lastly, the GEL was a list of products that were excluded from the national trade liberalization programme for security reasons.

Products that can benefit from the CEPT procedures were as listed below (ASEAN Secretariat 1992):

- The product should be in the inclusion list of both the exporter and importer country and the tariff should be either above 20 per cent or below 20 per cent.

- The product has experienced declining tariff progress that has been approved by the AFTA commission.
- The product should have, at least, 40 per cent ASEAN content.
- All products with tariffs between 0 per cent and 5 per cent are automatically included in the CEPT.

The CEPT-AFTA stipulated that all products from ASEAN country members must have at least 40 per cent ASEAN content. Narjoko and Amri (2007) indicated that the tariff under AFTA remained progressive. AFTA has hastened the zero tariff schedules as early as 2003, which ranged between 0 and 5 per cent in the fifteen years since 1993. AFTA responded to the Asian Financial Crisis of 1997 by accelerating the zero per cent tariff target, which was achieved in 2010 for ASEAN-6 and in 2015 for new country members.[9] This former objective has been met with the exception of commodities included in the SL of individual original members. In 2010, ASEAN-6 eliminated tariffs for 99.65 per cent of the tariff lines under the CEPT-AFTA, while the CLMV (Cambodia, Laos, Myanmar and Vietnam) countries have reduced 98.96 per cent of total tariff lines having 0 to 5 per cent import duties.[10]

Furthermore, the tariff reduction rate and schedule in AFTA are set by individual member countries. For example, the Fast Track Programme stipulated that products with a tariff higher than 20 per cent should be reduced to 0 to 5 per cent in ten years (in January 2003). Similarly, products below a 20 per cent tariff will be reduced to 0 to 5 per cent within seven years. Under the Normal Track Programme, products with tariffs above 20 per cent may be reduced to 20 per cent in five to eight years, and then further reduced to 0 to 5 per cent in the subsequent seven years. There was also a difference in scheduling deadlines for original and new member countries. The original members[11] achieved the deadline for a 5 per cent tariff reduction in 2002. Only those products which were included in the IL in 2002 were not reduced to 0 to 5 per cent (Octaviani, Rifin and Reinhardt 2007). Overall, in 2002 the CEPT product list's 2003 deadline was met and more than 99 per cent of the ASEAN six countries are now subject to a rate between 0 and 5 per cent.

Intra-regional trade was enhanced through the reduction and eventual elimination of trade barriers while allowing members to preserve domestic trade policies towards the rest of the world. Hence, AFTA was meant to be a rallying point for greater economic integration within the member countries. It was also intended to make the countries more competitive for FDI. Despite the tariff being lowered, export performance within ASEAN member countries remained at a low level coming in at 22.5 per cent in 2005, a slight increase over the 21.1 per cent in 1993 (Chandra 2008).

This chapter has demonstrated the multilevel effects of state restructuring as the institutional arrangements at state level and institutional trajectories at local level on local economic development. The following chapter introduces the institutional arrangements in the pre-state restructuring period, and illustrates the learning feedback and reproduction of institutions that influence local economic development.

Notes

1. Propulsive industry refers to the main industry that drives economic growth such as manufacturing industries in the 1950s (Hirschmann 1958; Perroux 1950).
2. Backward and forward linkages refers to the industry supply chain linkages. The backward linkages are industry linkages in industry that supplies raw and intermediate inputs sources of an industry, and the forward linkages are the industries that use the product produced by a particular industry.
3. Trade creation refers to shifts of domestic production to more efficient imports and cheaper goods, leading to welfare improvement through specializations in production. On the other hand, trade diversion happens when the lower cost of imports is replaced by higher import costs from member countries of the trade integration as a consequence of preferential trade agreements among member countries.
4. For more in-depth reading on Fordism and Post-Fordism debate, read Coe, Kelly and Yeung (2007) Chapter 5.1–5.3.
5. For more detail discussion on the post-Fordism and creative city literature, see Scott (2006).
6. Traded interdependency is a direct transaction between firms (supplier and inputs); thus, spatial proximity is important to reduce transport costs. Untraded interdependencies is considered to be a less tangible concept that regards production system depends on pool of labour, institutional arrangements, economic agglomeration with face to face (F2F) social and cultural interaction, and knowledge spillovers (Storper and Salais 1997).
7. Tacit knowledge refers to cultural and ideas sharing and the codified knowledge is know-how knowledge on tangible activities such as writings and diagram.
8. Tempo online news <http://www.tempo.co/read/news/2011/03/17/090320930/KPPOD-4741-Perda-Bermasalah-Hambat-Investasi-Daerah>.

9. "AFTA: An Update" <http://www.asean.org/communities/asean-economic-community/item/asean-free-trade-area-afta-an-update>.

10. ASEAN Trade and Facilitation Fact Sheet <http://www.asean.org/archive/Fact%20Sheet/AEC/AEC-01.pdf>.

11. The ASEAN original members include Indonesia, Malaysia, the Philippines, Singapore and Thailand.

3

INDONESIA AND ITS REGIONAL DEVELOPMENT SINCE THE 1980s
An Inheritance from the New Order Regime

The economic policy shift towards trade liberalization and decentralization has occurred globally. State restructuring should be viewed as a window of opportunity to promote regional development balance. However, presently there is a widening gap in regional developments due to the varied levels of local capacities. There were severe regional disparities between the eastern, western, and central regions. It is a reflection of the central government's imbalanced development policies which were put in place ever since the New Order regime had come into power.

This chapter documents the process of establishing institutions and looks at the transition period between the New Order regime and the decentralization period. This chapter explores institutional arrangements at the national level and between the central and regional hierarchies for the New Order regime. Consequently, the chapter elaborates on the political-economic changes towards the end of the New Order and the critical juncture at which institutional change could be seen as a possibility. Apart from examining the institutional arrangement for regional development in the New Order regime, this chapter argues that institutional arrangements between the central government and regions have influenced the economic divergence in terms of regional development as well as variations in the growth rate for the current regime. The long-standing authoritarian institutional arrangements have been institutionalized into the bureaucracy and political landscape, and this has altered the way politicians pursued policymaking at both the national and local levels. It is for this reason that the last part of this chapter expounds on the paradox of state restructuring decentralization processes. The paradox is that even as the government underwent decentralization, a certain level of centralized coordination was required in order to capitalize on AFTA agreements as a way to accelerate regional development.

THE LINEAGE OF REGIONAL CRITICAL ANTECEDENT INSTITUTIONS: THE NEW ORDER REGIME

Following the socio-political riots of 1965,[1] the new regime ruled Indonesia for more than thirty years (1966–98). The authoritarian New Order regime under President Suharto was enveloped by a political image which evoked a free pluralistic society, symbolized by the parliamentary (Dewan Perwakilan Rakyat or DPR) general elections every five years (Canonica-Walangitang 2004). The general election became a political theatre as the MPR re-elected President Suharto by acclamation in six consecutive elections. Early on during its reign, the new regime's political stance was one of strong anti-communism, economic stability, and inward-focused development. The New Order formulated a government regime that was centred on Pancasila and UUD 1945, which espoused constitutional order, political symbolism and cultural cohesion (Canonica-Walangitang 2004). These elements were employed to promote order, stability, security and economic development in order to protect against the potential repeat of the chaos that was 1965. During this period, the political ruling style immobilized any potential unrest. The controls it placed on institutions made it impossible to replace the President.

The roles that the military played throughout Indonesia's state policy history were extremely significant during Indonesia's various political periods, including in the old and New Order regimes. Under the Old Order regime, the military played an important role in maintaining national security and integration. Under the New Order, the military assumed the dual roles (*dwifungsi ABRI*) of being a military force as well as the political/ social overseer (Rosser 2001). This became the basic relationship between the military and economists — one which would later be institutionalized, with its factions who became known as "economic technocrats".

During the New Order, the state refashioned itself into an Integrated nation (*Negara Integralistik*) as a response to liberal and social-based state ideologies (Canonica-Walangitang 2004). The state advocated and emphasized unity as a concept, without divisions between the state and the people. In this concept, bureaucrats were the ones who controlled and made the decisions rather than the politicians since the state has autonomy in both policy and decision-making. As a result of this supreme power, the President is surrounded by advisors who were technocrats and nationalists/political bureaucrats.

The technocrats were a group of Western-trained economists supported by the IMF and other international agencies that secured development resources from the international economy. The nationalists on the other hand were bureaucrats focused on industrial development. This difference on development emphasis was a result of the different period of assignments. The economically minded technocrats began their strategies in the late 1960s during Suharto's first years. They reformed economic policies and led Indonesia to its first oil boom in the 1970s. This development boom allowed Suharto's idea of industrialization to be realized by the rise of the nationalist-bureaucrats such as that B.J. Habibie (Amir 2013). Suharto skilfully balanced the differences between the factions in the two contested institutions throughout the regime; BAPPENAS (Badan Perencanaan Pembangunan Nasional, or Agency for National Development Planning) became the grounds for the economically minded technocrats while BPPT (Badan Pengkajian and Penerapan Teknologi, or Agency for the Assessment and Application of Technology) became the grounds for the nationalist bureaucrats.

In the following discussion, I explored economic development periods and political system during the New Order regime.

Economic Development Periods

Economic development in the New Order regime began under a government regime now referred to as "Kabinet Pembangunan" (Development Cabinet).

The first cabinet's main aims revolved around tackling economic affairs with the following policies: reliance on oil, state revenues, export, foreign direct investment (FDI), and massive input on foreign aid. The period also witnessed a fundamental economic policy transformation at the hands of the Western-trained economic technocrats, with the assistance of IMF and the World Bank experts. There was also the establishment of an intergovernmental group on Indonesia (IGGI) and its successor, the consultative group on Indonesia (CGI), which were dominated by the United States and Japan.

The economic policy of the New Order was divided into four periods: 1967–73, 1974–81, 1982–86 and 1987–98. The first period, spanning 1967 through 1973, marked an initial acceleration of economic growth in terms of industrial development. The policies for this period emphasized an open door policy to foreign investment and foreign exchange, and accelerating import substitution industries. This policy was significant in that it went in opposition to the late Old Order regime, where Indonesia applied closed economic policies.

The second economic policy between 1974 and 1981 focused on regional cooperation and an inward-focused orientation, with a heavy reliance on high revenues from the oil-based industries. During this oil boom period, Indonesia's revenue improved significantly as the result of oil prices which appreciated seventeen times over a seven-year period (Canonica-Walangitang 2004). The emergence of public enterprises as part of the national economy was also a hallmark of this period. This period also witnessed the shift of the President Suharto's advisors from political bureaucrats to technocrats. In the 1970s, the nationalists and the engineers influenced national economic policy. This period witnessed the development of Indonesia's development of high-technology industries under the leadership of B.J. Habibie whose notions became known as the "habibienomics" (Canonica-Walangitang 2004). In his book, Amir (2013) introduces the period as a technological state regime where engineers and a wide range of modern technologies were utilized as a mechanism for development. The technocrats later drew a Programme for Stabilization and Rehabilitation as Decree No. 23, which became Indonesia's economic recovery and development guide (Winters 1996).

This period also saw the strengthening of centralized fiscal institutions which meant that local development budgets and directions were controlled by the central government. The development programme spent 80 per cent of their total public expenditure at the provincial level (disbursed from the national budget by departments and agencies in Jakarta), while the remaining 20 per cent was administered through the Presidential Decrees (Instruksi Presiden or Inpres) (which was designed for infrastructure and other development proposals) (Lewis 2005). From the 1970s through 1998, grant-supported development spending by local governments was channelled through the Inpres and Autonomous Region Subsidy (Subsidi Daerah Otonom or SDO) grants. The Inpres and SDO grants supported most of the components of local administration, infrastructure, and services, including local government officials, roads, schools, land preparation, soil conservation, markets, clean water, sanitation and drainage systems, health, regreening (planting trees along roadways), training, technical assistance, and planning (Silver, Azis and Schoeder 2001). These limited responsibilities and tasks at the provincial level indicated that local development was the function of the volume and structure of intergovernmental transfer grants.

The third period, spanning 1982 through 1986, marked the end of the oil boom with Indonesia's state revenues dropping as the result of plummeting oil receipts. The oil receipts had amounted to as much as three-quarters of export earnings and two-thirds of government revenue. This revenue decline became a huge problem; it was one that led to significant changes in the policy framework. In the post-oil economy, that framework structurally shifted to a state-led one through structural adaptation that included: (i) the devaluation of rupiah; (ii) the institutional adjustment of the financial and tax system; and (iii) the manufacturing industry deregulation packages on tariff and permits.

In the last period that spanned from 1987 to 1998, the economic policy gradually shifted from one of state-led protection to that of competitive and market oriented industries (Canonica-Walangitang 2004). The period also marked the first time that non-oil and gas exports exceeded oil and gas exports. This economic performance was evident with the rise of foreign expatriates and investments in the manufacturing industry. The policy shifted to a market-oriented economy in which the private sector became the driving sector. Various trade reforms followed in such a manner that Indonesia became one of the newly industrialized countries (NICs). Indonesia's foreign economic policy during the New Order was one of economic liberalization, growth in economic stability and a highly centralized government. In contrast to the previous periods where members of the cabinet who supported major social and political reforms were dominant, in this last period it was the technocrats who dominated the cabinet and advocated for economic- and market-driven reforms (Winters 1996). Following the shift in economic policy, the trade liberalization discourse was prevalent during the last years of the New Order in the early 1990s. This was marked with Indonesia's involvement with the ASEAN FTA that was launched in 1992.

The central government authoritarian style for governance also enabled targeted policymaking for certain regions. These specific policies were concentrated in regions designed as knowledge and economic growth hubs. In order to support these projects, development funds ranging from operational costs, project grants, and human resource improvement with enormous scholarship opportunities were allocated (Bruell 2003). As a result, these specific policies determined the variations for regional development and growth divergence. An illustration of this case is the knowledge and technology-based economic developments initiated in the various regions of Indonesia by the Minister of Research and Technology, B.J. Habibie, in the 1970s to the 1990s. These projects included the establishment of research agencies, for example, BPPT, LAPAN (Lembaga Penerbangan dan Antariksa Nasional, or Institute of National Aeronautics and Space), and BATAN (Badan Tenaga Nuklir Nasional, or Agency for National Nuclear Energy) in Jakarta and its suburb of Serpong; state-owned enterprises such as PINDAD (Perusahaan Industri Angkatan Darat, or Army Industry Company) and IPTN (Industri Pesawat Terbang Nasional, or Nusantara Aircraft Industry) in Bandung (Fromhold-Eisebith and Eisebith 2002); a ceramic centre in Bali; an agricultural centre in Lampung; and an industry-bounded zone in Batam City. Through the state-granted free trade zone (FTZ) status, Batam benefited from the central government's special development funding and policies such as tax holidays, longer land lease periods, and one-stop services which included the BIDA (Batam Industrial Development Authority), the Customs, and BKPM (Badan Koordinasi Penanaman Modal, or Investment Coordinating Board).

Political Arrangement

The main idea behind the New Order regime central–periphery relationship was one of unity and regional administration, which was considered an extension of the Jakarta bureaucracy (Canonica-Walangitang 2004). The nature of Indonesian bureaucracy institutions can be seen as a franchise

(McLeod 2005). The franchise refers to a system that has branches consisting of the legislative and executive bodies, legal bureaucracy, military, bureaucracy, and state-owned enterprises. The franchise analogy can be applied to the Indonesian case as the branch offices of the legislative body, legal bureaucrats, as well as state-owned enterprises existed at the provincial and district levels. Furthermore, the branch offices for bureaucrats and the military were also extended at the subdistrict and village level. These franchises provided strong incentives, both positive as well as negative, to the system. For example, key bureaucrats could be wealthy if they followed the regulations and would be ousted from the system if they failed to do so.

After the deregulation of industrial policies and the implementation of trade liberalization, the private sector had a more significant economic role. This deregulation of the industrial sector supported the emergence of the private sector and political openness in Indonesia. This can be illustrated with the rise of indigenous entrepreneurs and the burgeoning middle class, who were accustomed to economic development and were forced into political action. In the 1990s, a growing number of businessmen and activists then demanded access to economic and political opportunities, decision-making and human rights (Canonica-Walangitang 2004, p. 225). There were two important shift of Indonesia politics during the end of New Order regime; the shift in the socio-political landscape and decentralization demands.

First, the shift in the socio-political arrangement in the society led to the end of the strategy which combined repression with formal political institutions. The emergence of civic societies caused traditional government processes to come under pressure (Lim 2006). This shift introduced certain political latitude and pushed liberals a manner in which they could ensure a phase for openness (*masa keterbukaan*) (Canonica-Walangitang 2004). For instance, the economic prosperity introduced a new era of journalism which followed the removals of previous bans, and brought about the emergence of specialized new media. The phase for openness was then controlled through the ownership of members or people associated with the government. Even though on the surface the phase for openness seemed to have given a boost to the private sector, the rates at which the private sector benefited from the policies remained controlled by the government. This can be illustrated by the establishment of new television channels such as the Rajawali Citra Televisi (RCTI or Rajawali Citra Television) and Televisi

Pendidikan Indonesia (TPI or Indonesia Education Television), which ended the monopoly of the national television station broadcasting station Televisi Republik Indonesia (TVRI or Republic of Indonesia Television). These channels were owned by the relatives of regime leaders (Sen and Hill 2007).

The second important shift was the stronger demand and attempts for decentralization. The first attempt at decentralization was the issuance of Law 5/1974 which divided administrative districts into two types of regions: the autonomous region (bottom-up) and administrative region (top-down). The former was a region with its own legislative, executive and bureaucratic agencies (*dinas*), while in the latter region, both fiscal resources and bureaucrats were considered branches of central government ministries (*kantor wilayah*) under the supervision of regional executives and national government control. Furthermore, in the administrative regions, the head of regions, mayors and regents played dual roles: a regional political leader and a central government administrative representative. These roles provided them with enormous structural powers that surpassed those from the legislative levels.

Another spatial policy attempt at decentralization during this period was the Kabupaten programme where districts were given a sum of funding for infrastructure development (de Wit 1973). With this policy, the provincial role was one where the Kabupaten was the administrative level for supervision which represented the central government. Specifically, their main responsibility was to pass and explain instructions from Jakarta, and to check various national projects within their regional purview in order to ensure that they were on time and had sufficient preparation. At this time, the role of the central government was kept at a minimum level and thus, there were no specific directorates or agencies set up for this programme. The central government limited its role specifically by only drawing up the regulations and improving upon it annually, by determining the total budget allocated, and its effectiveness in order to provide guidance for the provinces and the overseeing districts administrative levels.

The divisions within the organization itself were uniformly similar. In the 1970s, an attempt at decentralizing power was attempted by a Presidential decree on the establishment of regional planning agencies (Badan Perencanaan Pembangunan Daerah or BAPPEDA) for each province. The importance of the agency gradually increased with the role to initiate and implement regional development budgets. The agency was funded by the government through Presidential Decrees (Inpres) which regulated grants and local OSR (own source revenue) from taxes of vehicle and ownership. Following this presidential decree, BAPPEDA agencies were also set up at the district levels. The agency had an important role in terms of designing the master plan and strategic plans, as well as implementing and auditing government expenditure in the region. This planning agency remained important for the decentralization period as it was the specific agency which held and administered the responsibility of planning both administrative and technical projects.

To support the above policy, in the 1980s planning bureaus held a much stronger role in most of the government ministries. Under Widjoyo, the Minister for National Development Planning, the ministry could oversee the coordination of any ministries and national planning agendas until 1983. However, after this period, each ministry was able to generate additional projects that strengthened their own authority as they would secure budgets for their pet projects in addition to the usual development budget sources. Booth (2005) further argued that these additional sources of budget were important as a supplement to the available state budget, as they represented a large part of the remuneration.

At this time, the local parliaments (Dewan Pewakilan Rakyat Daerah or DPRD) had very limited political authority due to a lack of control over local official appointments and resources. The provincial parliaments had 147 representatives in total, with each DPRD province represented by between four and eight members. The main task of these representatives was to elect the President. Their political power was limited in recommending a governor or mayoral candidate as it was the central government (with approval from the President) that had the power to appoint the heads of regions at the provincial and district level (Canonica-Walangitang 2004, p. 93). The Ministry of Home Affairs (MoHA) was responsible in providing recommendations on the gubernatorial candidate for the parliaments and appointed the regents and mayors. The first tier of the regional government was at the level of the provincial administration, headed by a governor, and the second tier was at the district level, which was governed by regents (*bupati*) for regencies and mayors (*walikota*) for municipalities. Another power that provincial parliaments had was the ability to elect regional delegates to represent their respective regions in the People's Consultative Assembly (Majelis Permusyawaratan Rakyat or MPR).

The previous discussion shows events and policies that occurred in the authoritarian regime and showcased potential political-economic shifts. The following section illustrates how these experiences will later influence the institutional path which was chosen during the critical juncture.

CRITICAL JUNCTURE AND INHERITED INSTITUTIONS

This section analyses the critical juncture as a transition period which illustrates the interaction between the new policy choices and previous inherited institutions. The global economy and financial crisis acted as exogenous factors that, when combined with domestic latent social situation, led to the fall of New Order regime. Following the historical institutionalism perspective, this study regards the resignation of President Suharto and the fall of New Order regime as the critical juncture. The financial crisis acted as the economic instigator along with severe regional disparities and income gaps, and led to massive social unrest which brought down the regime. The fall of the New Order regime provided the moment for Indonesia to determine institutional arrangements. Bertrand (2004) argued that despite exogenous factors, ethnic conflicts between races and religion created pressures for institutional change and were the main triggers in the fall of the Suharto regime. During this critical juncture, this socio-political situation allowed for the intensification of a decentralization discourse which emphasized regional demand for economic and political authority. At the same time, mobile capitalists were supported by the IMF in an effort to privatize Indonesia's economy. Policies during President Habibie's regime therefore reflected a commitment to accelerate economic liberalization and trade deregulation.

Hence, the fall of New Order regime should be seen as the critical juncture in which decentralization discourse grew and trade liberalization occurred. This transition period between regimes witnessed the emergence of various ideas for new institutional arrangements. The decentralization discourse was so powerful that within one year, two important laws on political and administrative decentralization and fiscal decentralization were released. Despite controversies and in contrast with the decentralization process in other countries, decentralization was conducted at the district level following political and government rationale of other courntries such as the United States, Mexico and India. One of the main political reasons to decentralize at the district level was to prevent provinces from claiming independence and breaking away from the republic once they had taken their physical size and natural resources into consideration. Meanwhile, the governmental efficiency supporters claimed that locals were more likely to immediately understand and have the knowledge of local needs.

The development pathway for decentralization at the district level was chosen with the legislation of decentralization Law No. 22 and 25/1999. The choice of decentralization type and legislation shaped the process of institutional change and feedback at the regional level (Rodríguez-Pose and Ezcurra 2010). Under decentralization, the delegation of policymaking and political authority remained as an institutional inheritance from the New Order regime.

First, the new fiscal arrangement continued with heavy influence of the central government into the decentralization period. For instance, just as in the pre-decentralization period, the provincial government continued to be delegated with the authority to decentralize; the provincial government could act as the representative of central government in the region, while the district government was delegated with the authority to decentralize. Second, the continuity of this organization and structure is also found in the programmes and functions of the provincial and district levels. For instance, when looking at a government officer's salary, the relative amount and the honorarium supplement from development budget systems remained the same. Thus, the notion that more incentive for civil servants to work in ministries that have large development budgets remained to be the case for the decentralization period.[2]

Third, three sources of local revenues for both provinces and districts under the fiscal decentralization remain the same: (i) local revenue, which was generated from local tax and retribution, locally owned enterprise profits, and other income resources; (ii) the Equalizing Fund, which consisted of the land and building tax, the DAU (Dana Alokasi Umum or General Allocation Fund), which amounted up to 25 per cent of domestic revenue (with 10 per cent allocated to the provincial government and 90 per cent to the districts), as well as the DAK (Dana Alokasi Khusus or Special Allocation Fund) for special projects in selected regions with the respective special development needs; and (iii) foreign loans, which had to be approved by the local assembly and the central government (Silver, Azis and Schoeder 2001). At present, the district governments rely primarily on intergovernmental transfers as the amount of their own local revenue sources only accounted for 5 per cent of total revenue. In addition, Fane (2003) showed that the source for 95 per cent of central government transfers were as follows: 79 per cent from the DAU, 5 per cent from tax sharing, and 12 per cent from natural resource share revenues. Therefore, the local governments are heavily dependent on the central government's intergovernmental transfers (IGT).

The decentralization process gradually altered intergovernmental fiscal transfers and administrative delegation in both direct and indirect ways. The direct delegation was funded by the funds allocated to individual regions via the fiscal decentralization process. Examples of funds allocated by direct distribution include DBH (Dana Bagi Hasil or natural resource revenue sharing fund), DAU and DAK. In addition, the central government funded each state's decentralization programmes and activities for the provinces. These direct allocation funds contributed to more than 38 per cent of the income for the regions, whilst indirect budget distribution for special programmes, such as the National Community Development Program (PNPM), amounted to 14.7 per cent of the central government budget in 2008 (BPS 2012).

While in the case of ASEAN, the loose system of governance under which ASEAN operated (and still operates today) emphasized the commitment of member countries. This governance approach was known as the ASEAN Way (Nesadurai 2003). The system was characterized by relaxing restrictions between trade for member countries and by placing external tariffs for non-members. With regards to dispute management, for example, ASEAN and AFTA disputes were rarely publicized and were largely settled through informal discussions between senior bureaucrats and politicians, unlike the EU and NAFTA, which leveraged legal mechanisms in courts and advice by technical experts (Stubbs 2000). When disputes could not be resolved, the problems were discussed at the AFTA council or the ASEAN Economic Ministers Meeting. These struggles between the desire for increased regionalism and over domestic concerns become a key characteristic for the region's economic dynamism (Nesadurai 2003). Details regarding how this loose system of governance was able to offset subnational gains received from the AFTA will be further discussed in Chapter 6.

The result of the above institutional arrangement is the influence of the Indonesian central government beyond the realm of domestic political-economy, but also in its implementation of ASEAN FTA. In this sense, the central government's role in solely making decisions on behalf of the regions as to which sectors would be affected by the AFTA industry sectors. For example, the selection of products included in the AFTA sensitive lists (SL) ought to have accommodated the concerns of major producers over the survivability of national products and labour. For instance, Octaviani, Rifin and Reinhardt (2007) explained that Indonesia's greatest advantage was in the automotive and electrical sectors. However, the Malaysian government's decision to include the automotive sector in their SL prevented Indonesia from further benefiting from trade in these sectors. The paper shows that the effect of the AFTA could be determined by the individual country's trade schedule and commitments. This finding was confirmed by Priantio (2011); as the AFTA tariff reductions in Indonesia were for the unskilled and rural manufacturing industries, the trade integration actually promoted economic disparities for those industries.

After the new institutional path is chosen during the critical juncture, institutional arrangements can be reproduced through adaption, feedback and learning even as the new institution is being implemented. The following section explores the effects of a decade-old decentralization process and the extent to which it may have benefited regions. The section highlights the effect of poor supranational institution on the reproduction of sectoral and regional institutional differences.

REGIONAL DIVERGENCE: REPRODUCTION OF REGIONAL INSTITUTIONS

In order to understand the process of economic growth variation, the historical institutionalism analytical framework advocates for the identification of the reproduction processes that reinforced government and political institutions over time.[3] In this sense, "reproduction" refers to the new institutional arrangement that resulted from the adjustment to new chosen institutions.

This section examines the reproduction of institutional change and the path reinforcement of state restructuring: local political empowerment, the fiscal decentralization scheme, and the governance of the AFTA implementation.

The decentralization laws of 1999 are the legal foundation of decentralization process that began in 2001 and became the building block in Indonesian political and economic dimensions. This leads Indonesia to significantly shift to a highly decentralized nation within a short period (Brodjonegoro 2006):

> Decentralization has been heralded as a landmark policy for advancing development, by giving local governments the ability to adopt locally appropriate regulation (Pepinsky and Widjaya 2011, p. 338).

The above statement emphasized the huge economic and political opportunities regional districts could gain from decentralization. However, the impact of decentralization on local development and public services has often been considered insignificant due to the many problems arising from decentralization: capacity building, regions unwilling to take the opportunities to develop, lack of communication between government levels, problematic fiscal arrangements, and poor local government institutions has been linked to the failure of decentralization.[4] The following discussion explored the reproduction of instutions into four issues; regional political shift, fiscal decentralization, local government capacities and ASEAN FTA impact.

Regional Political Shift

In the political arena, the organization of local governments shifted into different types of decentralization at the provincial and district levels. The political structure of deconcentration and devolution were found in the provinces, while only the devolution type was found in the districts. In Indonesia, provinces were seen as both a representation of the central government in the regions with some autonomy on their own politico-economic policies; on the other hand, districts were treated as a fully autonomous regions with devolution authority.

This difference in central government representation had several effects. Firstly, the local district governments only had administrative roles and oversaw the implementation of policies, rules and regulations. This bureaucratic administration shaped the hierarchical system in which governments at the national level were subordinate administration units that fell under Jakarta-based departments and agencies (*Dinas*). The central government outlined and directed local economic policies and development budgets through the regime's appointed political leaders; the government also heavily depended on central government budget allocations. This financial dependence guaranteed the continued dominance of the central government over major policymaking decisions. About 80 per cent of the total public expenditure in the provinces was disbursed from the national budget by the central government's departments and agencies while the remaining 20 per cent was administered through instructions from the President (Inpres) for infrastructure and other development purposes (Lewis 2005). In addition, resource exploitation and administration were under the purview of the state. As a result, Jakarta as a special administrative district exhibited exponential economic and political growth throughout the New Order regime (Lewis 2005).

The political system also altered parliamentary elections and political roles. After decentralization, provincial and district parliament members were elected every five years using the same regulations as those of the national parliament. Currently, the local parliaments have more responsibilities and control over laws, which include initiatives and rejecting new laws. An illustration of the effect of the new political order was the decentralized design of Batam city. In 2004, there was much debate when the parliament (DPR) legalized the entire island of Batam as having FTZ status without agreement from the central government (Phelps 2004). The parliament argued that designating the entire island with FTZ status avoided additional bureaucratic hindrances as compared to designating only certain enclaves with FTZ classification, as the government had originally proposed.[5] The debate officially ended with the issuance of Law 44/2007 on Batam Island as a Free Trade and Port Zone. Following this new legal status, the Batam authority was renamed from Batam Industrial Development Authority (BIDA) to Batam Indonesia Free Zone Authority (BIFZA).

In addition, the ambiguity and unclear regulations as to the required qualifications and political experiences of the candidates also jeopardized the quality of public administration and service. The law only stated that candidates only needed to meet certain basic criteria, such as being of sound mental health, possessing a secondary school education, and the ambitious statement that "the candidate should understand the region and be known by the community".[6] As the candidates were recruited and nominated by political parties, they had limited knowledge and understanding of the bureaucratic process. Furthermore, these candidates were also considered to be loyal towards the political party's elites as the elites were the ones who supported them during their own election campaign (Sarundajang 2011 p. 7).

As a result, leadership quality varied across regions with some areas having clear and target-driven development visions, whilst other regions had acquired incompetent local leaders who had ill-targeted development trajectories. This variation caused a vast diversity in local policies and development programmes, as has been emphasized by other researchers (Heinelt and Zimmermann 2010; von Luebke 2009). Furthermore, competent leaders were able to obtain political support from the local parliament, civic societies, and communities. The ability and capacity to build political coalitions and societal support afforded them better odds to increase the possibility of their programmes being implemented. As there were no hierarchical relationships, the inequality of bureaucracy and regional government was guided by electoral preferences. Bureaucrats and members of the leadership who were unable to meet public demands would be ousted in the following elections. This continued to be true even in 2012. For instance, the incumbent Jakarta province governor, Fauzi Bowo failed to continue his leadership for a second term following the public outcry over his first term's unsatisfactory performance rating.[7]

Furthermore, following political rearrangements, decentralization has also shed light on the important role of community-based groups and non-governmental societies. These community groups and societies included NGOs, community leaders, and business societies that had channels of participation in the governance process. The local strategic plan (Rencana Strategik Daerah or Renstrada) enabled the implementation of the new development model, which was designed as a bottom-up scheme to evaluate local government performance (Peraturan Pemerintah No. 108/2000). Following the rapid institutional shift of decentralization and the numerous local governments, civic society has important role to improve local government capacities as follows:

> Civic societies believe that citizen empowerment is crucial in local development. Our main project is to improve local actor's network capacities to support local growth. A solid local collaboration is expected to generate effective regulations and policies. (Senior researcher for a multinational NGO, 23 November 2009.)

However, the MoHA was concerned over the effectiveness of these civic societies and viewed these organizations as pressure groups. In this sense, civic society groups were merely headline news seekers rather than those who were supportive of improvements made in the public service sector:

> The question is to what extent the role of other actors such as NGO and civic society ... they have not been successful to act as a pressure groups as [might be] found in advance[d] democratic countries ... they are only interested with issues that involve "media attention" such as smear campaign and race and ethnic-related regional splitting, rather than pushing the government to provide better public services. (Director at the MoHA, 4 December 2009.)

Given that these civic groups have largely put on pressure regarding certain policies which benefit their own vested interests, focusing on short-term gains, their effectiveness in pushing broad-based policies which would benefit public service as a whole are likely to be reduced in the long run.

Fiscal Decentralization System

Decentralization also changed the implementation of institutional budgetary planning scheme through multi-stakeholder governance; this included the involvement of citizens and the participation of NGOs and community-based organizations (CBOs) in the Annual Activities Planning Forum (Musyawarah Perencanaan Kegiatan Tahunan or MPKT). The role of civic societies in local planning remains limited and has not penetrated the decision-making process, as is illustrated in the dotted box in Figure 3.1. Given that the NGOs/CBOs were rarely involved in the budgetary decision-making process, these organizations advocated for citizen participation in several development forum tiers at the district, subdistrict, and villages levels (*musyawarah kabupaten/kota, kecamatan, dan desa*).

Another institutional reproduction of governmental and political institution is the DAK. This fund requires active lobbying by the heads of regions so that they may be allocated additional development budgets. This shows the "informality" of DAK on economic development process.

> If you want to develop a particular sectoral product, you can purpose [propose] sectoral development[s] with the DAK ... the more sectoral products you have, the more DAK funding you receive. (Director at the MoHA, 4 December 2009.)

> There [are] considerably [numbers of] head of regional heads that spend more time in Jakarta rather than in [his/her own] region ... I think it is a common sense because the lobbying activities and authorize [authorizations can only be] are found in Jakarta including the

FIGURE 3.1
Budgetary Processes in Indonesian Post-Decentralization

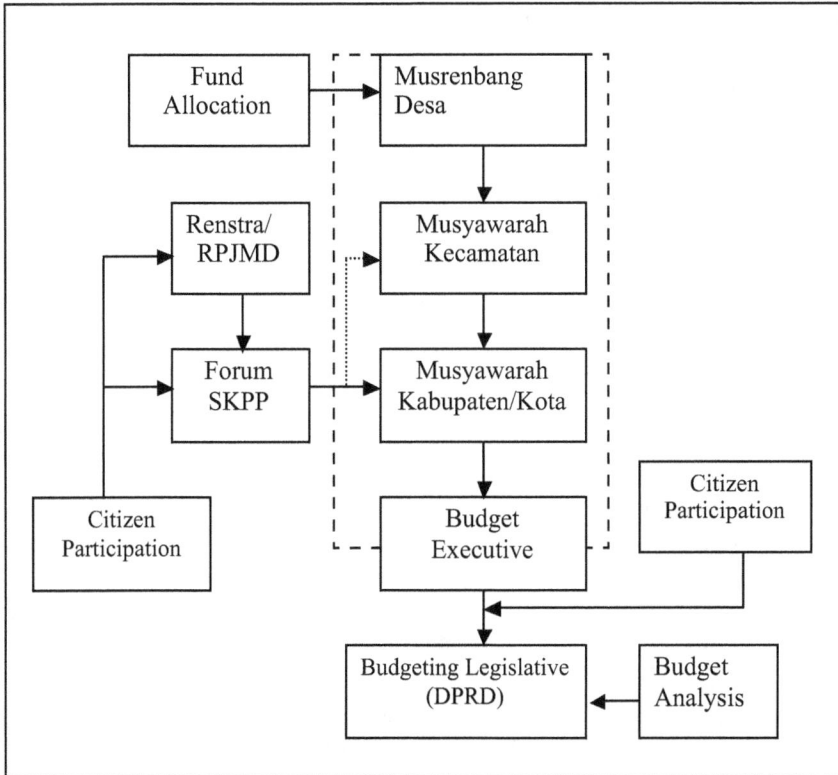

Source: Author's analysis of regional budget proposal in the decentralization period.

Parliament, MoHA, and MoF. (Senior researcher for a multinational NGO, 23 November 2009.)

As a result of ambiguity ambiguous and loosely worded regulations, the DAK was exploited by both central and local government officers:

This fund management is a less transparent process and depends on lobby [rent] seeking and political connection[s] with central government offices in Jakarta … we found that there are head of regions who spend more time in Jakarta to lobby for DAK and other additional funding, compared with their time in[to] their [own] respective regions. (Executive Director of KPPOD, 24 November 2009.)

The DAK distribution tended to increase disparities as it was skewed for regions with low populations and low-density areas (Lewis 2001). For example, Papua received per capita allocations at a rate which was tenfold higher than those that of West Java, the most populated province, because of the complex mathematical formula adopted by the MoF. Unfortunately, the revenue sharing funds (DBH), from taxes and natural resources revenue, could not close the fiscal gap amongst the regions, especially considering the uneven economic level and natural resources among provinces and districts. The OSR rates were also highly variable when one compares the highest and lowest achievers. For example, in 2002 the ratio of the highest and lowest OSR size was 510 and 47, for the districts and provinces respectively.

The political institutional changes also introduced shift to business and investment regulation that led to local regulations that harms business climate (Goodspaster 2003, p. 83). For instance, Undang-undang 34/2000 on Regional Government Taxes and Charges led to many distortions (Kuncoro 2009, p. 239). The provincial governments did not have a clear understanding of their responsibilities and tasks, and instead projected high revenues by imposing high taxes and new levies in order to meet the revenue targets for each local agency. Moreover, the mindset of the local officers had to change as they were no longer subservient to, and dependent on, the central government. As a result, for example, regional officers and members of local parliament regarded this as an opportunity for personal enrichment through tax exceptions or reductions;[8] these opportunities used to be found largely at the level of the central government. Thus, various studies named this phenomenon as the emergence of "local kings".

One way to achieve this was the imposition of a range of taxes in the regional provinces. However, the net result of this tax imposition on regional development was the harmful effect to regional investment competitiveness and attractiveness. The study conducted by Komite Pemantauan Pelaksanaan Otonomi Daerah (KPPOD or Committee Monitoring the Implementation of Regional Autonomy) showed that out of 4,000 local regulations on business and investment procedures reviewed by the MoHA, 25 per cent of them were eliminated as they threatened local investment and economic development. The number of local regulations had increased to this number as there was a law which allowed the local district governments to pass regulations without the central government's approval if there was no response within fifteen days of submission.[9]

> We need to review all local regulations and ensuring cooperation between central and local government in formulating good local regulations … the way forward is to change the bureaucrats' mindset and culture to improve government capabilities as facilitator for private sectors whilst [minimizing] and [erasing] the government administration[s] malpractices and grease monies. (Senior researcher for a multinational NGO, 23 November 2009.)

At the company level, various conflicts with the state and other regions leading to unnecessary and inefficient development (Seymour and Turner 2002). For instance, newly established provinces are willing to claim ownership of state-owned enterprises (SOEs) in an attempt to secure higher local revenue, causing potential inefficiency and zero-sum competition among regions. In the case of PT Semen Gresik, a major cement manufacturing firm in Indonesia, two provincial governments, from the regions where the company had major manufacturing plants, seized control of the central government's stake of the company and blocked its sale to Cemex, a Mexican company (Nasution 2001). There was also some quarrel between the State and Banten Province regarding the management of the port, addressing that the state is inefficient. This leads to the establishment of a local government enterprise, Pelabuhan Mandiri, to compete with PT. Pelindo, an SOE that manages the port (Matsui 2005).

The above attempts at increasing revenues through taxes and levies, and seizure of SOEs reflected the struggle of the regional provinces to increase revenue sources following the limited amounts of IGT and locally generated revenues. Currently, one-third of the central government budget goes to the regional governments and its expenditure is still controlled by the sectoral ministries via the share allocation of development expenditures. In order to explain this multi-level government conflict, it is important to acknowledge that tax administration is controlled by each state. The regional government tax authorities are regulated, with the provincial government responsible for vehicle tax whilst the district governments impose land and business taxes (districts). The deficiencies in tax collection also determined regional differences. Regions with more economic activities and business activities had higher local revenues than regions with fewer economic activities did, as:

The provincial government do not receive local revenue from the industries as the industries are listed in Jakarta ... this has disadvantaged our province because of losing potential revenue from the industry taxes. (Deputy Head of Regional Planning Agency, Province of West Java, 13 November 2009.)

Local Government Capacities

On the other hand, there was a need to improve local government institutional capacities for bureaucrats and the government officers. The bureaucrats simply shifted from top-down "instructions" and an authoritarian mindset inherited in the New Order regime, to one where they seek top-down "instructions from the centre". The inadequacy of public sector institutions is reflective of the New Order regime as it may encourage its franchise officers to exploit their positions (McLeod 2005). Thus, as officers at the top rank were appointed with a limited period, they were more likely to focus on the immediate opportunities they would have to increase their income from the franchise, rather than the long-term goal, such as policies that benefitted economic development.

There have been several attempts to tackle the lack of institutional capacities, which are as follows: the development of strategic plans for institutional development; insight and knowledge development for all staff; upgrading of skill and technical expertise; the development of organization through standard operational procedures (SOPs) and minimum standard of services (SPMs) under PP. 65/2005 on Guideline for Preparation and Implementation of Minimum Service Standard. However, together with PP. 41/2007 on Regional Government Organization, these regulations are regarded as more bureaucratic rather than those that focus on improving the public service. The reason for this critique is that the regulation focused on the organizational structure and number of units as opposed to the organization's function and quality. The regulation also caused confusion among administrators as to how to follow its ambiguous guidelines (Triana 2011).

Local empowerment led to local competition through the adjustment and innovation of local regulations based on development strategies. The study by the Lee Kuan Yew School of Public Policy on thirty-three provinces suggested that the quality of infrastructure played a small role when one considers the relatively low infrastructure development and governance across Indonesia's regions (Tan et al. 2013). For instance, despite having a lower rank of infrastructure, the province of West Java remained as the main manufacturing hub compared to other provinces. This provides evidence that the location proximity to Jakarta and geographical proximity of Bogor, Tangerang, and Bekasi were more attractive than infrastructure governance per se.

Another case in Batam shows that with its inherited centralized policy legacy, the city neglected linkages potential links with surrounding regions in terms of inter-regional competitiveness. This had a great impact on inter-regional relations, as argued below:

> The competitiveness are [was] felt very strongly ... for example, currently Batam Island are [is] competing with other Riau province districts in terms of city tidiness, investment attraction, [as well as] and social facilities [and] services. (Vice Mayor, Municipality of Batam, 20 November 2009.)

As a result of such competition, there was a lack of inter-regional cooperation and economic integration in the post-decentralization period.

> There are communication[s] regarding FTZ's but [there is a] lack of cooperation by Batam Island with its neighbouring areas [districts] [in order] to improve regional competitiveness. (Head of Centre of Data and Information System BIFZA, 21 November 2009.)

The above discussion shows how decentralization law highlighted the lack of spatial integration policies, which may have been caused by the inadequacy of the provincial government as a spatial coordinator and development monitor. This caused local policies to become inward looking and lack integrated development plans. This limitation of inter-local governance network is illustrated as follows:

> There has been no cooperation between Batam Island with neighbouring areas ... of course this might improve regional competitiveness. (Head of Centre of Data and Information System BIFZA, 21 November 2009.)

The strong Batam–Jakarta relationship was also reflected in the cooperation with the Customs and BKPM as Batam was the only local entity that were promoted by the central government, as explained below:

> Batam progress is promoted as a part of ASEAN FTA and also has an exclusive FTA with Singapore, which both has benefited from each other

on the investment and businesses. (Former Deputy of BIFZA Chairman, 20 November 2009.)

ASEAN FTA Impact

Now we turn to the institutional changes which resulted from the ASEAN FTA. In the AFTA implementation, poor ASEAN governance has allowed the central government to neglect the consultation with local authorities regarding their plans for the national trade liberalization policy, which showed a lack of intra-national developmental cooperation. The local government officers also argued about the lack of consultation and discussion on the AFTA trade agreements, as follows:

> The agreements fail[ed] to acknowledge local diversities on business licence range and regulations, environment standards, urban zoning, and employee trainings ... only regions with products included in the agreements gain advantage from AFTA. (Head of Industry and Trade Agency, West Java Province, 26 November 2009.)

Unfortunately, the ASEAN Way has highlighted the weakness of ASEAN as a supranational institution in that it allowed the central governments of member countries to control their own AFTA implementation. The relationship and networks amongst the state ministries influenced Indonesia's national trade policies through trade line track schedules, tariff lines, and AFTA agreement adjustments.

The ASEAN Way highlighted the dominant role the Ministry of Trade (MoT) played as the coordinator of the AFTA implementation in Indonesia, and compelled other actors to implement and comply with the AFTA agreements. However, there was resistance from several stakeholders on the MoT's insistence to include products which were not ready for liberalization and did not afford Indonesia much benefit. For example, the AFTA commodity lines compelled other ministries to satisfy the modalities decided by the MoT, regardless of sectoral readiness. AFTA modalities at a rate of 90 to 10 per cent indicated that 90 per cent of the products should be free and have zero tariffs, whilst the remaining 10 per cent would be taxed.

> Because MoT is the frontrunner for the AFTA, other central government departments and agencies are constrained to support the free trade agreements that were signed by the Department of Trade ... however, in its implementation different department views and technical schedules

may be differ with what MoT has agree[d] [up]on. For example, in the case of open sky policy, Ministry of Transportation [is] still reluctant to agree, whilst Ministry of Tourism fully support the policy ... hence, conflicts amongst [various] state departments inevitably occurred. (Expert Staff for the Minister of Transportation, 24 November 2009.)

The above quotation highlighted the importance of inter-ministry coordination on the effectiveness of international trade and cooperation. Policies regarding international trade and cooperation were more effective in supporting development when there was better understanding among related ministries.

The institutional changes instigated by state restructuring also introduced conflicts of interest between actors that had disagreements, particularly between the provincial governments and sectoral business societies. For example, enforcement to AFTA policies was found largely by civic societies playing their role and by the chamber of commerce at the national level. It was only after the Department of Trade reached sectoral agreement at the ASEAN level that the various sectoral departments or agencies coordinated internal discussions, which typically involved related stakeholders. The Indonesian transportation sector, for instance, held regular meetings to disseminate trade policies and received feedback from transportation actors, associations, and independent transportation communities, such as the Indonesian Transportation Forum (Masyarakat Transportasi Indonesia or MTI), in which academics, NGOs, and researchers participated). These meetings were seen merely as a policy briefing forum for the stakeholders over policies the government had decided, as described below:

In the case of [the] open-sky in AFTA aviation policy that concerns national security, the Ministry of Transportation held discussion sectoral forums with stakeholders including the Association of transportation operators, transportation experts and academics, NGO (transport society), and the Chamber of Commerce ... whilst at local level, such as the consortium of monorail in Jakarta, include other actors such as the media and local government. (Expert Staff for the Minister of Transportation, 24 November 2009.)

Another example of a conflict of interest is the central government's absolute authority in continuing trade agreement implementations with modified objectives, despite demands from the Indonesian Chamber of

Commerce and Industry (KADIN) to postpone the plans (Stubbs 2000). The Indonesian government is fully committed to the AFTA schedules and has never requested a delay, thereby neglecting the demands of local producers and business actors with regards to Indonesia's involvement in AFTA and ASEAN-China.[10] The government defended its policy to follow the schedule and responded with additional campaigns for trade liberalization through the Ministry of Economic Coordination with the launch of the "white campaign" which promoted the assurance of import quality from AFTA as well as consumer protection.[11] Again, this showed the supremacy of the government and the lack of involvement by other stakeholders when it came to the formulation and decision-making process of the AFTA national policies in Indonesia.

The last reproduction factor of institutional change is the management of Form D by the state; a lack of management has meant that the local governments were neglected when it came to form distribution. The previous chapter explained that AFTA implemented the Common Effective Preferential Tariff (CEPT) scheme in order to increase the international competitiveness of ASEAN industries and the region as an investment destination. However, in order to gain tariff reduction from CEPT AFTA, exporters needed to present a Form D certification from its national government confirming that the goods have met the 40 per cent requirement.[12]

Exporters could use Form D in order to improve their economic advantages through AFTA by benefiting from tariff reductions and exemptions on exports and imports for certain industries. Form D could also be used as a gauge to determine AFTA's effectiveness and progress, as the AFTA commission was determined to extend Form D's utilization. However, in Indonesia's case, there were concerns that the form had been underused by the business sector. This has been acknowledged by the ASEAN Secretariat. As an example, this can be seen in the lack of AFTA members' authority to promote and conduct the distribution and promotion of Form D.

> There are possibly [many] reasons of [for] the low export from Form D
> … first is due to the rareness of Form D, hence it is worth to be used by
> the exporters … and second, perhaps the local exporters do not know
> about the form due to lack of promotion. (Head of Data at the ASEAN
> Secretariat, 2 December 2009.)

This issue was also acknowledged by the Ministry of Industry (MoI) as follows:

> The volume of trade with Form D also has not increased significantly ... it seems that the form has not been distributed and promoted well, this should be DoT's responsibilities, also with the training and guidance regarding the form utilization. (Head of Centre of Regional Trade Cooperation at MoI, 2 December 2009.)

Despite the shifting of blame, it was clear from the statements above that Form D was not distributed equally to the Indonesian regions. Fieldwork survey has shown that the regions which were unfamiliar with the form only promoted its use for a limited period, thereby undermining its use. The following statement showed that regional authorities were merely participants with no role in the decision-making role in for AFTA:

> I have never seen the form and it is very rare to obtain ... but there has been promotion by the DoT to our district. (Head of Industry and Trade Agency, Province of West Java, 26 November 2009.)

Furthermore, there were doubts from the MoI, which were detailed as follows:

> Has the form been utilized correctly? Does the Directorate of Customs and Excise have the capacity and competencies to supervise the process? ... the distribution and promotion of Form D is beyond our responsibilities, hence MoI and other ministries could not controlled although we are responsible to [for] the products and communicate with the industries. (Deputy for the Minister of Industry, 2 December 2009.)

To sum up, Form D had not been widely used as there was a lack of promotion by the Indonesian authorities at both the provincial and central government level. Thus, there was lack of data on Form D implementation at the ASEAN Secretariat and researchers will find it quite difficult to obtain an accurate overview of AFTA's actual effect on Indonesia and its regions.

This chapter has examined the institutional lineages, the critical juncture at which changes could be made, and the path for state restructuring. It is apparent from the discussions above that new institutions which were adopted during the state restructuring were inherited from the previous regime as they had similar government organizational structures and the central government still retained a central role post- decentralization. Furthermore, the persistent lack of institutional capacities of other stakeholders (for example, NGOs, local governments, and community groups) illustrates the extensive period of authoritarian regime that has curtailed the development of these stakeholders. This reflects the path dependence of Indonesia decentralization process.

The following chapter uses quantitative analysis to analyse how regional economic development has progressed between the different periods. The chapter highlights different local economic development growth patterns, both economic and geographic.

Notes

1. The coup d'état attempted by Indonesian Communist Party (Partai Komunis Indonesia or PKI) with the assassination of several high-rank Army generals that led to a state of emergency in 1965.
2. See Booth (2005) for the analysis of central government spending after decentralization.
3. For more readings on the process of reproduction, see Thelen (1999) and Eaton (2004).
4. For further readings, see Triana (2011), Macleod (2005), Pepinsky and Widjaya (2013), McCulloch and Malesky (2011), Brodjonegoro (2006), and Lewis (2013).
5. <http://us.finance.detik.com/read/2004/09/15/010152/207835/4/dpr-nekat-sahkan-ruu-ftz-batam>.
6. Law 32/2004 article 58.
7. <http://nasional.kompas.com/read/2012/02/23/17494547/JK.Gagal.Bangun.Jakarta>; <http://news.detik.com/read/2011/03/27/125249/1602150/10/foke-dinilai-gagal-pimpin jakarta?nd771104bcj>.
8. See Macleod (2005) for an in-depth study on civil services after decentralization.
9. Law No. 34/2000.
10. Interview with the Director of Promotion, BKPM.
11. Kompas Print edition online, <http://www.kompas.com/read/xml/2009/12/28/12362833/white.campaign.untuk.hadapi.fta> (accessed 29 December 2009).
12. The ASEAN Agreement on the Common Effective Preferential Tariff (CEPT) Scheme for the ASEAN Free Trade Area (AFTA).

4

DYNAMICS OF REGIONAL
ECONOMIC CONVERGENCE

In the last two decades, international theory and econometric analysis have linked regional disparities with decentralization and trade liberalization policies. This can be measured via local economic welfare mobility following trade liberalization (Quah 1993), local endowments (Martin and Sunley 1998) and local economic convergence rates (Barro and Sala-I-Martin 1991).

Furthermore, empirical studies have resulted in varied perspectives over the impact of these state restructuring. The regional disparity studies in Indonesia during the New Order period were mainly studied at the provincial levels (Akita and Lukman 1995; Garcia and Soelistianingsih 1998), while there are emerging studies on the regional disparities at the district level for the post-decentralization period (McCulloch and Syahrir 2008; McCulloch and Malesky 2011; Aritenang 2012).

The analysis of industry types (Fan and Scott 2003), industry concentration (Sjöberg and Sjöholm 2004), main economic sectors and the existing political order (Shankar and Shah 2003) have all affected the level of disparities between and within countries and the trade liberalization policy regime in particular (Petrakos, Rodríguez-Pose and Rovolis 2005). There are also a growing number of studies on the local impact of state restructuring, such as the impact of trade liberation on regions with borders (Logan 2008; Rodríguez-Pose and Sanchez-Reaza 2005) and the local infrastructure (Rivas 2007). These studies confirmed Heng's (2012) argument that the most significant impact of the globalized economy was at the local level, rather than national or provincial level. This study examined the impact of decentralization and the ASEAN Free Trade Agreement (AFTA) on districts in Indonesia.

This chapter is organized as follows: the first section is a short description of data and spatial unit of analysis and followed by a section on exploratory analysis of economic growth in terms of time series and geography between 1993 and 2010. The next section examines spatial distribution of economic growth and manufacturing industries. The final section discusses the research findings from this chapter.

RESEARCH DATA DESCRIPTION

This chapter uses the BPS publication of regional list in 1997[1] based on the number of districts before the decentralization. In the 1997 regional list there are 26 provinces and 292 districts[2] with 4,088 overall observations for the period between 1993 and 2010. As this chapter uses the district level as the spatial unit of analysis, it is expected that the results will be different from that of previous papers (Akita and Lukman 1995; Garcia and Soelistianingsih 1998; Hill, Resosudarmo and Vidyattama 2008; Viddyatama 2013). The Gross Regional Domestic Product (GRDP) in constant price 2000 Indonesian rupiah is used to proximate district per capita income.[3] The spatial unit is the district level as the devolution is at this level of government.

REGIONAL ECONOMIC DISTRIBUTION INDICES

This research analyses regional economic growth process occurring at the provincial level in order to capture the inequality distribution located within provinces. Systematic inequality variations are meant to measure regional economic distribution (Fan and Casetti 1994).[4]

Variations in systematic inequality can be seen via the Lorenz graphs,[5] which depict the inequality level among Indonesian districts using GRDP. The non-natural resource figures, such as GRDP per capita, has a larger Lorenz curve area. This suggests higher disparities as compared to one which included the natural resources, which is shown in the second graph in Figure 4.1). By using the natural resource GDP as the concentration of natural resources for a few districts, the graphs confirmed the disparity measurement bias. On the other hand, Figure 4.2 shows a more balanced local economic growth with the declining disparity GRDP per capita between 1993 and 2010. This is an important initial finding, as in the following sections, this book examines the economic factors of uneven development between districts.

Next we turn to the annual convergence rate as shown by the sigma convergence analysis; one can derive these figures by using the standard deviation of log-transformed provincial GDP per capita for the period 1993–2010 (Figure 4.3). The graph reflects the political-economic impact on regional and manufacturing industry policies. First, following the oil boom period in 1984, in the early 1990s the regional dispersion of provincial GDP per capita was about 0.62. It fell and hit its lowest value in 1995 when it reached 0.4.

Afterwards, the 1997 Asian Financial Crisis (AFC) caused a sharp provincial inequality that reached 0.65 at the height of the crisis in 1999 and the sigma convergence reached the same levels as the periods before the AFC. This had a significant effect on Indonesian disparity as in the post decentralization period the figure continuosly increased and peaked to 0.88 in 2008. In the following years, the figure declined sharply to 0.74 in 2010. The disparity increased because several provinces — such as Jakarta, Riau, and East Kalimantan — had high economic growth rates as they gained greater financial authority in the post-decentralization period.

Further detailed analysis on inter-district inequalities using three measurement graphs — the Theil Index, CV, and Gini Coefficient — indicated a decline in inequality during the period of observation (Figure 4.4). The three reference lines in 1998, 2001 and 2006 in the graph represented the political-economic shift during these years. Inequality increased rapidly between 1993 and 1997 before it fluctuated during the AFC between 1998 and 2001. Figure 4.4 shows that as AFC occurs in 1997, the Theil index increase proportionally in both between and within provinces. During the transition period, inter-district inequality dropped slightly. However, after the decentralization took place in 2001, the between province Theil index decline faster than the within province. Interestingly, districts disparity has continue to decline after the elimination of hold harmless regulation in 2006.[6]

FIGURE 4.1
Lorenz Curve GRDP per capita and GRDP per capita (non-natural resource)

GRDP per capita (Non-natural resources)

GRDP per capita (Natural resources included)

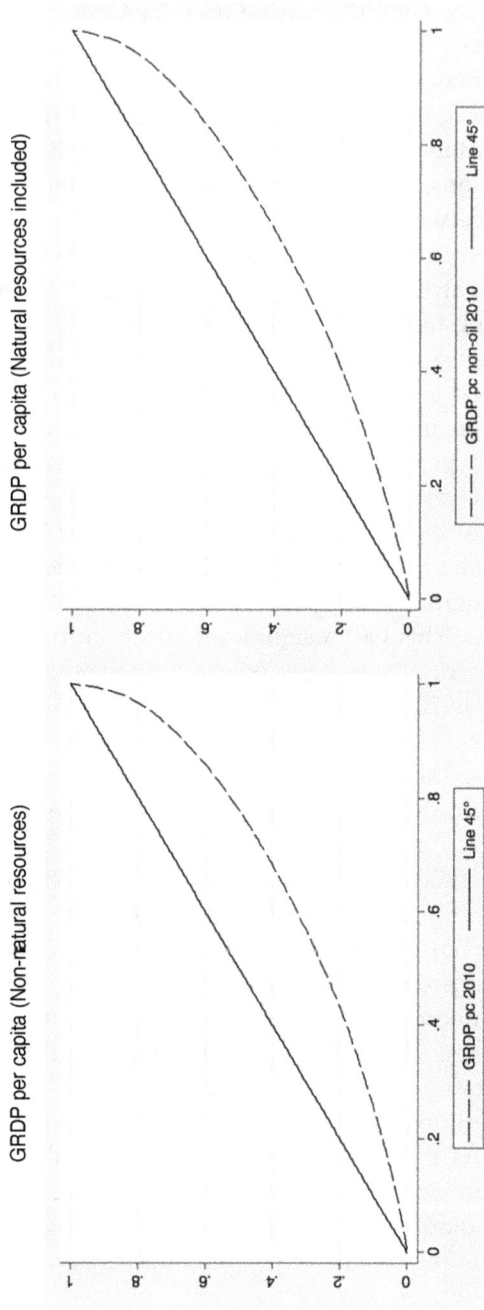

Source: Author's calculation.

FIGURE 4.2
Lorenz Curve GRDP per capita, 1993 and 2010

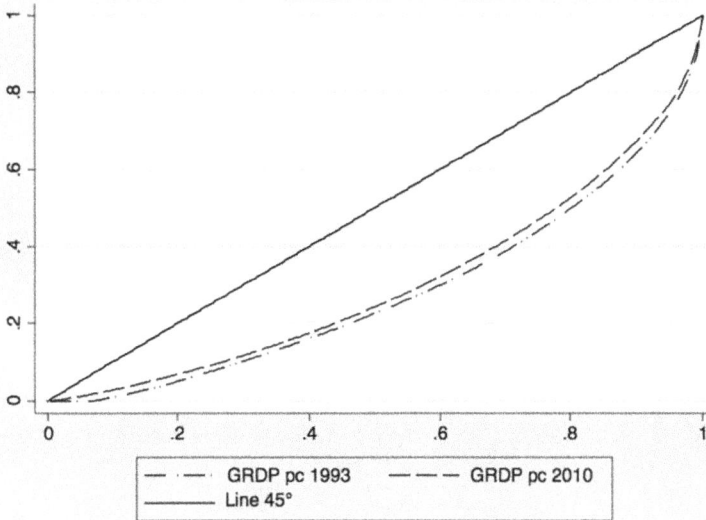

- · - GRDP pc 1993   - - - GRDP pc 2010
——— Line 45°

FIGURE 4.3
Dispersion of per capita Provincial Incomes, 1971–2010

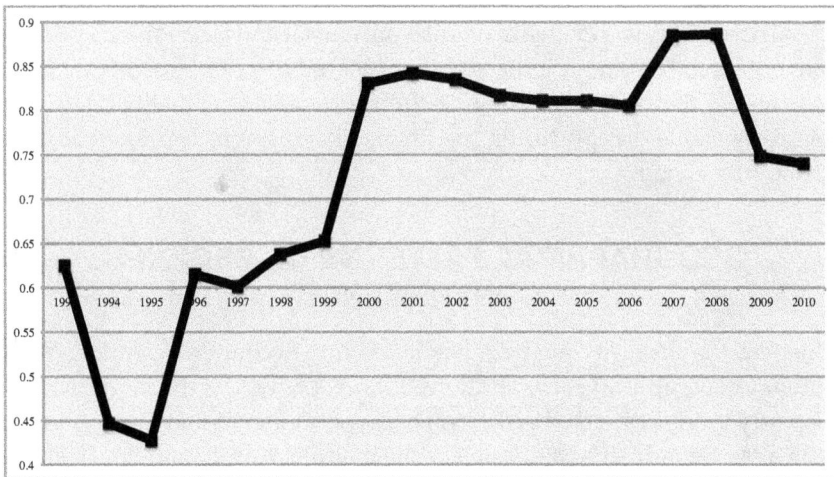

Source: Author's calculation.

FIGURE 4.4
Inter-district Inequality per capita GDP, 1993–2010

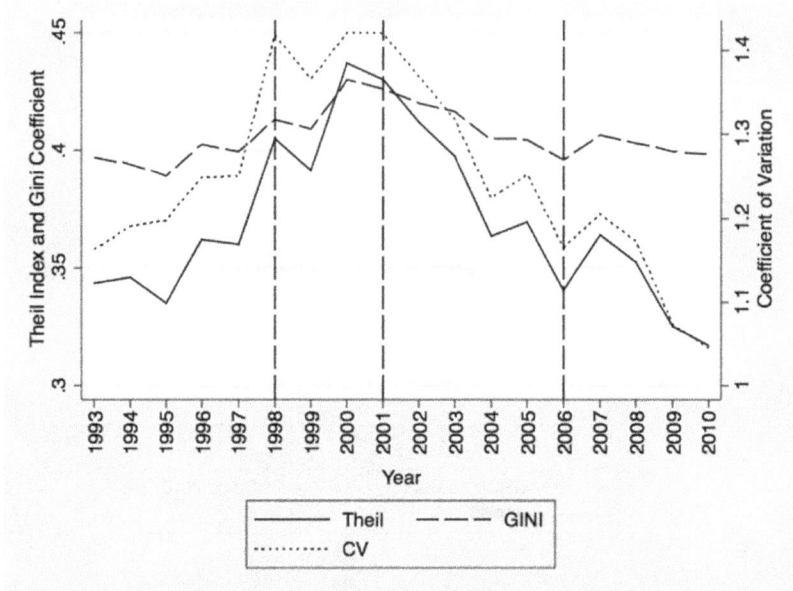

Figure 4.5 shows evidence of inter-provincial and inter-district growth convergence. The graph indicated that inequality rates between districts were higher than between provinces. Inter-provincial inequality rates were relatively stable except during the financial crisis, which peaked at 0.32, before it declined.

GEOGRAPHICAL PATTERNS OF REGIONAL CONVERGENCE

Thus far, the disparity analysis has taken into account economic indices without geographical considerations. Figure 4.6 depicts the inter-districts disparity levels at selected districts. There was evidence that rich provinces with a strong industrial base such as the manufacturing industry (Jakarta, West Java, and East Java) and the oil and gas industry (Riau, East Kalimantan and Papua) had higher inter-provincial disparity rates. On the

FIGURE 4.5
GRDP Province and District Inequality Index, 1993–2010

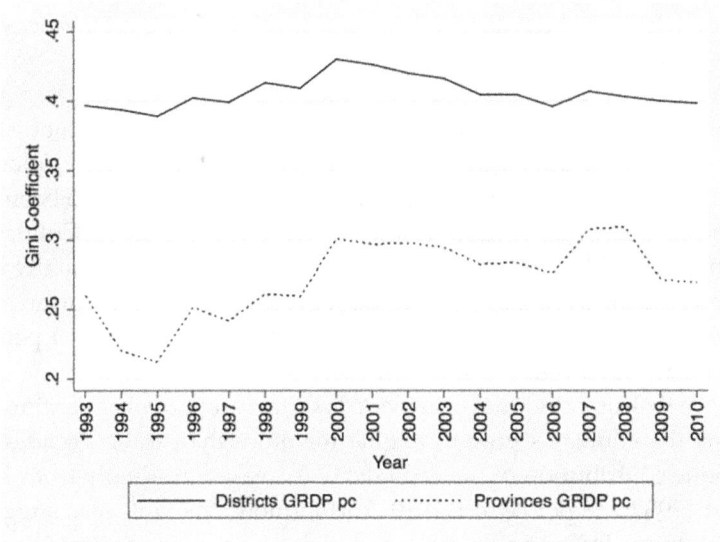

Source: Author's calculation.

FIGURE 4.6
Inter-district Inequality per capita GDP, 1993–2010

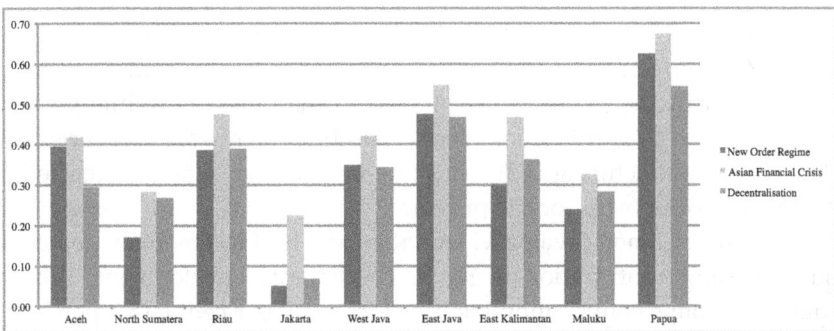

Source: Author's calculation.

other hand, poorer provinces such as Aceh and Maluku had relatively low inter-district disparity levels. This suggests that economic concentration and development within rich provinces were imbalanced, a few districts were privileged, whilst district economic levels in lagging provinces were relatively more even.

In order to capture a more accurate depiction of the Indonesian regional economic distribution, the provinces were divided into five major islands groups; Java-Bali, Sumatra, Kalimantan, Sulawesi and Eastern Indonesia. This method in analysing the regional economic level has also been used by other studies (Hill, Resosudarmo and Vidyattama 2008; McCulloch and Syahrir 2008). Table 4.1 shows that the Java-Bali region persistently made up more than 60 per cent of the Indonesian economy. The Sumatran region followed at 20 per cent, Kalimantan at 9 per cent, Sulawesi at 4 per cent, and eastern Indonesia at 3 per cent.

If we look at individual provinces, Jakarta's economy has continuously become the country's growth engine for more than three decades. The economic contribution of the capital city increased gradually from 16 per cent in 1993 to 18 per cent in 2010. Furthermore, the table also suggested that the move by manufacturing industries from more central locales in Jakarta to more suburban districts in the neighbouring West Javanese provinces had not contracted Jakarta's non-mining GRDP contribution. The establishment of industrial zones and parks following deregulation in the 1980s witnessed the reallocation of manufacturing industries from central Jakarta to the districts of Bogor, Tangerang and Bekasi (Hudalah et al. 2013). Unexpectedly, the GRDP contribution was higher in Jakarta compared with West Java. One possible explanation for this phenomenon was that manufacturing headquarters remained in Jakarta, and it was only the manufacturing plants which moved to the outskirts. While Jakarta and West Java's contributions were expanding, there was evidence of a declining manufacturing industry share in East Java, which suggested a stagnant development for the province.

The two rich non-Java provinces, Riau and East Kalimantan, depicted an increasing contribution to national economic development. Whilst Riau's economic contribution increased from 1.9 per cent to 6.3 per cent, Kalimantan's richest province had increased its contribution from 5 per cent to 5.5 per cent between the same years. For Riau's case, this suggested that Batam Island's role as a manufacturing hub and export zone was significant. The East Kalimantan economy was driven by the abundance

TABLE 4.1
Provincial GRDP: Shares of National Totals (%)

	1993	1998	2001	2005	2010
Aceh	3.59	2.64	2.39	2.02	1.50
North Sumatera	6.01	5.77	5.23	5.30	5.32
West Sumatera	2.41	1.97	1.74	1.78	1.83
Riau	1.90	4.97	6.83	6.60	6.28
Jambi	0.81	0.80	0.73	0.74	0.77
South Sumatera	3.50	3.38	3.54	3.54	3.49
Bengkulu	0.35	0.45	0.36	0.37	0.37
Lampung	1.80	1.66	1.71	1.74	1.38
Sumatra	*20.38*	*21.64*	*22.68*	*22.09*	*20.94*
Jakarta	16.77	14.44	17.17	17.69	18.10
West Java	18.87	17.92	17.59	17.84	18.34
Central Java	7.90	10.11	8.05	8.04	7.72
Jogjakarta	1.36	1.22	1.02	1.02	0.97
East Java	15.32	14.52	14.50	14.41	15.46
Bali	1.89	1.84	1.22	1.22	1.24
Java-Bali	*62.10*	*60.06*	*59.46*	*60.23*	*61.82*
Java-Bali non Jakarta	*45.33*	*45.61*	*42.27*	*42.53*	*43.73*
West Kalimantan	1.73	1.82	1.34	1.35	1.39
Central Kalimantan	1.31	1.17	0.84	0.82	0.83
South Kalimantan	1.50	1.50	1.37	1.36	1.40
East Kalimantan	4.98	5.24	6.51	6.21	5.48
Kalimantan	*9.51*	*9.73*	*9.98*	*9.73*	*9.09*
North Sulawesi	0.90	0.97	0.90	0.91	0.98
Central Sulawesi	0.53	0.51	0.60	0.65	0.80
South Sulawesi	2.48	2.38	2.31	2.40	2.59
Southeast Sulawesi	0.42	0.39	0.44	0.49	0.54
Sulawesi	*4.33*	*4.25*	*4.26*	*4.44*	*4.90*
Maluku	0.68	0.63	0.36	0.35	0.33
Irian Jaya	1.46	2.16	1.75	1.68	1.49
West Nusa Tenggara	0.84	0.83	0.95	0.92	0.93
East Nusa Tenggara	0.70	0.70	0.56	0.56	0.48
Eastern Indonesia	*3.68*	*4.33*	*3.61*	*3.51*	*3.24*

Source: Author's calculation based on provincial and districts BPS data from various years, in 1993 constant prices.

of oil exploitation and natural resources-related manufacturing and related processing industries.

When the national average is set to 100, the gap between the richest and poorest provinces remained very high (Table 4.2). The highest GRDP per capita (Jakarta) was 17.9 times higher than that of East Nusa Tenggara; this difference had increased compared to 1993 when the difference ratio was 13.4. Why was this be so? A comparison and analysis of the main manufacturing regions is needed in order to answer that question. Firstly, the economy of Jakarta showed the highest contraction as a result of the AFC compared to Riau, West Java and East Kalimantan. This suggests that the province's share of financial and service sector centres was the highest compared to other provinces. Secondly, the gradual growth of manufacturing centres after decentralization shows the mobility of resources and authority delegation to the regions, while at the same time shows warning of persistent economic disparity.

Another case to consider was that of persistently poor regions, which consisted of the two Nusa Tenggara provinces and Southeast Sulawesi. They have 33 to 50 per cent of the national average GRDP. On the other hand, the two provinces that have experienced conflicts, Maluku and Aceh, had a sharp drop in GRDP during the observation period.

The Theil index indicated that overall disparities among districts in Indonesia declined (Table 4.3). When the index is broken down into three types of regional division, which are the within province, between province, and within parts of Indonesia, the disparity levels are various. The disparities among districts have declined sharply between the years, while the disparity between provinces had declined at a lower rate. An interesting finding was that disparities between three parts of Indonesia, the western, central and eastern regions, increased significantly during the pre-decentralization period of the 1990s and peaked during the early 2000s before it reached its current position. This finding confirmed that eastern Indonesian regions were severely left behind in terms of economic development and welfare.

To give a more detailed analysis, provincial and major island distribution indices have depicted a similar outlook (Table 4.4). An interesting analysis result was that after the financial crisis in 1997, Indonesian regions experienced a higher economic divergence. For instance, within the transition period, between 1997 and 2001, there is an increase of inequality level in each measurement between 10 and 20 per cent.

TABLE 4.2
Provincial GRDP per Capita (Indonesia = 100)

	1993	1998	2001	2005	2010
Aceh	9.508503	7.430134	7.017318	6.236695	4.807072
North Sumatera	5.39229	5.500054	5.203272	5.526779	5.794368
West Sumatera	5.700006	4.951845	4.549147	4.89302	5.244488
Riau	3.844782	10.65502	15.28666	15.49997	15.38551
Jambi	3.241011	3.401429	3.219053	3.431464	3.746889
South Sumatera	4.990473	5.121238	5.590066	5.873485	6.042363
Bengkulu	2.496002	3.325775	2.844559	3.01664	3.192095
Lampung	2.743253	2.69018	2.897042	3.08808	2.567671
Sumatra	*97.03177*	*105.3328*	*109.8261*	*105.6175*	*99.81506*
Jakarta	20.54362	18.79916	23.32647	25.21452	26.9097
West Java	4.35944	4.398943	4.506351	4.795337	5.14278
Central Java	2.62682	3.569388	2.968151	3.105988	3.115158
Jogjakarta	4.410541	4.200376	3.669323	3.854098	3.821684
East Java	4.495735	4.526879	4.71727	4.920463	5.505958
Bali	6.098595	6.334209	4.359887	4.593753	4.877435
Java-Bali	*101.8023*	*98.27432*	*97.80015*	*99.88625*	*101.8587*
Java-Bali non Jakarta	*79.67617*	*80.00002*	*74.48466*	*75.62192*	*77.27682*
West Kalimantan	4.71879	5.28695	4.059838	4.279085	4.608412
Central Kalimantan	6.912251	6.578298	4.938109	5.047542	5.316167
South Kalimantan	5.035525	5.343383	5.090565	5.320816	5.69291
East Kalimantan	19.79241	22.1477	28.69712	28.71059	26.44281
Kalimantan	*172.7403*	*176.7462*	*180.4722*	*175.9487*	*165.9655*
North Sulawesi	3.282526	3.745269	3.662866	3.859723	4.335523
Central Sulawesi	2.605488	2.682932	3.299852	3.719089	4.762381
South Sulawesi	3.210321	3.27557	3.317063	3.607917	4.066126
Southeast Sulawesi	2.474746	2.41834	2.842123	3.306218	3.846388
Sulawesi	*61.3658*	*60.4019*	*60.04616*	*61.48975*	*71.03282*
Maluku	3.83063	3.800594	2.261194	2.32654	2.286077
Irian Jaya	6.358812	10.04522	8.480392	8.526499	7.926829
West Nusa Tenggara	2.210993	2.313157	2.776981	2.829211	2.972604
East Nusa Tenggara	1.811037	1.918091	1.589039	1.661878	1.503543
Eastern Indonesia	*67.7121*	*74.50263*	*60.97976*	*58.13815*	*54.51138*

Source: Author's calculation based on provincial and districts BPS data from various years, in 1993 constant prices.

TABLE 4.3
Rate of Theil Index

Year	Province Level		Region Level (West-Central-East)		Total Theil Index
	Within Province	Between Province	Within Region	Between Region	
1993	0.23	0.12			0.34
1994	0.25	0.10			0.35
1995	0.24	0.10			0.34
1996	0.25	0.11			0.36
1997	0.25	0.11			0.36
1998	0.27	0.14	0.381	0.024	0.40
1999	0.26	0.13	0.375	0.016	0.39
2000	0.27	0.17	0.429	0.008	0.44
2001	0.27	0.16	0.423	0.007	0.43
2002	0.26	0.15	0.406	0.006	0.41
2003	0.25	0.15	0.393	0.005	0.40
2004	0.22	0.14	0.362	0.001	0.36
2005	0.23	0.14	0.366	0.004	0.37
2006	0.21	0.13	0.339	0.001	0.34
2007	0.22	0.15	0.357	0.007	0.36
2008	0.21	0.15	0.348	0.004	0.35
2009	0.20	0.12	0.324	0.002	0.33
2010	0.20	0.12	0.316	0.001	0.32

Source: Author's calculation.

In the advanced decentralization period, the regional disparities gradually converged, although not to the same degree as before the crisis, as it had about 5 to 7 per cent convergence rate in the log variance of regional GRDP between 2001 and 2010. A different picture is seen between parts of Indonesia and Java–non-Java analysis during this period. While there is evidence of significant decline of regional disparity in each parts of Indonesia, the regional disparity remains the similar. This suggested that whilst the regional economy within parts of Indonesia converged, there is persistent regional economic gap between Java and non-Java districts.

Figure 4.7 shows the dynamics of Theil index between 1995 and 2010. It shows an increasing trend of inequality level in 2001 as a result of AFC

Districts GDP per Capita Variation of Log, Theil Index, and Gini Coefficient

	1995			1997			2001			2005			2010		
	Theil	CV	GC	Theil	CV	GC	Theil	CV	GC	Theil	CV	GC	Theil	CV	GC
Aceh	0.28	0.92	0.35	0.23	0.82	0.33	0.24	0.85	0.31	0.14	0.56	0.28	0.08	0.42	0.20
North Sumatra	0.04	0.27	0.15	0.04	0.28	0.16	0.05	0.33	0.18	0.05	0.33	0.17	0.47	1.26	0.47
West Sumatra	0.09	0.47	0.23	0.08	0.43	0.22	0.04	0.30	0.16	0.04	0.28	0.15	0.10	0.43	0.23
Riau	0.29	0.89	0.35	0.27	0.87	0.35	0.24	0.71	0.37	0.21	0.67	0.34	0.13	0.54	0.28
Jambi	0.00	0.00	0.00	0.02	0.20	0.10	0.02	0.20	0.11	0.02	0.22	0.12	0.06	0.35	0.18
South Sumatra	0.05	0.32	0.18	0.04	0.29	0.17	0.07	0.36	0.21	0.06	0.33	0.19	0.05	0.31	0.17
Bengkulu	0.06	0.33	0.16	0.04	0.30	0.16	0.05	0.33	0.17	0.07	0.38	0.21	0.07	0.37	0.20
Lampung	0.11	0.51	0.22	0.12	0.54	0.24	0.02	0.21	0.11	0.03	0.23	0.12	0.10	0.43	0.24
Jakarta	0.00	0.00	0.00	0.00	0.00	0.00	0.00	0.00	0.00	0.00	0.00	0.00	0.00	0.00	0.00
West Java	0.20	0.70	0.34	0.22	0.74	0.36	0.21	0.72	0.35	0.20	0.71	0.35	0.18	0.66	0.32
Central Java	0.21	0.73	0.35	0.19	0.71	0.32	0.18	0.66	0.32	0.18	0.69	0.32	0.17	0.66	0.31
Jogjakarta	0.11	0.50	0.23	0.12	0.53	0.25	0.09	0.47	0.22	0.09	0.45	0.21	0.08	0.44	0.21
East Java	0.56	0.51	0.47	0.63	0.56	0.49	0.63	0.56	0.48	0.56	0.51	0.47	0.47	1.41	0.44
Bali	0.10	0.49	0.22	0.10	0.48	0.22	0.06	0.38	0.19	0.06	0.36	0.18	0.06	0.35	0.18
West Nusa Tenggara	0.02	0.21	0.11	0.02	0.21	0.12	0.24	0.80	0.34	0.21	0.74	0.33	0.33	0.95	0.40
East Nusa Tenggara	0.10	0.51	0.21	0.11	0.55	0.22	0.09	0.47	0.20	0.09	0.48	0.21	0.06	0.31	0.16
West Kalimantan	0.11	0.51	0.25	0.11	0.51	0.25	0.07	0.39	0.20	0.07	0.40	0.19	0.04	0.31	0.14
Central Kalimantan	0.19	0.67	0.31	0.18	0.67	0.31	0.04	0.26	0.12	0.02	0.21	0.12	0.03	0.23	0.12
South Kalimantan	0.06	0.35	0.19	0.07	0.39	0.21	0.09	0.43	0.23	0.09	0.43	0.23	0.11	0.51	0.25
East Kalimantan	0.06	0.35	0.18	0.17	0.63	0.32	0.31	0.90	0.40	0.28	0.84	0.38	0.15	0.58	0.29
North Sulawesi	0.06	0.35	0.19	0.06	0.36	0.20	0.17	0.59	0.32	0.16	0.57	0.31	0.12	0.48	0.27
Central Sulawesi	0.05	0.32	0.17	0.05	0.30	0.17	0.05	0.30	0.16	0.05	0.30	0.16	0.02	0.18	0.10
South Sulawesi	0.05	0.33	0.16	0.05	0.33	0.15	0.06	0.38	0.19	0.07	0.41	0.21	0.09	0.45	0.23
Southeast Sulawesi	0.03	0.24	0.13	0.03	0.27	0.14	0.05	0.33	0.18	0.08	0.41	0.22	0.08	0.42	0.21
Maluku	0.10	0.46	0.24	0.10	0.48	0.25	0.09	0.41	0.23	0.08	0.41	0.23	0.07	0.40	0.21
Papua	0.87	1.65	0.63	0.83	1.70	0.60	1.00	1.93	0.64	0.78	1.67	0.58	0.28	0.85	0.40
Sumatra	0.15	0.64	0.27	0.13	0.60	0.27	0.24	0.88	0.33	0.18	0.75	0.30	0.24	0.84	0.35
Java & Bali	0.34	1.14	0.41	0.37	1.24	0.41	0.40	1.35	0.41	0.37	1.26	0.41	0.34	1.17	0.39
Kalimantan	0.18	0.65	0.33	0.30	0.93	0.40	0.45	1.34	0.45	0.41	1.23	0.43	0.29	0.93	0.39
Sulawesi	0.05	0.35	0.18	0.06	0.35	0.18	0.09	0.45	0.24	0.10	0.46	0.24	0.10	0.45	0.25
Maluku and Nusa Tenggara	0.15	0.61	0.29	0.14	0.60	0.28	0.19	0.73	0.31	0.17	0.69	0.30	0.27	0.95	0.34
Papua	0.87	0.52	0.63	0.83	0.54	0.60	1.00	0.61	0.64	0.78	0.53	0.58	0.28	0.85	0.40
West Indonesia	0.28	1.00	0.36	0.29	1.07	0.37	0.34	1.17	0.39	0.31	1.08	0.38	0.31	1.05	0.39
Central Indonesia	0.23	0.80	0.36	0.32	1.06	0.40	0.43	1.44	0.43	0.38	1.31	0.41	0.31	1.03	0.40
East Indonesia	0.84	1.81	0.59	0.79	1.81	0.56	1.01	2.14	0.62	0.81	1.85	0.57	0.36	1.01	0.45
Off Java	0.32	1.19	0.37	0.34	1.22	0.38	0.43	0.45	0.42	0.35	1.22	0.39	0.29	0.96	0.39
Java	0.37	1.21	0.42	0.40	1.30	0.42	0.43	1.40	0.43	0.40	1.31	0.42	0.36	1.21	0.40

Source: Author's calculation based on provincial and districts BPS data from various years, in 1993 constant price.

FIGURE 4.7
Theil Index of GRDP per Capita, 1995–2010

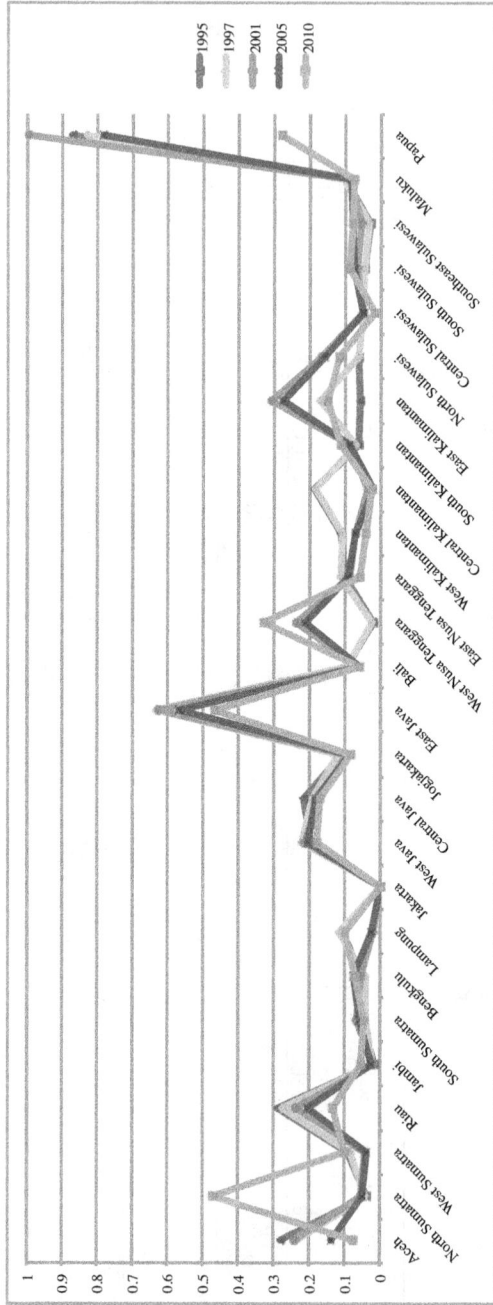

such as found in East Java, East Kalimantan, and Papua provinces. Similarly, Figure 4.8 compares the disparity level between provinces and districts in Indonesia between 1993 and 2010. The figure suggest that disparities in both administration level peaked during the Asian Financial Crisis (AFC) between 1998 and 2002. However, the disparity level among districts declined significantly in the post-decentralization period compared with the provinces.

The final graph (Figure 4.9) showed that districts in Java and Sumatra had a similar disparity level at 0.5, after decentralization between 2002 and 2010, compared with earlier years especially in Sumatra. This new trend may be due to growth in manufacturing sector in Batam and the declining of mining sector in Dumai. Furthermore, the conflict-prone Aceh province and the lack of new emerging economy centre in Sumatra also contributed to the increase of disparity in Sumatra. The increasing inequality in Java was likely due to Jakarta's economic growth and larger manufacturing activities in West Java provinces. The last bar depicts a lower disparity in Java Island by omitting Jakarta, indicating the manufacturing industries located in Jakarta had primary roles which were significant to the economy of the Island. The stable inequality rates over the period confirm that Jakarta was the main source of Javanese inequality.[7]

FIGURE 4.8
Coefficient Variation of GRDP per Capita, 1993–2010

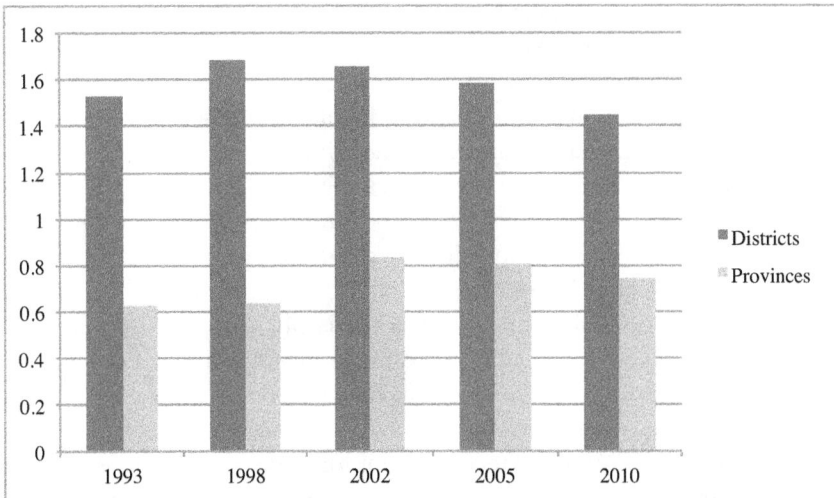

FIGURE 4.9
Coefficient Variation of GRDP per capita in Java and Sumatra, 1993–2010

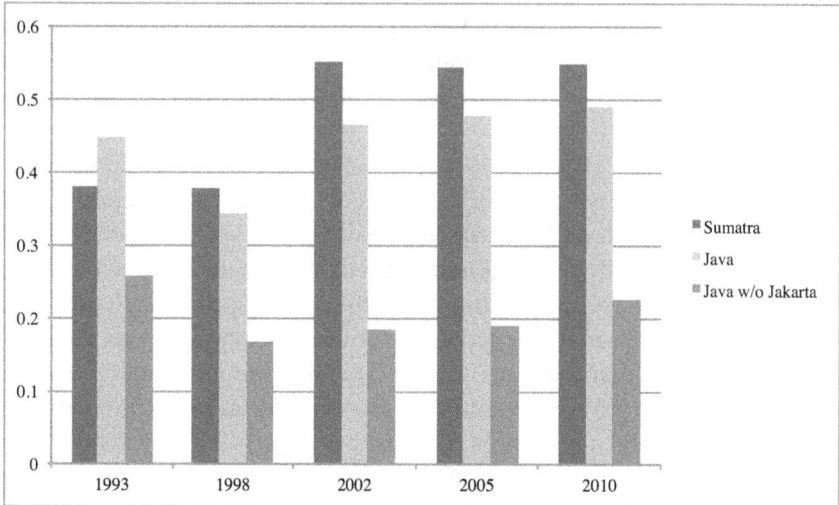

Furthermore, if we deconstructed the inequality levels to look at district-level data within provinces, a very different picture can be seen. For instance, Batam's growing export-based manufacturing and Kutai Kertanegara's oil and natural resources-based development have led Riau and East Kalimantan provinces (respectively) to be depicted as districts with rich natural resources, and subsequently, as having high economic disparities. The intra-province inequality for Riau had been in decline over the years following the decrease in oil production. On the other hand, disparities in East Kalimantan had increased, following oil and gas exploitation in a few districts. Interestingly, the new decentralization law, No. 33/2004, with which it afforded provinces a higher proportion of share revenue sharing proportions from natural resources exploitation has only had a small impact on the district-level development for the provinces. One possible explanation for this phenomenon may be that the increased revenue amounts were insignificant amount for regional development. Another explanation was that after the discreet expenditure of the natural resources revenue shares, those particular revenues were spent on salary and maintenance, and not for development expenditure.[8] On the other hand, in Java the disparities levels remained persistent and higher compared with to other islands. The comparison between Indonesian regions showed that the disparity levels for central Indonesia the former was three times compared with western Indonesia. Overall, the disparities among districts were seen as steadily increasing, after having previously reached its peak during the AFC period.

I will now discuss the inequality levels between provinces and districts. Quah's (1993, 1996) cross-section dynamics model presented the mobility of regional welfare mobility levels during one five-year transition between 2000 and 2005.[9] The first column in Table 4.5 represents the total number of transitions with normalized initial levels from the income of the provinces. The table shows the mobilization of provincial welfare according to the percentage of welfare level. For example, the second row shows that for the overall sample — across twenty-six provinces, for the period during one five-year transition between 2000 and 2005 — fifteen provinces were in level 2, with incomes between 40 per cent and 80 per cent of the Indonesian GRDP per capita average. The next columns in the same row indicated that 80 per cent of these fifteen provinces remained at the same level, while the other 20 per cent became wealthier and transitioned to state 1 and above.

The analysis showed that the economic level of the provinces was stagnant since less than 80 per cent of the provinces in states 2 and 4 stayed at the same level. Interestingly, there were more provinces in the middle-income range which had moved into different state levels than the

TABLE 4.5
Real GRDP per capita (Relative to National Average)
First order (2000 to 2005)
Grid: (0,0.4,0.8,1 and ∞)

	Upper Limit			
(Number)	*40*	*80*	*1*	*∞*
(2)	50	50	0	0
(15)	0	80	13.3	6.7
(4)	0	50	25	25
(5)	0	20	20	60

Source: Author's calculation.

number of provinces that which remained in the same state. As higher-income provinces moved to lower-income states, and low- and middle-income state provinces transitioned to higher-income states, this provides evidence of convergence process among Indonesian regions.

SPATIAL DISTRIBUTION AND CONCENTRATION OF MANUFACTURING INDUSTRY

The geographical distribution of manufacturing in Indonesia at the provincial levels indicated that the highest concentration of the manufacturing sector was in Java (see Table 4.6). Similar to the explanation for Table 4.1, it should be noted that the AFC and political unrest might have resulted in a sharp swings for the data. In 1993, the island of Java accounted for more than 80 per cent of the total shares of employment and value-added in for Indonesia's manufacturing sector. In 2010, the employment and value-added shares decreased to 73.1 per cent and 65.2 per cent, respectively. The table indicated that the domination of the island of Java in the manufacturing sector in Indonesia has declined significantly.

Table 4.6 also confirms that a significant increase in employment and value-added shares in the West Java province was due to structural changes in the manufacturing sector, and this influenced the fluctuation. From this analysis, it can be seen that although employment shares increased in the post state-restructuring period, the value-added share decreased to 33.5 per cent in 2010. The figures also suggested that the province of West Java had an increasing share of employment and value since the suburbanization of manufacturing industries since the early 1990s. The shift in the manufacturing sector showed labour moving from Jakarta to West Java, as indicated by a decrease in Jakarta's employment share from 11.7 per cent in 1993 to 6.9 per cent. This is also found in value-added shares that declined slightly, to 14.3 per cent from 20.3 per cent, in the same period.

Two other provinces with a substantial amount of manufacturing were the North Sumatra and Riau provinces. In North Sumatra, there was a decreasing trend for the study period in terms of both employment and value-added shares, from about 5.3 per cent to 3.2 per cent, and 3.6 per cent to 3.6 per cent, respectively. The Riau province provided an interesting finding, as there was evidence of a persistent increase in the value-added

TABLE 4.6

Spatial Distribution of Manufacturing (Share of Total Labour and Value Added Percentages)

Province	Share of Employment					Share of Value Added				
	1993	1997	2001	2005	2010	1993	1997	2001	2005	2010
Aceh	0.0047	0.0038	0.0023	0.0014	0.0014	0.0098	0.0068	0.0060	0.0030	0.0041
North Sumatra	0.0530	0.0419	0.0361	0.0352	0.0311	0.0362	0.0361	0.0446	0.0335	0.0331
West Sumatra	0.0047	0.0039	0.0042	0.0040	0.0034	0.0043	0.0057	0.0030	0.0070	0.0028
Riau	0.0194	0.0348	0.0373	0.0471	0.0473	0.0254	0.0503	0.0864	0.0755	0.0768
Jambi	0.0067	0.0079	0.0075	0.0056	0.0054	0.0043	0.0111	0.0172	0.0138	0.0089
South Sumatra	0.0149	0.0139	0.0099	0.0108	0.0126	0.0099	0.0120	0.0133	0.0218	0.0396
Bengkulu	0.0009	0.0005	0.0006	0.0006	0.0006	0.0002	0.0005	0.0005	0.0004	0.0003
Lampung	0.0092	0.0104	0.0135	0.0137	0.0128	0.0088	0.0087	0.0103	0.0146	0.0120
Jakarta	0.1169	0.0960	0.0908	0.0881	0.0701	0.2023	0.1642	0.1447	0.1808	0.1441
West Java	0.3469	0.3696	0.3854	0.3707	0.3851	0.2986	0.3554	0.3196	0.3255	0.3827
Central Java	0.1262	0.1311	0.1379	0.1475	0.1647	0.1051	0.0573	0.0745	0.0550	0.0651
Yogyakarta	0.0085	0.0088	0.0095	0.0106	0.0118	0.0039	0.0040	0.0030	0.0046	0.0030
East Java	0.2109	0.2041	0.1981	0.1996	0.2067	0.2204	0.2184	0.1999	0.2030	0.1651
Bali	0.0073	0.0071	0.0065	0.0059	0.0063	0.0024	0.0019	0.0040	0.0015	0.0013
West Nusa Tenggara	0.0016	0.0019	0.0015	0.0014	0.0014	0.0003	0.0005	0.0003	0.0002	0.0001
East Nusa Tenggara	0.0004	0.0006	0.0003	0.0005	0.0003	0.0002	0.0002	0.0004	0.0002	0.0001
West Kalimantan	0.0119	0.0103	0.0099	0.0114	0.0050	0.0094	0.0122	0.0098	0.0083	0.0050
Central Kalimantan	0.0046	0.0035	0.0025	0.0038	0.0044	0.0042	0.0050	0.0048	0.0024	0.0094
South Kalimantan	0.0122	0.0126	0.0119	0.0096	0.0055	0.0162	0.0123	0.0106	0.0078	0.0104
East Kalimantan	0.0158	0.0141	0.0131	0.0130	0.0071	0.0217	0.0198	0.0213	0.0236	0.0168
North Sulawesi	0.0039	0.0036	0.0037	0.0029	0.0028	0.0020	0.0015	0.0030	0.0036	0.0054
Central Sulawesi	0.0014	0.0012	0.0007	0.0008	0.0010	0.0005	0.0005	0.0004	0.0005	0.0019
South Sulawesi	0.0084	0.0087	0.0090	0.0100	0.0085	0.0058	0.0065	0.0151	0.0087	0.0075
Southeast Sulawesi	0.0007	0.0019	0.0017	0.0012	0.0010	0.0003	0.0037	0.0021	0.0012	0.0015
Maluku	0.0049	0.0047	0.0021	0.0011	0.0006	0.0042	0.0036	0.0016	0.0005	0.0001
Papua	0.0034	0.0033	0.0041	0.0034	0.0031	0.0037	0.0017	0.0038	0.0028	0.0028

Source: Author's calculation and adapted from Sjöberg and Sjöholm (2004).

shares from 2.5 per cent in 1993 to 7.6 per cent in 2010. Interestingly, the Riau province employment shares increased from 1.9 per cent to 4.7 per cent; however value-added shares increased to twice its initial levels. This confirmed the high technology and knowledge levels for the province's manufacturing sector, especially in Batam as a Free Trade Zone (FTZ) for manufacturing and export-oriented process. This might also suggest the technological advances of manufacturing industries in Batam were related to the concentrated presence of Singaporean manufacturing firms through economic and technology spillover effects.

The negative effect of conflict provinces were as expected, with declining employment and value-added shares of employment between 1993 and 2010. Employment in the Maluku province increased between 1993 and 1997 before it significantly declined to 0.1 per cent in 2010. On the value-added shares, there was evidence to indicate that Jakarta's share is in fact lower than West Java. This suggested that industrial parks are dominated by foreign manufacturing firms, while industrial zones have more domestic firms (Hudalah et al. 2013).

The intra-province concentration pattern indicated which districts were the largest districts within the provinces and as well as that district's manufacturing employment and value-added shares between 1993 and 2010 (Table 4.7). First, the largest districts reflected differences in employment and value-added shares; the situation illustrated different spatial distributions and manufacturing industries. Second, the largest districts were dynamic over time, with fifteen of twenty-six provinces having different districts named as largest in terms of manufacturing employment and/or value-added shares. Third, the manufacturing employment and/or value-added shares in the largest districts decreased in thirteen provinces. The case of West Java showed that industries had expanded and moved from the traditional provincial capital to the bordering districts. For instance, the figures showed that the highest employment and value-added shares shifted from Bandung and Serang to Bekasi, which borders Jakarta. This suggests that these industries sought to gain infrastructure and market access by locating near Jakarta, and also sought the relatively lower land leases in the suburbs.

I will now turn to examine the industrial dispersion and concentration within provinces. This research follows other studies that have used the H-index to study industrial contributions to spatial disparities, with different concentration measurements such as income, population land

TABLE 4.7
District with Largest Share of Total Manufacturing, by Province (Employment and Value Added)

	Employment						Value Added					
	1993	%	2005	%	2010	%	1993	%	2005	%	2010	%
Aceh	East Aceh	53.9	East Aceh	36.0	East Aceh	30.2	North Aceh	47.6	North Aceh	63.9	North Aceh	64.4
North Sumatra	Dairi	31.3	Deli Serdang	35.8	Deli Serdang	41.7	North Tapanuli	30.8	Medan	27.4	Asahan	27.7
West Sumatra	Padang	60.5	Padang	51.1	Padang	44.2	Padang	72.9	Padang	85.5	Padang	56.3
Riau	Batam	37.7	Batam	61.4	Batam	70.8	Batam	57.3	Batam	34.1	Batam	46.4
Jambi	Batang Hari	42.0	Batang Hari	60.0	Tanjung Jambung	51	Batang Hari	51.9	Batang Hari	85.7	Tanjung Jambung	52.7
South Sumatra	Palembang	39.4	Palembang	41.4	Palembang	28.9	Palembang	53.1	Palembang	65.8	Bangka	30.5
Bengkulu	South Bengkulu	63.3	South Bengkulu	59.4	South Bengkulu	62	South Bengkulu	42.1	South Bengkulu	45.9	South Bengkulu	70
Lampung	Central Lampung	40.2	Tanggamus	32.8	Tanggamus	37.1	Tanggamus	46.5	Tanggamus	32.8	Tanggamus	51.5
Jakarta	DKI Jakarta	100.0	DKI Jakarta	100.0	DKI Jakarta	100.0	DKI Jakarta	100.0	DKI Jakarta	100.0	DKI Jakarta	100.0
West Java	Bandung	18.6	Bekasi	30.3	Bekasi	31.3	Serang	17.2	Bekasi	29.4	Bekasi	28.4
Central Java	Semarang	14.9	Semarang	12.6	Kudus	13.1	Semarang	50.3	Semarang	25.1	Kudus	23.5
Yogyakarta	Sleman	46.4	Sleman	43.3	Sleman	43.6	Yogyakarta	43.8	Yogyakarta	58.7	Yogyakarta	39.7
East Java	Sidoarjo	19.2	Surabaya	18.0	Surabaya	14.4	Surabaya	30.1	Kediri	24.1	Kediri	19.9
Bali	Denpasar	46.5	Denpasar	34.3	Badung	29.0	Denpasar	52.1	Denpasar	33.9	Denpasar	33.9
West Nusa Tenggara	West Lombok	44.2	East Lombok	30.8	East Lombok	41.0	West Lombok	34.3	Central Lombok	32.4	Mataram	37.3
East Nusa Tenggara	Kupang	58.4	Kupang	51.4	Kupang	44.4	Kupang	77.1	Kupang	55.1	Kupang	59.8
West Kalimantan	Pontianak	65.7	Sambas	53.4	Sintang	36.2	Pontianak	65.3	Sambas	46.9	Pontianak	37.1
Central Kalimantan	East Kotawaringin	48.7	West Kotawaringin	50.7	West Kotawaringin	42.2	West Kotawaringin	52.6	West Kotawaringin	73.2	East Kotawaringin	51.1
South Kalimantan	Barito Kuala	41.8	Banjarmasin	42.2	Kotabaru	43.7	Barito Kuala	48.1	Kotabaru	35.7	Kotabaru	70.3
East Kalimantan	Samarinda	61.6	Samarinda	39.4	Samarinda	28.5	Samarinda	44.5	Kutai	64.5	Kutai	50.05
North Sulawesi	Bitung	49.2	Minahasa	58.2	Manado	48	Bitung	54.5	Minahasa	87.5	Manado	74
Central Sulawesi	Donggala	49.5	Palu	50.5	Palu	59.4	Donggala	54.4	Banggai	46.8	Toli-Toli	29.7
South Sulawesi	Ujung Pandang	48.0	Ujung Pandang	44.4	Ujung Pandang	48.7	Ujung Pandang	33.1	Pangkajene	38.0	Pangkajene Islands	41.0
Southeast Sulawesi	Kendari	53.7	Kendari	38.8	Kendari	34.1	Kendari	51.0	Kolaka	81.1	Kolaka	92.2
Maluku	North Maluku	51.1	Ambon	52.9	North Maluku	54	North Maluku	58.5	Ambon	64.8	North Maluku	37.7
Papua	Sorong	40.4	Sorong	28.8	Merauke	43	Sorong	47.3	Merauke	37.2	Merauke	70.6

Source: Author's calculation and adapted from Sjöberg and Sjöholm (2004).

use, worker productivity and value-added rates (Fan and Scott 2003; Sjöberg and Sjöholm 2004).

The Herfindahl index for the total manufacturing sector at the provincial and district levels is compared in Table 4.8. The table shows a constant increase of manufacturing concentrations at the districts level. For example, the employment data revealed that the Herfindahl index value was 0.059 in 1993 and increased to 0.062 in 2010. The figure for value-added data reveals similar results: although the figure increased before the financial crisis, it returned to its initial value in 2010. These results indicated increased regional manufacturing growth divergence at the district level.

The provincial Herfindahl index for the three periods suggests that after trade liberalization and decentralization, manufacturing concentration remained high in a few districts (Table 4.9). A high concentration of manufacturing industries was located in provinces with small number of manufacturing firms, while a contrasting result was that manufacturing industries are more dispersed in the industrial provinces.[10] For example, there were lower concentration rates for manufacturing industries in notable industry industrial provinces such as East Java, Central Java, West Java and Riau.

The analysis also revealed an interesting finding: although some provinces showed signs of industrial dispersal, concentration rates increased for several other provinces. The main manufacturing provinces in Java Island had increasing concentration rates during the period under study, except for the East Java province. In the duration of the study, employment concentration for East Java province decreased slightly, while the value-added concentration peaked before the financial crisis; and it

TABLE 4.8
Concentration of Manufacturing — National Level (Herfindahl Index)

Administration Level	Employment		Value Added	
	Province	District	Province	District
1993	0.009	0.059	0.068	0.151
1997	0.008	0.051	0.050	0.137
2001	0.008	0.049	0.052	0.122
2005	0.009	0.056	0.049	0.124
2010	0.009	0.062	0.048	0.154

Source: Author's calculation.

TABLE 4.9
Concentration of Manufacturing — Provincial Level (Herfindahl Index)

Province	Employment					Value Added				
	1993	1997	2001	2005	2010	1993	1997	2001	2005	2010
Aceh	0.056	0.052	0.074	0.106	0.082	0.186	0.175	0.199	0.417	0.403
North Sumatra	0.006	0.005	0.006	0.005	0.005	0.022	0.019	0.041	0.027	0.032
West Sumatra	0.042	0.041	0.037	0.038	0.038	0.090	0.508	0.094	0.194	0.070
Riau	0.021	0.012	0.011	0.012	0.048	0.074	0.037	0.069	0.047	0.080
Jambi	0.053	0.050	0.061	0.090	0.048	0.073	0.283	0.202	0.209	0.062
South Sumatra	0.027	0.028	0.017	0.023	0.027	0.115	0.156	0.169	0.141	0.072
Bengkulu	0.276	0.060	0.236	0.238	0.135	0.170	0.181	0.150	0.158	0.254
Lampung	0.035	0.068	0.058	0.052	0.041	0.058	0.079	0.088	0.099	0.083
Jakarta	0.002	0.002	0.003	0.004	0.006	0.038	0.038	0.050	0.079	0.099
West Java	0.001	0.002	0.002	0.002	0.002	0.015	0.008	0.004	0.005	0.023
Central Java	0.004	0.003	0.004	0.008	0.003	0.177	0.015	0.011	0.012	0.009
Yogyakarta	0.020	0.016	0.014	0.013	0.014	0.085	0.167	0.091	0.271	0.066
East Java	0.008	0.005	0.005	0.005	0.005	0.067	0.074	0.079	0.070	0.046
Bali	0.011	0.006	0.010	0.013	0.017	0.018	0.013	0.161	0.047	0.024
West Nusa Tenggara	0.020	0.012	0.014	0.013	0.011	0.078	0.215	0.165	0.077	0.038
East Nusa Tenggara	0.057	0.044	0.063	0.042	0.057	0.390	0.349	0.759	0.073	0.101
West Kalimantan	0.034	0.038	0.041	0.042	0.081	0.041	0.068	0.125	0.042	0.055
Central Kalimantan	0.038	0.039	0.053	0.079	0.082	0.122	0.271	0.320	0.109	0.076
South Kalimantan	0.026	0.035	0.036	0.035	0.053	0.055	0.070	0.054	0.060	0.102
East Kalimantan	0.029	0.030	0.028	0.029	0.040	0.127	0.089	0.171	0.153	0.199
North Sulawesi	0.049	0.031	0.045	0.024	0.043	0.098	0.049	0.088	0.263	0.407
Central Sulawesi	0.036	0.028	0.052	0.052	0.024	0.037	0.072	0.147	0.152	0.230
South Sulawesi	0.025	0.014	0.025	0.022	0.028	0.122	0.062	0.176	0.091	0.126
Southeast Sulawesi	0.042	0.133	0.073	0.087	0.074	0.052	0.737	0.727	0.658	0.825
Maluku	0.166	0.149	0.198	0.171	0.105	0.206	0.131	0.232	0.190	0.101
Papua	0.126	0.117	0.083	0.101	0.072	0.187	0.278	0.216	0.132	0.242

Source: Author's calculation and adapted from Sjöberg and Sjöholm (2004).

then decreased slightly in 2010. Meanwhile, West Java province shows an increasing trend for both employment and value-added rates confirmed that they had increasing concentrations for the post-decentralization period. The province showed increased value-added concentration rates by sixfolds between 2001 and 2010. The concentrations of firms were mainly found in Bogor, Tangerang, and Bekasi in the West Java provinces and in Semarang, Kudus, and Surakarta in the Central Java province. However, in contrast, there was a decline in both employment and value-added concentrations in the province with a stable concentration in Surabaya, Gresik, Sidoarjo, Mojokerto and Pasuruan districts. This suggested a stagnant manufacturing industry growth in East Java compared to West Java.

The Sumatran provinces showed contrasting concentration developments, with an increase in the employment concentration rate and a decrease in the value-added concentration rate. An exception is Riau province where its employment concentration increased threefolds and the value-added concentration rate increased by almost 16 per cent after decentralization. However, it should be noted that slightly after decentralization, the value-added level declined before increasing again after 2005. This decline in Riau's concentration rates suggested increasing employment concentration, even as there was a dispersal of technical capabilities across firms in the province, which led to the decline of value-added concentration (Kuncoro 2002). This trend was uniquely found in the Riau province following the relatively advanced manufacturing sector in Batam where it was dominated by export-oriented industries and the large share of foreign-related manufacturing plants. Furthermore, the proximity to Singapore enhanced knowledge and technical spillovers that might have induced higher manufacturing value-added rates as argued by Kuncoro (2002).

This finding suggested that foreign firms tended to be concentrated in terms of production and networks. The presence of FDI bolstered the productivity of domestic firms through inter-firm worker mobility. Furthermore, it was common for foreign firms to be concentrated in areas such as the Jababeka industrial park in West Java, which once hosted 1,500 multinational companies from 30 countries, and Batamindo in Batam, which hosted more than 100 companies from more than two countries. There were several incentives to locate in Jababeka, which included the proximity to Jakarta as a market and high infrastructure quality. On the other hand, Batam, which was supported by its status as an FTZ, provided infrastructure and unique policies, such as tax holidays and the elimination of export levies.

Another factor that determined manufacturing industry growth was the region's availability and policies on land supply. Jakarta's land availability for the manufacturing sector had declined sharply from 2,050 hectares to 300 hectares between 1990 and 2010, while a contrary picture was illustrated in West Java where there was an increase from 50 hectares to 8,000 hectares in for the same period.[11] In Batam, for instance, foreign investors are allowed to establish 100 per cent foreign ownership, long leases of up to eighty years and investment licence for thirty years.[12]

REGIONAL ECONOMY DYNAMICS IN THE AFTA AND DECENTRALIZATION PERIOD

The above discussions have elaborated and explored the geographical and sectoral distribution of the Indonesian economy. Indonesia's economic distribution remained highly unequal with concentrations in only a few districts and provinces. This chapter examined uneven development and economic locations that may have been the cause for persistent continual regional disparities. This chapter gave evidence of regional disparities which persisted during the period under observation.

This study has showed that economic development is sensitive to political and institutional changes. The analysis shows a growing district economic disparity during the AFTA and pre-decentralization period. This period bore witness to the deregulation of manufacturing policies and as well as the initial attempts for decentralization having led to economic boom and increasing disparity at both provincial and district levels. The analysis indicated that there were patterns of increasing regional disparities during the height of economic growth between 1993 and 1997. The disparity peaked during the transition years of the AFC as economic development contracted in a significant manner. The contraction can be seen geographically with the decline of the economic sector within districts.

However, an analysis of the decentralization period suggested an unexpected finding; there was an increased regional disparity in the following decade since its implementation. The first five years showed that persistent regional disparity could not be referred to as the immediate impact of decentralization; rather, regions were still recovering from the AFC. The analysis after the mid-2000s until 2010 depicted a declining disparity, which suggested a catching-up period with regards to wealth by the poorer regions. This implicated a stable national economy that has accelerated the role of decentralization and trade liberalization on regional economic growth. For instance, the cross-section analysis by geographic region indicated that at the provincial level, there was a mobilization of economic welfare, with lower-income regions transferring to higher-income states and vice versa; this depicted the convergence process. Consequently, this confirmed that manufacturing regions, such as Riau, West Java and East Java provinces, had higher economic growth than rich natural resource provinces, such as Papua and East Kalimantan. This confirmed the importance of the local government's ability to accelerate endogenous industries, which would have significantly determined regional competitive capacities and development; this has also been argued elsewhere (Lucas 1986; Romer 1988, 1994; Barca, McCann and Rodríguez-Pose 2011).

Thus, it is important to study the dynamics and determinants of economic disparity, not only in the post-decentralization period, but also in the period leading up to decentralization, so as to capture the role of the political economy and institutions of the particular period. In the following chapter I will examine the determinants of regional economic growth at the district level. I will examine both the decentralization attempts during the New Order regime as well as the implementation of decentralization. The analysis will highlight the impact of decentralization and AFTA on regional disparity. Specifically, I will also examine the role of the local government in the provision of public goods and services, as well as the districts' trade performance.

Notes

1. Available at <www.bps.go.id>.
2. The Special Region of Capital Jakarta is province with five non-autonomous districts.
3. The base year 2000 is used for the statistics data between 1993 and 2010.
4. The equations and detailed information on these indices are presented in Appendix A.
5. The Lorenz curve consisted of two lines, the diagonal line represents perfect balance of development, and the curve line represents the level of development. The area between diagonal and curve lines refers to the level of inequality. The further the Lorenz curve is from the diagonal line, the higher the disparity level is between those districts.

6. The hold harmless policy states that the intergovernmental transfer revenues (IGT) for districts and provinces should not be lower than the previous year's amount. This regulation was in effect between 2002 and 2008. (Law 33/2004).

7. This study continues and confirms the finding of similar studies (Hill, Resosudarmo and Vidyattama 2008; Akita, Kurniawan and Miyata 2011; Vidyattama 2013).

8. For instance, the paper by Lewis (2013) revealed that an additional Rp1 of natural resources revenue only led to an increase of Rp0.02 of districts expenditure, compared to an additional Rp1 special allocation fund (DAK) which led to Rp1.02 of district expenditure. This indicates low development benefits despite having higher share revenue funds.

9. The years of analysis are from 2000 through 2005 using provincial GRDP per capita and the national average. The results of the estimations are reflected in the graph, in which the GRDP per capita is compared with the annual averages of Indonesian regions (standardized to 100).

10. Balisacan and Fuwa (2004) acknowledged this result may be biased by the number of districts within a province, affecting the measured rate of concentration; provinces with a small number of districts tended to score higher in concentration levels.

11. For a reading on manufacturing industry development in Jakarta and West Java, see Hudalah et al. 2013.

12. Investment guide in Batam, BIFZA website <http://www.bpbatam.go.id>.

5

DECENTRALIZATION AND THE ASEAN FTA IMPACT ON REGIONAL ECONOMIC CONVERGENCE

There are limited studies on developing countries that question the impact of devolution and trade liberalization on regional economic growth (Logan 2008; Rivas 2007; Rodríguez-Pose and Sanchez-Reaza 2005). This study thus aims to complement existing literature by analysing the economic impact of devolution and trade liberalization during the state-restructuring period in Indonesia between 1993 and 2010. The effects of devolution, ASEAN FTA variables, and selected control variables on the growth of district GRDP are observed using econometric analysis. The research finds that there is evidence of regional convergence throughout the periods under observation, but while devolution has significantly increased economic divergence, the ASEAN FTA appears to have an insignificant impact on Indonesia regional economic growth.

This chapter is divided into five sections. The next section discusses the econometrics model and data construction. The third analyses the ordinary least square (OLS) and panel regressions for four periods: the pre-decentralization period (1993–97), transition period (1998–2001), early decentralization period (2001–05), and advanced decentralization period

(2005–10). The final section presents discussion and debates on regional disparities in Indonesia.

STUDIES ON INDONESIAN REGIONAL ECONOMIC CONVERGENCE

Decentralization proponent literature emphasizes that decentralization promote efficiency on decision-making and planning (Calamai 2009). For instance, Tiebout (1956) argues decentralization brought citizen participation into planning and decision-making through the ability of people to move between regions to choose the public service and taxes that suit them. Thus, decentralization introduces market-like solution to local public goods problems and the provision of public goods and services through the preferences of individual by market mechanism. As a result, efficiency of public goods is achieved as there is a large variety of local institutions, not merely the central government (Rondinelli 1989, p. 59).

Many studies of convergence determinants seem to point to similar findings (Akita and Alisjahbana 2002; McCulloch and Syahrir 2008; Resosudarmo and Vidyattama 2006; Vidyattama 2013). First, the Asian Financial Crisis (AFC) was found to contract economic growth and to cause persistent economic disparities. The divergence of regional development continues after the fall of the New Order regime in 1998 to the early period of the AFC as poorer regions were badly affected and hindered in its development growth.

Second, the unconditional convergence model studies (Garcia and Soelistianingsih 1998; Akita and Alisjahbana 2002; Akita, Kurniawan and Miyata 2011) show the presence of convergence. While the effect of AFTA is debatable as insignificant on the district's economic growth, despite the evidence of economic convergence (Aritenang 2011; Aritenang forthcoming). While using the computable general equilibrium (CGE), Feridhanusetyawan and Pangestu (2003) found a small effect of AFTA on economic growth. Furthermore, the convergence of regional development occurs as lagging regions are catching up to the advanced regions, particularly after the mid-2000s, with the exception the Java Island where the districts' economic growths are diverging in this period. The major districts in Java such as Jakarta, Bandung, and Surabaya have become primate cities that hinder smaller districts from gaining economic growth in decentralization (McCulloch and Syahrir 2008; Hill, Resosudarmo and Vidyattama 2008; Aritenang, 2012; Vidyattama, 2013).

However, it should be noted that differences on local endowments, government policy, spatial plan, political decisions and fiscal expenditure and consequently local economic growth occurs between districts. As a result, studies with spatial unit at the provincial level (Akita and Lukman, 1995; Akita and Alisjahbana, 2002; Garcia and Soelistianingsih, 1998, McCulloch and Syahrir, 2008; McCulloch and Malesky, 2011, Hill, Resosudarmo and Vidyattama 2008, Vidyattama 2013) have different research findings and policy implications with this book.

In the following econometrics analysis, the fiscal decentralization is approximated using the amount of its own source revenue and intergovernmental transfers. The institutional and political boundaries are represented using dummy variables on Java and non-Java districts, municipalities or regencies, and the head of region's political party.[1] Others studies have attempted to provide alternative explanatory variables such as manufacturing TFP (Aritenang 2013) and governance (McCulloch and Malesky 2011).

THE STATE RESTRUCTURING IMPACT: ECONOMETRICS MODEL AND DATA CONSTRUCTION

Traditional convergence analysis uses spatial dependence effect with the GDP per capita growth rate in each districts as the most common variables to measure economic growth, as indicated in non-spatial (Barro 2000; Fan and Casetti 1994; Sánchez-Reaza and Rodríguez-Pose 2002; Rivas 2007; Fujita and Hu 2001; Garcia and Soelistianingsih 1998; Resosudarmo and Vidyattama 2006) and spatial literature (Arbia and Piras 2005; Rey and Montouri 1999; Rey 1991).[2]

The next econometrics model is the panel (data) analysis that collects data from repeated observations over the same unit (district) over a period of time. The availability of two-dimensional (cross sectional/times series) panel data from repeated observations allows the specification and estimation of complex and more realistic models than a single cross-section of time series data (Verbeek 2008). The panel data offers an opportunity to address unobserved heterogeneity related to economic growth in individual districts. Panel data eliminates variable bias when the omitted variables are constant over time within a given state. However, when the observations are repeated for each individual region, the data may suffer from missing values and heterogeneity.

The general formulation of a panel data model is expressed by the following equation:

$$y_{it} = \alpha_i + X'_{it} \beta + \upsilon_{it} + \varepsilon_{it} \tag{1}$$

With i ($i = 1,...,n$) representing individual districts and t ($t = 1,...,t$) representing time periods. The X'_{it} is the observation of explanatory variables in district i and at time t. The α_i is time invariant and denotes district-specific effects that are included in the equation. The error term is a composite error, $\varepsilon_{it} = \alpha_i + \upsilon_{it}$, combining individual heterogeneity (α_i) and an idiosyncratic error term (υ_{it}) that is independent across all observations.

The α_i interpretation can be approached by two different types of panel data estimations: (1) fixed-effect, and (2) random-effect estimation. If the α_i is assumed to be a fixed parameter estimate, the equation's estimate is termed as a fixed-effect panel data model. The fixed-effect model is used to capture all unobserved time-invariant district factors such as geographic areas, institutions, interregional heterogeneity and cultures (Suwanan and Sulistiani 2009). This model eliminates endogeneity problems and demonstrates unobserved characteristics of a district. However, if the α_i is assumed to be random in its error, ε_{it}, the estimation is then termed as a random-effect panel data model. The fixed-effect model is used in a regression analysis that is limited to precise individuals, districts, or firms, whereas a random-effect model is used if we are interested in drawing certain individuals randomly from a large population of reference (Arbia and Piras 2005). After a Hausman test, the fixed-effect model is suggested for this analysis.

The use of panel data and a fixed-effect model in a convergence study has been common since Islam (2003). Convergence rate using panel data that uses fixed-effects tends to have larger coefficient estimation than a cross-sectional model, with estimates of 2 per cent per year (Barro and Sala-i-Martin 1991).

The model that I estimated is expressed in the following equation:

$$\ln\left(\frac{y_{it} - y_{it-1}}{y_{it-1}}\right) = \alpha_i + \beta \ln y_{it} + \varepsilon_{it} \tag{2}$$

Where the dependent variable is the annual growth rate per capita GDP, the regressor is the (log) GDP per capita for region I, at time t, and α_i represents a parameter to be estimated in the panel model.

Raw statistics data were collected from various government and international institutions — the central bureau of statistics (Badan Pusat Statistik or BPS), Ministry of Finance (MoF), Ministry of Trade, and the ASEAN Secretariat. The BPS data include gross domestic and national products (GRDP and GNP), population, plant-level data, revenue from oil and gas. The BPS data also provide the data on input and output costs, productivity, and labour from Indonesian large and medium manufacturing industries. The MoF website provides data on regional budgets, local revenue, block grant (dana alokasi umum or DAU), as well as routine and development expenditures. The tariff trade data were obtained from the Ministry of Trade for the MFN tariff, and from the ASEAN Secretary for the AFTA-CEPT tariff. Finally, geographical map data were purchased from a private mapping firm.

To construct regional variables, this research uses the BPS publication of regional list in 1997[3] that includes regions before the decentralization in 1998, and time-series data to provide the analysis of impact trade to regions between 1993 and 2005. The 1997 regional list consisted of 26 provinces (after the separation of East Timor in 1999) and 292 districts,[4] made up of 232 regencies and 60 municipalities, with 4,088 overall observations for the period between 1993 and 2010. After decentralization, there was a significant regional splitting into 542 districts with 98 municipalities and 410 regencies in 34 provinces (Booth 20011; Fitrani, Hofman and Kaiser 2005).[5] All data are available for these districts in the observation period, except for the regional budget data, which are available only from 1994.

Since the Indonesian statistical bureau only publishes data at the provincial level and does not publish annual GDP and population data at the district level, the data have to be exclusively ordered and purchased from the BPS. The dependent variables are the GDP and population data. The constant data base year is the year 2000 for the whole analysis.

Fiscal Decentralization Impact Measurement

The research uses data of government budgets — consisting of local budget and expenditure (APBD), local revenue, and intergovernmental grants — from the Ministry of Finance website.[6] Note that the data had to be modified due to some technical problems such as duplications of codes and aggregates of districts before decentralization.

There are two fiscal decentralization measurements: district fiscal dependency and financial capacity (Darise 2009). The district fiscal dependency is calculated as the annual percentage change of DAU transfer amount from the central government. As DAU transfer amount is based on the formulation of development indicators, a decline in the annual percentage of DAU transfer amount indicates a decline in the transfer fund and improvement in economic performance. The local financial capacity refers to the region's own source revenue (OSR). The OSR represents two local capacities — the level of local economy and local revenue institutions.

Export Import Measurement

The value of export and import of the manufacturing sector in a district is used to approximate a district's integration and openness into ASEAN FTA, as it reflects changes in trade restrictions such as tariff quotes, licensing, non-tariff barriers, and labour dynamics. Rivas (2007) has argued that this variable also represents non-trade policy influences including transport cost, production, and global trade levels. Due to its diverse array of influencing factors, this variable should be used carefully as an alternative variable to approximate ASEAN FTA. This alternative openness variable is constructed as the sum of exports and imports divided by GDP within a year (Rivas 2007). The export and import data are based on firm-level data for municipalities with plants, and on national trade liberalization for municipalities without plants. This variable has a negative correlation value with the tariff impact variable because both variables show opposite behaviours to economic growth. Regional economic growth increases following lower tariff and higher trade activities.

Tariff Impact Measurements

The tariff variable measures direct impact of a trade liberalization by calculating AFTA CEPT tariff reduction. This analysis assumes that the increase in imports due to the lower trade barrier in AFTA CEPT tariff increases trade activities and manufacturing productivity, which eventually will affect the regions where the manufacturers are located. However, focusing only on the tariff as the sole variable neglects other trade restrictions and non-trade policies that determine the level of openness. This gap is thus addressed by the export-import measurement above.

The AFTA CEPT tariff data, collected from the ASEAN Secretariat, are used to analyse the impact of tariff on local economic development.[7] By combining the tariff data and the proportion of industries within a region, we obtain the approximate profits of the region from the AFTA tariff within a particular industry. The measurement is obtained using three statistics data on the shares of a district's manufacturing plants, specifically of industry output, industry productivity, and export value of the district.

Following Amiti and Cameron (2004), and Amiti and Konings (2007), this research requested the BPS to make data on each industry available, including intermediate inputs and the amount on each in rupiah from its SI questionnaire.[8] Note, however, that this information is not routinely prepared, and thus this research uses the data from 1998 and 2002. For all other years, the SI data provide total expenditure on domestic and imported inputs, but not by any individual type of input. The 1998 and 2002 data are available for five-digit industries, and are used to create a 228 manufacturing input/output table. The mix of inputs by industries is assumed to be fixed over time.[9]

In trade liberalization, there are output and input tariffs, where the output tariff measures the import value of a product, and the input tariff measures the import value of raw materials of manufacturing industries within a district.[10] Following Amiti and Konings (2007), the input tariff calculation uses the MFN tariff. The available dataset is an unbalanced panel of around 21,000 firms per year with a total of 274,061 observations.

Regional Control Variables

Following McCulloch and Syahrir (2008), the share of people in urban areas is used to observe the effect of agglomeration in regional control variables. In measuring the impact of human capital, this study defines its stock for human capital in economic activities as the share of people who have at least attained a junior high school level of education. Infrastructure data is approximated using infrastructure data availability such as water debit, road length, and road ratio (Rivas 2007). This research uses the road access variable because it serves as a proxy for the spatial connectivity and access for economic activities in a district. The road access variable may also be perceived as a factor for industry location (Balisacan and Fuwa 2004).

Lobbying Capacity Variable

Following Rodríguez-Pose and Gill (2005) and Rodríguez-Pose, Tijmstra and Bwire (2009), a lobbying capacity variable is constructed as an interaction between the sums of an earmarked fund that a district receives with a dummy that represent the district's level of revenue. A district is considered rich if it has an above-average GRDP value, with its dummy value accorded as 1; if it is a poor district, its dummy value is accorded as 0. For example, the state ministry of forestry provides an earmarked budget for districts dedicated to local forests management and development. Thus, this variable demonstrates the influence of a district's fiscal resources and political power on lobbying the central government to earn additional development budget.

Industrial Control Variables

ASEAN FTA tariffs target manufacturing industries, but contrary to other Indonesian regional studies (McCulloch and Sjahrir 2008; McCulloch and Malesky 2011), this research does not include the presences of natural resources (oil, gas, and minerals). Instead, it uses the share of manufacturing activities in the GRDP. Since the labour productivity variable is measured by the ratio of labour per output, this variable is expected to have a negative association with the economic growth. The higher ratio of the number of labour to produce one unit output implies inefficiency of factor of production and thus, lower economic growth.

Total Factor Productivity (TFP) Variable

The TFP is an important measure to examine the technology level. The Indonesian manufacturing TFP, from varying periods, has been widely studied (Aritenang 2013; Amiti and Konings 2007; Prihawantoro, Hutapea and Suryawijaya 2012; Topalova and Khandelwal 2011). These studies show that higher manufacturing TFP contributes significantly on regional development. Studies in the topic show that the TFP growth and level have significant effects on the role of manufacturing with high technology contents such as metal and machinery materials.[11] The level of technological availability is approximated by TFP, an approach widely used to estimate the role industry technological level on economic growth such as in India and Indonesia (Amiti and Konings 2007; Topalova and Khandelwal 2011).

To construct the firm-level TFP, the approach by Levinsohn and Petrin (2003) deploys manufacturing data on capital, investment, labour, and energy. The construction of this follows a Cobb-Douglas production function which requires the data on physical quantities of output, capital and intermediate inputs. In the absence of firm-specific price deflators, industry-specific deflators are used. Thus, the TFP measure captures both technical efficiency and price-cost mark-ups (Topalova and Khandelwal 2011). The TFP is constructed by subtracting firm's i predicted output from its actual output at time t.[12] Following the endogenous growth model, a positive sign of the industry TFP implies that a regional industries' technology level is associated with a higher economic growth (Romer 1986, 1990, 1994).

Dummy Variable of Bordering Regions

To capture the spatial effect of location proximity, this research constructed a dummy variable of bordering regions. Literature suggests that with their proximity to markets, these regions have location advantage to seize trade liberalization (Logan 2008; Sanchez-Reaza and Rodríguez-Pose 2002). To capture the effects of spatial locations, I use dummy variables for international borders. The bordering districts are listed as prioritized regions based on Undang-undang No. 43/2008 and Government Regulation (Peraturan Pemerintah) No. 26/2008. The research aggregates the regions to the number before decentralization with a total of twenty-five bordering districts. The dummy variable has a value of zero if it is a bordering region, and a value of one if otherwise. The trade spatial effect variable is constructed as an interaction between bordering districts and import tariff.

Indices Variable Construction and Pattern

To observe the impact of decentralization and AFTA, I have constructed indices.[13] The decentralization index variable is constructed as the combination of district fiscal dependency and financial capacity. Both fiscal decentralization measurements have been discussed in the fiscal decentralization impact variables in Chapter 2. A positive sign of this variable shows that decentralization accelerates regional convergence. Meanwhile, the ASEAN FTA index is a combination of ASEAN CEPT output and input tariff with trade integration. The output tariff measures the import value of a product and the input tariff measures the import value of raw material of manufacturing industry within a districts.

Descriptive Statistics

Descriptive statistics of variables used in economic growth regression are displayed in Table 5.1. The explanatory variables are grouped into four types of variables. First, the local endowment variables that includes shares of people in school, of people in urban areas, and of roads that are accessible by four-wheeled vehicles. Second, the economic structure group that includes the share of non-natural resources industries, the size of manufacturing activities, and the district type (either a municipality or regency). The decentralization is approximated by variables that shift significantly during the period such as a ratio of local revenue and GRDP, and the amount of central government transfer funds. The ASEAN FTA variables include CEPT tariff reduction and bordering regions, with regions in the border tend to benefit more from the free trade agreements.

TABLE 5.1
Statistics of Variables in Economic Growth

	Mean	SD	Min	Max
GRDP growth annual	0.1	0.28	−2.80	2.27
GRDP pc Initial	1.1	0.88	−1.64	4.41
Decentralization Index	0	0.08	−0.17	2.02
AFTA Index	0	1	−4.59	2.63
Urban Population	0.37	0.42	0	1
Share pop in junior school	0.06	0.07	0	0.86
Road Access	0.91	0.14	0.04	1
Share of Manufacturing	0.15	0.15	0	0.84
Tariff*border	−0.15	0.53	−2.65	0
Lobby	25.7	5.8	15.53	40.91
Labour	7.89	2.04	3	13.3
Technology	7.97	1.14	1.63	15.35

Source: Author's analysis using data from BPS, MoF, and ASEAN Secretariat.

EMPIRICAL ANALYSIS AND FINDINGS

The regression analysis includes three regressions: OLS regression, cross-section spatial analysis, and fixed-effect panel regression analysis. To provide an integrated and comparable analysis, I present the exact same variables and models for these three regressions through a technical econometrics manipulation, performed by following a spatial analysis that requires a balanced panel data. The missing data is replaced with the mean value of the variable in its respective period.

The β Convergence Analysis on State-restructuring Impact

This subsection conducts β convergence analysis, which demonstrates that the faster the poor regions grow relative to the rich regions, the sooner they catch up, thus resulting in a faster convergence. Neoclassical economic theories argue that economic growth convergence with low initial economic regional levels will have higher economic growth rate, and will eventually catch up with rich regions. However, an analysis by Barro and Sala-i-Martin (1991) reveals that convergence is conditional, as the growth rate of an economy does not depend on initial levels, but on local endowments and economic structure.

Absolute β Convergence Analysis. The absolute β Convergence is measured with regression analysis, and then calculated to determine whether what takes place is an absolute convergence (where poorer regions grow faster than rich regions) or a conditional convergence (where poorer regions grow faster than rich regions if other variables are taken into account beside initial income level).

Table 5.2 (column 1) shows that the evolution of absolute convergence between periods with regressions has a very low R^2 variant between 0.001 per cent and 0.281 per cent. The speed of convergence rate has increased from 2.5 per cent in the pre-decentralization period compared to the decentralization period at 27.2 per cent, despite this rate decline in the advance decentralization period after 2005. This shows the early decentralization period demonstrated the highest convergence rate as the decline in the national economic growth had reduced the district disparities level.

TABLE 5.2
Absolute and Conditional Regression

	1993–97			1998–2001			2001–05			2005–10		
	I	II	III	I	II	III	I	II	III	I	II	III
GRDP pc Initial	-0.025**	-0.029**	-0.017	-0.024	-0.01	-0.061*	-0.272**	-0.195**	-0.258**	-0.028**	-0.008	-0.019*
	-0.01	-0.01	-0.01	-0.03	-0.01	-0.03	-0.01	-0.01	-0.02	-0.01	-0.01	-0.01
Decentralization		0.095	0.449		-8.695**	-9.223**		-2.980**	-7.106**		-0.008	-0.135
		-0.5	-0.7		-0.14	-0.2		-0.31	-0.46		-0.12	-0.19
AFTA		-0.007	0.013		0.033**	-0.023		-0.116**	-0.143**		0.006	0.0001
		-0.01	-0.01		-0.01	-0.02		-0.01	-0.02		0.0001	-0.01
Urban Population			-0.018			0.028			0.117**			0.01
			-0.01			-0.03			-0.03			-0.01
Share pop in junior school			0.514**			0.389			-0.662+			-0.198
			-0.07			-0.32			-0.38			-0.15
Road Access			-0.102*			-0.029			-0.526**			-0.008
			-0.05			-0.1			-0.09			-0.03
Share of Manufacturing			0.011			0.118			0.569**			-0.043
			-0.05			-0.1			-0.1			-0.04
Tariff*border			0.061**			-0.032			0.052*			0.004
			-0.02			-0.05			-0.03			-0.01
Lobby			0.003			0.050**			0.103**			0.002
			-0.01			-0.01			-0.01			0
Labour			-0.013**			0.020*			0.014			0.003
			0.0001			-0.01			-0.01			0
Technology			0.003			0.013			0.056**			0.005
			-0.01			-0.02			-0.01			0
Constant	0.042**	0.040**	0.087	0.347**	0.184**	-1.312**	0.558**	0.329**	-2.316**	0.091**	0.051**	-0.033
	0	-0.01	-0.17	-0.02	-0.01	-0.27	-0.02	-0.03	-0.28	-0.01	-0.01	-0.13
No. Obs	1.354	989	339	870	585	324	1.751	1.256	556	1.752	404	370
R2	0.013	0.018	0.248	0.001	0.87	0.887	0.281	0.396	0.757	0.011	0.008	0.036

Notes: Significance at * $p < 0.05$; ** $p < 0.01$; *** $p < 0.001$, $N = 338$, $T = 13$; *t*-values in parenthesis.
Growth rates for 1993–2000 and 1993–2010 are based on constant 1993 prices; growth rate for 2001–05 is based on constant 2000 prices.
Source: Author's analysis using data from BPS, MoF, and ASEAN Secretariat.

Figure 5.1 illustrates the log annual change of real GDP per capita (1993–2010) with the log of initial GDP per capita (1993). The speed of convergence is about 1.3 per cent per annum, which is slower compared to Barro and Sala-I-Martin (1991).[14] Figure 5.2 shows a wide range of growth district rates for two periods: before the financial crisis, and after decentralization. The central line on each axis indicates mean growth rate, whilst the lines on the other part of the axis shows one standard deviation above and below the mean.

Conditional β Convergence Analysis. Using three econometric models, this research provides an extensive analysis of Indonesian regional growth (Table 5.2, columns 2 and 3). With the original variables, this research test has found no evidence of either heteroscedasticity or multicollinearity.

The variables that are consistently significant, between the models and throughout the periods, are the initial GRDP, index variable of decentralization, lobbying capacities and level of technology (TFP).

FIGURE 5.1
The ß Convergence between Log Annual Change of real GDP per capita and Initial GDP per capita (1993–2010)

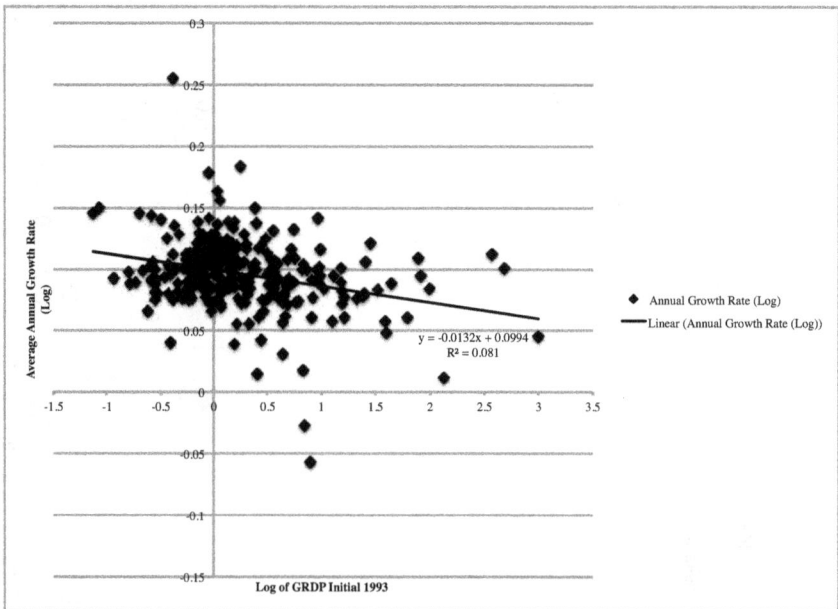

$$y = -0.0132x + 0.0994$$
$$R^2 = 0.081$$

Source: Author's analysis using GRDP districts' data from BPS.

FIGURE 5.2
Districts Growth Rate between 1993–97 and 2001–10

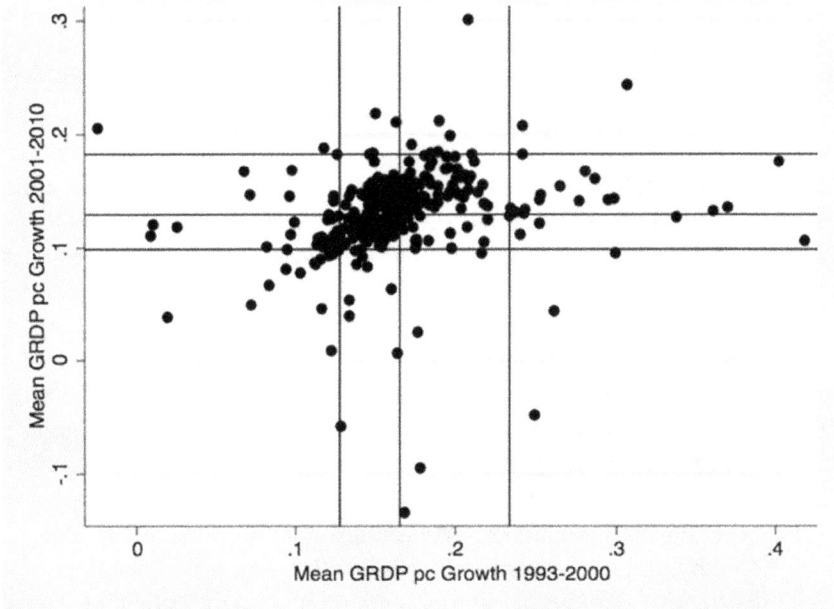

Source: Author's analysis using GRDP districts' data from BPS.

The initial GRDP and decentralization index variables are significant in explaining the diversity in regional economic growth. The result confirms that the annual convergence speed in the early decentralization period is 25.8 per cent, which is faster than during the pre-state restructuring (1.7 per cent) and advance decentralization (1.9 per cent). The consistent negative sign of the decentralization index indicates that decentralization actually contracts economic growth, thus confirming the negative impact of decentralization on regional disparities (Rodríguez-Pose and Gill 2006; McCulloch and Syahrir 2008). The AFTA index has significantly negative effects throughout in the decentralization period, suggesting that in the transition period AFTA became the source of economic growth as the lack of fiscal decentralization support. A reduction of 1 per cent AFTA index demonstrated an increase in economic growth by 1.16 per cent, a finding in contrast to other studies that argue trade liberalization has benefited regional economic growth (cf. Feridhanusetyawan and Pangestu 2003; Logan 2008; Rivas 2007).

The following detailed analyses of significant variables provide more insights. The population share in urban areas variable remains insignificant in all three sub-periods. This finding suggested that economy concentration does not necessarily lead to a cumulative economic growth as argued by neoclassical economic literatures (Perroux 1950; Myrdal 1957; Hirschman 1958; Krugman 1991). Contrary to the general expectation, the education variable has an insignificant effect on economic growth. However, as Rivas (2007) explains, this result has actually been widely found in the growth literature — that a negative effect on the initial level of human capital refers to an exogenous change in its return (Krueger and Lindhal 2001). The road accessibility variable is also negatively significant throughout the whole periods, in contrast to the general expectation that road accessibility should associate with higher economic growth. This can be explained by the presence of a backwash effect of regional development as argued by Myrdal (1957), that these regions absorb the economy of neighbouring regions that have an average road accessibility and poor market access.

The lobbying capability variable shows that additional development funding has positive effect on regional economic growth for richer regions. This additional development funding, which significantly determines economic performance, reflects the rich local government's capacity to lobby the central government. This sign is in contrast to the pre-decentralization and advance decentralization periods where lobbying were insignificant on economic growth. This confirms that earmarked fund was distributed only to poor and lagging regions through the Inpres Fund and the DAK (Dana Alokasi Khusus or Special Allocation Fund) after 2005, respectively. The research also finds that trade liberalization has insignificant effect on bordering regions, thus rejecting findings from other research (Logan 2008; Sanchez-Reaza and Rodríguez-Pose 2002).

The analysis shows that a higher share of manufacturing industries is associated with higher economic growth. As the manufacturing industry is more capital-intensive than agricultural and natural resources industries, this might imply that the technological level in manufacturing industries consequently influence regional growth. However, the research finds that manufacturing share variable in the decentralization period has lower positive effect on economic growth than that in the centralized regime. The level of technology variable, represented by the TFP, also has insignificant effect on development for the whole periods. These findings might indicate that the TFP of Indonesian industries do not determine regional growth.

The labour productivity variable, approximated as a ratio of labour and output, shows that the variable has a negative and significant supporting effect on economic growth, implying that a lower ratio of labour is required to produce a certain output that leads to a higher economic growth. The significance of these variables provides evidence for the endogenous growth model that emphasizes on human capital, technology and the role of manufacturing for economic growth (Lucas 1988; Romer 1986, 1990).

The R^2 size in Table 5.2 shows that the OLS models explained more variation in regional economic growth in the transition and early decentralization periods (1998–2005) than in the advance decentralization period (2005–10). The advance decentralization period analysis has the lowest R^2 calculation, indicating that other significant variables — such as the shift in political and administration issues — that have not been included within this analysis but crucially determine regional economic growth within the seventeen years of observation.

In the pre-decentralization period, the findings confirm results from the OLS analysis that labour productivity is associated with higher economic growth (Table 5.2, column III). The significant sign of manufacturing variable shows a high dependence on manufacturing contracts economic growth. However, the analysis found that the role of industrial technology is geographically significant and positively influences regional economic growth. This finding confirms that endogenous growth theory that distance positively influences regional technology spillover (Lucas 1988; Romer 1986, 1990). The opposite, however, is found during the state restructuring period, as there is a lack of significant explanatory and control variables.

Panel Analysis on State Restructuring Impact

To demonstrate how economic growth and explanatory variables change over time, similar to the OLS analysis above, a panel data analysis is conducted over three periods of observation: pre-decentralization (1993–97), transition period (1998–2001) early decentralization (2001–05), and advance decentralization (2005–10). The Hausmann test result suggests a fixed-effect panel analysis rather than a random-effect model. The analysis does not suffer from heteroscedasticity or autocorrelation, as in the methods developed by Wooldridge (2002), but there are missing data in almost all control variables that lead to a reduced number of observations in the OLS and panel data analysis. For example, whilst there are 5,256 observations in the full dataset, there were only 416 observations for 292 districts over the advance decentralization period. The panel analysis use variables in Model 1 in the OLS regression, and are presented in Table 5.3.

The panel regression analysis confirms that there is, statistically, a significant convergence of regional economic growth for the whole periods, providing evidence that poorer districts grow faster than rich ones. This result confirms the distribution analysis in the previous chapter and the OLS results.

In sum, panel analysis on state-restructuring impact yields the following results. First, the decentralization index has a negative effect only in the transition period, implying that decentralization significantly contracts economic growth. The finding also confirms OLS result that there is an insignificant effect of fiscal autonomy from the AFTA variable in the pre-decentralization period.

Second, the local economic structure such as manufacturing output and labour productivity determines regional economic growth only in certain periods. For instance, the share of manufacturing is only significant in the pre-decentralization period, suggesting a declining importance of manufacturing industry on regional development.

Third, the analysis shows that bordering regions are insignificant for the pre-decentralization period, rejecting the idea that economic gains are promoted by political and fiscal devolution (cf. Rodríguez-Pose and Bwire 2004; Rodríguez-Pose and Gill 2005). However, this result is expected in Indonesia, as the bordering regions — except for Batam — are economically lagging and remote, and challenged by persistent socio-political conflicts (Hill, Resosudarmo and Vidyattama 2008; Eilenberg 2012).

Fourth, the lobbying capability variable has a positive significant impact on economic growth in this period, confirming that additional development funding is crucial to the regional development. Last, the panel analysis also confirms the OLS finding that the TFP that represents the level of technology is insignificant for economic growth, mainly due to the poor technological level and progress in Indonesia manufacturing industries.

TABLE 5.3
Fixed Effects Regression of per capita GRDP Growth

	1993–1997		1998–2001		2001–2005		2005–2010	
	I	II	I	II	I	II	I	II
GRDP pc Initial	-0.729**	-0.640**	-0.969**	-1.022**	-0.943**	-0.906**	-0.302**	-0.813**
	-0.03	-0.03	-0.07	-0.12	-0.01	-0.01	-0.03	-0.06
Decentralization	1.701*	0.763	-8.673**	-8.836**	0.874**	0.359**	0.061	0.252
	-0.76	-0.68	-0.1	-0.13	-0.07	-0.13	-0.05	-0.23
AFTA	0.043**	0.033**	0.01	-0.011	-0.001	0	0.005	-0.004
	-0.01	-0.01	-0.02	-0.02	0	-0.01	-0.03	-0.01
Urban Population		-0.006		0.086*		0.006		0.021
		-0.01		-0.04		-0.01		-0.01
Share pop in junior school		0.296**		1.018+		-0.631**		-0.195
		-0.05		-0.56		-0.22		-0.45
Road Access		-0.205		-0.398		0.002		-0.017
		-0.26		-0.31		-0.08		-0.02
Share of Manufacturing		-1.395**		0.049		-0.342		0.526
		-0.17		-0.74		-0.23		-0.71
Tariff*border		0.194**		-1.666*		0.165**		0.037
		-0.07		-0.73		-0.05		-0.19
Lobby		0.012		0.039**		0.009**		0.010*
		-0.01		-0.01		0		0
Labour		0.023		-0.015		0.006		0.003
		-0.01		-0.02		-0.01		-0.01
Technology		0.006		-0.001		0.010*		0.007
		-0.01		-0.02		0		-0.01
Constant	0.319**	0.139	0.586**	-0.056	1.531**	1.182**	0.549**	0.950**
	-0.02	-0.3	-0.03	-0.44	-0.01	-0.11	-0.05	-0.18
No. Obs	1.105	946	757	608.000	1.552	1.045	1.415	416
Groups	250	225	259	240	271	245	275	241
Adj. R2	0.414	0.514	0.937	0.947	0.977	0.98	0.104	0.543

Source: Author's analysis using data from BPS, MoF, and ASEAN Secretariat.

Overall, the panel fixed-effects model explains more variations in Indonesia's economic growth during the early decentralization (98 per cent) compared to the pre-decentralization and advance decentralization periods, 51 per cent and 54 per cent. This high R^2 in the post-decentralization period might indicate that the model and the variables are appropriate to estimate the determinant factors of regional economic growth in the post-decentralization than for other periods.

State Restructuring Impact on Regional Convergence: A Discussion

The OLS and panel econometrics analysis provide evidence that regional convergence were operating in Indonesia between 1993 and 2010. The regional convergence rate was higher in decentralization period than that in pre-decentralization period. This implies two important findings. First, the process of catching up by lagging regions to advanced regions is evident in Indonesia in the post-decentralization period, as the GDP per capita in lagging regions have higher growth rate than that in advanced regions. Second, lower convergence rate for the pre-decentralization period, compared to after decentralization, signifies the presence of economic and political shifts within the periods (McCulloch and Syahrir 2008).

Second, the decentralization index demonstrates a negative sign in the OLS analysis, which indicates decentralization contracts the regional economic growth (Table 5.2). However, if we isolate the characteristics of districts, the panel fixed-effects analysis shows that decentralization has a postive effect on regional economic growth (Table 5.3). This finding rejects literature that limited fiscal decentralization authority hinders economic growth (McCulloch and Syahrir 2008; Suwanan and Sulistiani 2009).

The OLS analysis confirms that labour, technology and share of manufacture have positive association with regional economic growth. However, if we isolate individual regions with the fixed-effects panel analysis, the labour productivity is the only variable that has positive significance on economic growth. This confirms endogenous model literatures (Lucas 1988; Romer 1986, 1990) that emphasize the role of labour and technological progress as the action of economic agents that positively determine economic growth.

A positive sign in the lobbying variable suggests that the lobbying capacity promotes further economic growth for richer regions, but further research is needed since starting in 2008, the law on public finance (Undang-undang No. 33/2004) has eliminated the "no hold harmless" policy, to ensure that funds are allocated to poorer regions (Brodjonegoro 2003).

Specific studies on the role of fiscal decentralization (Lewis 2013; Booth 2006) reveal that the DAK has a more significant effect on regional development compared to other types of revenues, since DAK is specifically used only for social or infrastructure development. As a comparison, an additional rupiah in DAK will increase the government expenditure by Rp1.21, while an additional rupiah in DAU only contribute to Rp0.09.[15] Other IGT fund components have a much lower contribution to economic growth; for instance, the size of tax and non-tax revenues depend on the economic structure of individual district and province to generate these taxes. The DAU by default follows the fiscal history of an individual district and is predominantly allocated for government officers' salaries and maintenance of government facilities.

A spatial analysis by Vidyatamma (2013) shows that most newly founded districts initially demonstrate high growths before the growth stagnates and fades, owing to the abundant investment and infrastructure funds from the government in its first years. The neighbouring regions also appear as an influential factor due to the spatial concentration of economic growth and spillover. Districts with higher economic growth tend to be located close to other high economic level districts.

The analysis also confirms that trade liberalization does not always benefit regions. First, manufacturing industries tends to exacerbate regional disparity (Rodríguez-Pose and Bwire 2004). The findings suggest that trade liberalization may have affected convergence through the high concentration of manufacturing industries. Second, the institutional approach claims that the effects of trade liberalization are determined by preferential trade agreement, the agreement's capacity to produce trade creation, trade diversion, and the economic power of nation-states (Baldwin and Wyplosz 2006). Third, in the economic impact analysis, regions with abundant natural endowments and infrastructure accessibility are more able to attract investments and economic activities (Elliott and Ikemoto 2004; Paelinck and Polèse 2000). This leads to divergence among regions until the economy finds its equilibrium and creates a balanced economy where poorer regions can experience economic development.

The regional initial economic level and standard deviation (SD) growth for the three periods are presented Figures 5.3 to 5.8. A darker colour represents higher district economic growth effect of decentralization and ASEAN FTA. First, the district initial GRDP 1993 map (Figure 5.3) shows that districts in Java have higher economic level than districts in other islands. This illustrates that disparities in regional economic growth have occurred prior to decentralization. The standard deviation (SD) growth map between 1993 and 2001 (Figure 5.4) also depicts a similar picture, showing that the rate of economic growth in the districts of Java approximates closely to national average, while districts in Sumatra, Kalimantan and Sulawesi have more dynamic growth rates. Specifically, districts in Riau, East Kalimantan and West Sulawesi provinces had higher economic growth during the pre-decentralization period.

FIGURE 5.3
Districts Initial GRDP per capita, 1993

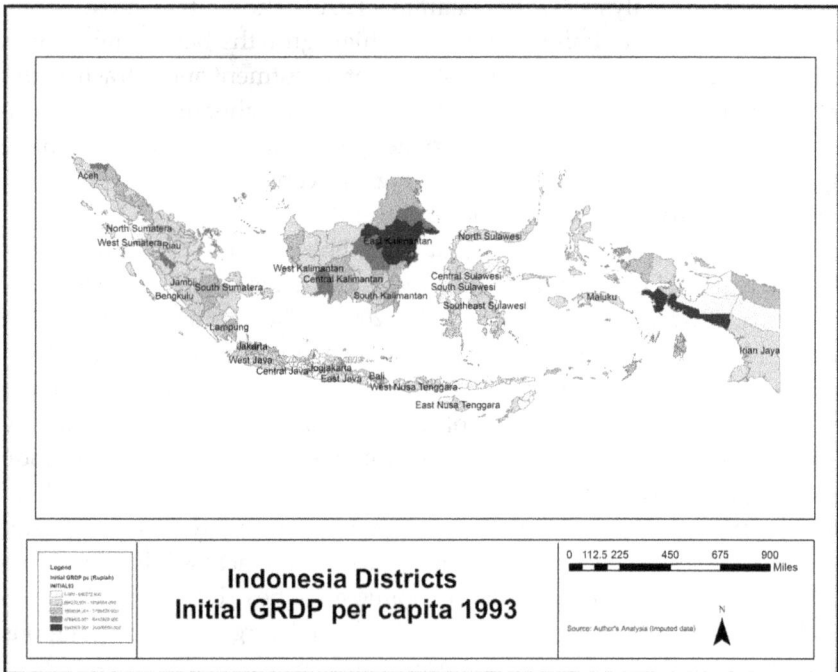

Source: Author's analysis using GRDP data from BPS.

FIGURE 5.4
Districts Growth, 1993–2001 (Standard Deviation)

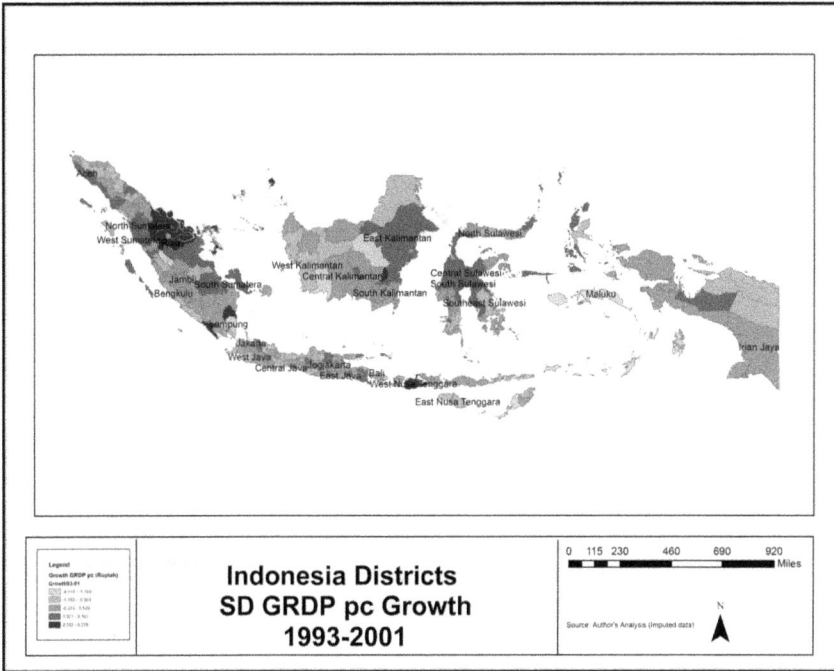

Source: Author's analysis using GRDP data from BPS.

In the beginning of decentralization in 2001 (Figure 5.5), districts in Java have lower economic level than other regions as a result of economic growth in the authoritarian regime. This low performance of economic growth continues throughout the state restructuring period (Figure 5.6). The economic growth of these districts is similar to the national average, with the exception of Jakarta and several districts in Central Java that have higher economic growth rate. The economic growths of districts in Sumatra, Kalimantan and Sulawesi throughout the state-restructuring period are similar to that in the pre-decentralization period, although there is a higher economic growth in Papua Island districts. Thus, Figure 5.6 illustrates the econometric analysis findings that there is a higher rate of catch-up growth by lagging regions. The figure also reveals a positive

FIGURE 5.5
Districts Initial GRDP per capita, 2001

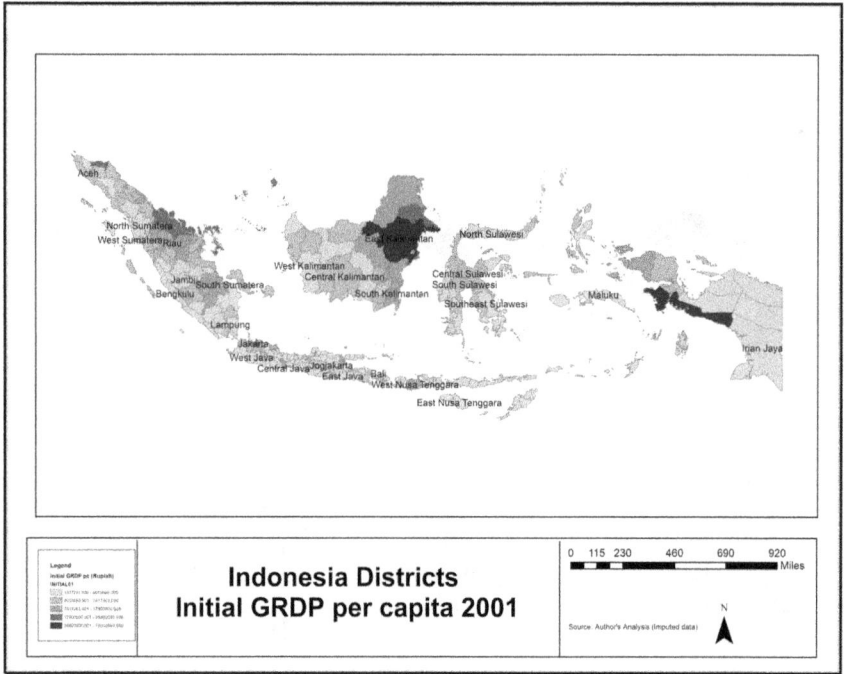

Source: Author's analysis using GRDP data from BPS.

effect of state restructuring on regions located at the borders — these regions have higher economic growth than other regions, although the growth rate is lower than that in the pre-decentralization period.

The economic level map in 2010 (Figure 5.7) shows that there are variations in the economic levels between districts in Sumatra and Kalimantan, where even some districts have higher economic level than the districts in Java. This confirms the convergence of economic development between districts. This is also shown in the SD district economic growth over the period between 1993 and 2010 (Figure 5.8) that districts in Java have lower economic growth rate than districts in other islands. For instance, districts with rich natural resources and manufacturing provinces (such as Riau, East Kalimantan and West Sulawesi) had higher economic growths

FIGURE 5.6
Districts Growth, 2001–10 (Standard Deviation)

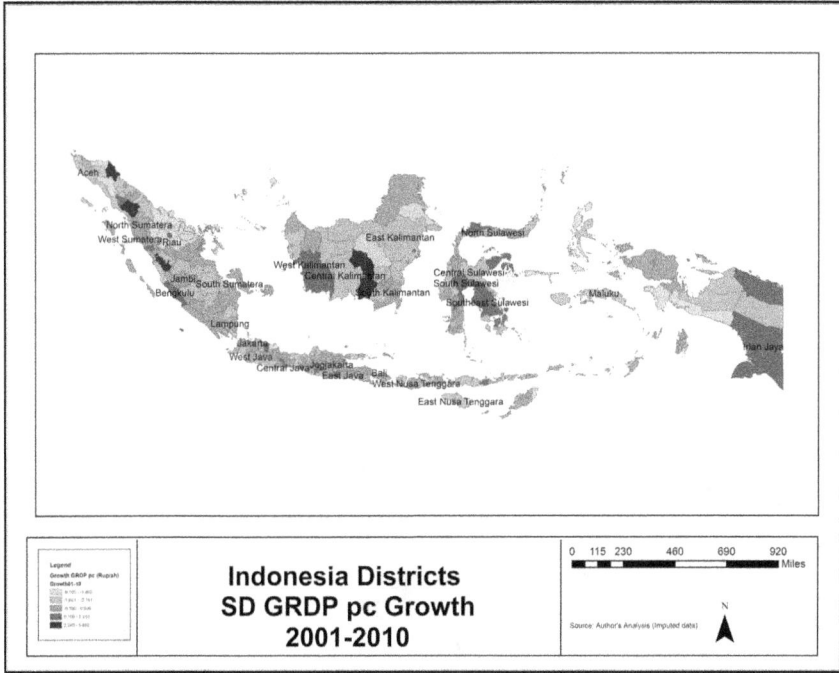

Source: Author's analysis using GRDP data from BPS.

than lagging provinces between 1993 and 2010. Districts at the borders in Sumatra have higher SD economic growth rates than bordering districts in Kalimantan and Sulawesi islands, suggesting higher variations of economic growth in Sumatra. The maps also show that districts in Papua and Java have economic growth at the national average.

DISCUSSION

Devolution and trade liberalization are commonly seen as policies to promote regional economic growth (Musgrave 1959; Juan-Ramón and Rivera-Batiz 1996; Paelinck and Polèse 2000; Elliott and Ikemoto 2004; Rodríguez-Pose and Gill 2005; Calamai 2009). However, by analysing the

FIGURE 5.7
Districts GRDP per capita, 2010

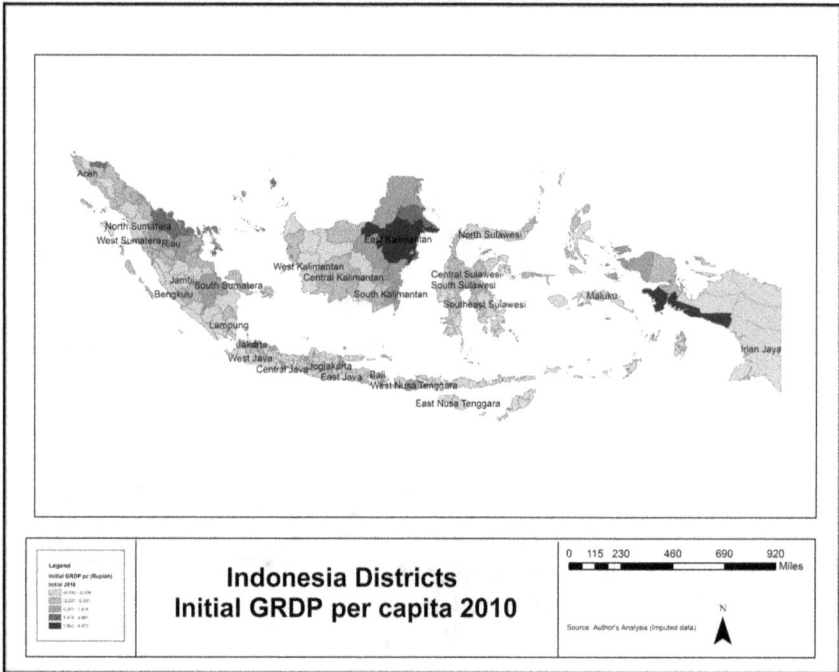

Source: Author's analysis using GRDP data from BPS.

regional development in decentralized Indonesia after the Asian Financial Crisis, this study argues that devolution and trade liberalization do not necessarily accelerate regional economic growth, as each region has different local endowments, institutions, and economic structures. With more than 290 districts of varying cultural and economic endowments, Indonesia is an interesting case study to explore the determining factors of sub-national growths.

Decentralization introduces higher transaction cost and regulatory burdens (including bribes) that hinder knowledge spillover and manufacturing R&D (Asia Foundation 2002; Kuncoro 2004*a*). The fixed cost brought about by regulations imposes more burdens on small firms, thus encouraging the growth of informal sectors to avoid these costs. A

FIGURE 5.8
Districts Growth, 1993–2010 (Standard Deviation)

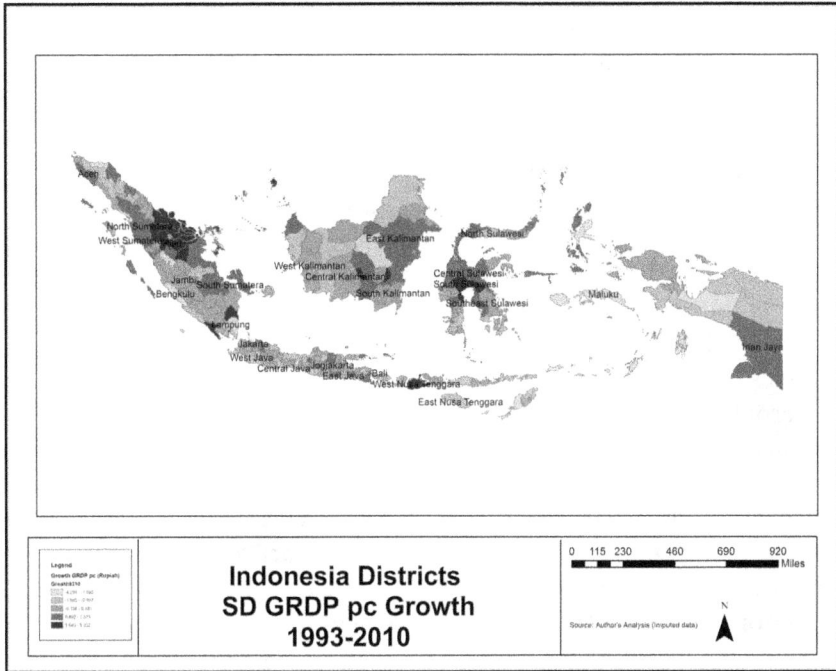

Indonesia Districts
SD GRDP pc Growth
1993-2010

Source: Author's analysis using GRDP data from BPS.

study by the Asian Development Bank (2008) showed that firms spent 10 per cent of their time completing forms and more than half of their time dealing with local government's regulations. Lengthy liquidation procedures imposed additional costs on the process of reallocating resources to more productive uses. According to the World Bank (2008) report, Indonesia ranked 135 out of 175 countries in terms of the ease of closing a business. Beside regulatory burdens, manufacturing firms in Indonesia face domestic challenges of trade tariffs and non-tariff barriers elimination in ASEAN FTA. As trade barriers have been lifted, the regions are also under competitive pressure as local products struggle to compete with the flux of cheap, readily available imported products flooding the market.

Studies using unconditional convergence models have been conducted to examine regional economic disparity in Indonesia, such as Akita and Alisjahbana (2002) and McCulloch and Syahrir (2008) that studies convergence rate at provincial and district level, respectively. This chapter finding confirms that economic disparity remains high between districts despite evidence of regional convergence, specifically after decentralization.

Further analysis of local explanatory variables and policy determinants are necessary to gain more insights and explanations of the economic trends. In addition, the econometrics analysis omitted the administration type of local governments and their location, as this is insignificant for analysis throughout the period. This result differs from McCulloch and Syahrir (2008) who found districts located in Java had lower economic growths.

From the conditional empirical studies, we can draw several conclusions. First, all regression conducted in this chapter shows a significant convergence rate indicating poorer districts grow faster than advanced districts, especially more pronounced in the decentralization period than in other periods. Second, the impact of decentralization is significantly different from research findings in Italy (Calamai 2009). In Indonesia, decentralization has a negative impact on economic growth, suggesting that although these gaps have existed even before the decentralization period, autonomy and self-government have led to increased growth gaps between districts.

The negative association between decentralization and economic growth, however, has declined in the decentralization period. The study suggests that decentralization by itself can have negative impacts, but coupled with external events such as trade liberalization, governance capacities, and good social policies, decentralization can potentially promote local economic growth. Thus, central governments should plan additional policies that support the implementation of decentralization in order to improve local development. The absence of central government intervention has further hindered a balanced development between regions. The low R^2 econometrics analysis suggests that the model for the pre-decentralization period explains less variation of economic growth compared with in other periods. This implies the variables in this study are appropriate to represent political and social dynamics that determine the variations of district economic growth in the decentralization period.

Third, the share of manufacturing and infrastructure availability have positive effects on regional development, but the level of technology has insignificant impact, both in the pre- and the post-state restructuring periods. The infrastructure, approximated by the proportion of roads that are accessible and paved within districts, is associated with higher economic performance. A 1 per cent increase in the road access leads to a higher economic performance by 0.5 per cent. Thus, this variable should be considered and included in each local government's development plan. In the long run, beside infrastructure and technology level in manufacturing industries, the share of population also shows positive relation, suggesting that these variables determine regional development, as growths are more prominent in regions that have advancement in these variables. This result shows the significance of circular cumulative causation theory (Myrdal 1957) that argues regions with more local endowments attract more investment and economic activities. In addition, this study also captures the effect of non-tangible political variables, such as the lobbying capacities by the local government, on economic growth. However, the availability of such political and institutional variable is limited and requires specific assumptions that are unique between countries and regions.

Fourth, ASEAN FTA tariff elimination has a positive impact on economic growth. However, the variable's insignificant value demonstrates AFTA's small contribution to regional economic performance, as found by Feridhanusetyawan and Pangestu (2003) using the CGE model. This research finding agrees with Rodríguez-Pose and Gil (2006) that there is a weak positive effect of trade on regional disparity and low intra-trade performances in AFTA. This is different from other studies such as Rivas (2007) that found trade liberalization, through NAFTA, promotes convergence in Mexico. Additionally, if it is combined with other variables such as infrastructure and worker's income, it will exacerbate disparity. In NAFTA, there was less convergence effect, and much less gain for Mexico than in the GATT era (Sanchez-Reaza and Rodríguez-Pose 2002). The study of MERCOSUR FTA shows that economic growth and convergence occurred during the stable macroeconomic era between 1994 and 2002 (Madariaga, Montout and Ollivaud 2004).

The chapter also shows the significance of path-dependence theory (Krugman 1991) that trade liberalization promotes exploitation of peripheral economies by advanced regions. High economic growth is found in regions with high percentages of exports, labour productivity, and value-added, and those that are included within the global trade integration such as Batam, West Java and East Java. The positive effect of labour productivity also confirms this argument as found with regions that has higher AFTA impact in Table 5.2.

Based on this econometrics analysis, I argue that Indonesian economic growth has not witnessed the hollowing out of the state. On the contrary, the sub-national districts and provinces remain heavily dependent on the transfer of funds from the central government. The importance of intergovernmental processes, governance between different actors, and how these processes impact local economic performances and disparities will be discussed in-depth in the next qualitative chapter.

Notes

1. For recent publication at the provincial level see Resosudarmo and Viddyatama (2011) and Viddyatama (2013); and for district levels see McCulloch and Syahrir (2008), and McCulloch and Malesky (2011).
2. The method derivation is presented in Appendix B and C.
3. Available at <www.bps.go.id>.
4. The Special Region of Capital Jakarta is a province with five non-autonomous districts.
5. The data is available at <http://www.kppod.org/datapdf/daerah/daerah-indonesia-2013.pdf>.
6. Available at <http://djpk.depkeu.go.id/data-series/data-keuangan-daerah>.
7. The method derivation is presented at Appendix D.
8. The available data are number of labours, wage, manufacturing capital, investment, energy utilized for production, and value-added.
9. Assuming a Cobb-Douglas technology (Amiti and Konings 2007).
10. See Appendix F for the construction of tariff data.
11. For studies on general studies on Indonesia manufacturing TFP, see Vial (2006) and Timmer (1999). For a study on the effect of manufacturing TFP on selected Indonesia districts, see Aritenang (2013).
12. All of these technical procedures are performed using the STATA software command "levpet" with all variables are in the logarithms form.
13. The method derivation is presented at Appendix F.

14. Barro and Sala-I-Martin (1991) found that convergence for U.S. states (from 1880 to 1990) to be on the order of 2 per cent per year.
15. Intergovernmental transfers are divided into the general allocation fund, special allocation fund, and the share of tax and non-tax (natural resources) revenues. For dedicated studies on fiscal decentralization, see Lewis (2013); Booth (2006).

6

THE INSTITUTIONAL EFFECTS ON REGIONAL POLICIES AND DEVELOPMENT
A Historical Institutionalist Perspective

This chapter explains the findings obtained from the quantitative study through a regional institutional analytical tool, which combines economic performance and historical institutionalist approaches to investigate institutional antecedents, path dependences, and political shocks.[1] There is a difference on the manufacturing analysis scope in Batam and Bandung based on the type of economic structure that is under observation. In Batam, the manufacturing industries are historically spillovers from Singapore and other countries and are dominated by medium and large manufacturing firms. In Bandung, the creative city analysis focuses on creative industries that are dominantly small and emerging firms.

From the findings in this chapter, I argue that regional disparities and variations in Indonesia, inherited from the past institutions, have shaped current institutions through path dependence, and were further disparaged by the state restructuring.

Using case studies from Batam and Bandung to illustrate my findings, the chapter is organized as follows. The first section discusses institutional changes and adaptations during the post-decentralization period that have occurred in the forms of dispersed institutional layering in relation to politics, economics, and ethnics. The second section examines the development of manufacturing and creative industries in Indonesia, by discussing the antecedent institutions and developments in the manufacturing city of Batam and the creative city of Bandung. Using these two case studies, I analysed the impacts of decentralization and ASEAN FTA on regional development.

THE TALE OF TWO SECTORS: MANUFACTURING AND CREATIVE INDUSTRIES

Manufacturing in Indonesia

The impact of state restructuring institutional change on manufacturing industry is an important study because decentralization changes the manufacturing policies and AFTA trade tariff directly affect the manufacturing production. Since the pre-decentralization period, the industry faces ongoing problems that include: (1) persistent high degree of labour intensity, (2) inconsistent policies, and (3) land acquisition issues.

First, while the high degree of labour intensity in manufacturing may increase labour absorption rate, its value-added is insignificant, and has little impact on technological and knowledge spillover in Indonesia. Wages and consumption also remain low for the workers.

Second, the changing policies meant inconsistency and insecurity for foreign direct investments (FDIs). For instance, the report by KPPOD (2007) points out that decentralization has not improved public services at the district level despite the shifts in business and investment procedures. Except for the municipality of Batam that is supported by the national act of FTZ status designation, studies have shown the importance of foreign investment manufacturing firms in accelerating local productivity through industrial linkages and technological spillovers. However, there is no evidence of such effects of FDI on research and development (R&D) in Indonesia. This can be explained by two factors: (1) research and development are mostly still conducted in countries equipped with advanced, highly skilled workers and infrastructures; and (2) the capacities of local firms to tap into the technology and knowledge base of these foreign firms are still limited.

Third, land acquisition, entangled within the convoluted systems of land and rent-seeking institutional arrangements in Indonesia, is further complicated by multi-layered authorities where the local government administered the business documents but BKPM (Badan Koordinasi Penanaman Modal or Investment Coordinating Board) decides the business permit, and the land permit remains controlled by BPN (Badan Pertanahan Nasional or National Land Agency).

Three decades of centralized regime have led to severe regional disparities. Indonesia had experienced its most rapid development during the New Order regime, with income per capita increasing from US$50 to US$1,000 between 1965 and 1997. Indonesia's GNP during this same timeframe increased 7–8 per cent annually and 3–4 per cent in the following decade. Because Indonesia is an open economy, external factors, such as the decline in oil prices and recession in the world economy, affect the economy significantly.

A study in pre-state restructuring period in Indonesia regional development using a neoclassical convergence analysis by Garcia and Soelistianingsih (1998) showed that convergence had declined from 0.39 in 1975 to 0.28 in 1993. Meanwhile the σ convergence analysis showed that the annual converging rate is 2.4 per cent for absolute convergence and 4.5 per cent for conditional convergence. These results suggested that income distribution in Indonesia was converging across time and thus heading towards Kuznets' curve (Tambunan 2006). Another study by Akita and Lukman (1995), however, confirmed opposite evidence, showing widening disparities with a comparison of coefficient of variation (CV) between the richest and poorest provinces increasing from 5.6 in 1975 to 7.7 in 2002. This study also revealed that government investment and expenditure was uneven, with investment in Riau being thirty times that in the East Nusa Tenggara province.

The most significant disparity existed between Java-Bali and the rest of the country (Hill 2000, p. 230). Java Island comprises only 6 per cent of the total island area in Indonesia, but it dominates the nation's economy. During the transition period between 1998 and 2001, Java constituted 58.6 per cent of the population and produced 54.1 per cent of the non-oil GDP, while Papua Island, with 20 per cent of the total island area, had only 1.0 per cent of the population and 1.6 per cent of the non-oil GDP

(Akita and Alisjahbana 2002). The leading sector in Indonesia, the footloose manufacturing industrial activities, is concentrated in Java and Bali, where both export-oriented and import-substituting activities take place. Land prices, wage levels, the roles played in commercial assets, and the proximity to national political powers are higher in these islands. Java and Bali are also the main providers of high-value services such as finance, education, health, and international transportation. The BPS provincial data in 2004 showed that poverty rate in Jakarta was 3.18 per cent compared to 38.69 per cent in Papua. The education rate was 9.7 years in Jakarta but 5.8 years in the province of West Nusa Tenggara/Nusa Tenggara Barat (NTB). The study by National Planning Agency (Badan Perencanaan Pembangunan Nasional or BAPPENAS) (2006) shows evidence that metropolitan regions led to economic disparities following high concentration of economic activities and labour.

Sectorial analysis showed that changes in industrial structures in Indonesia corresponded with those in global industrial structures, exhibiting decreasing agriculture on one hand and increasing manufacturing and service industries on the other (Kuncoro 2004*b*). Agriculture's share in the GNP had declined from 51 per cent in 1968 to only 15.4 per cent in 2004, while, the share in manufacturing sector increased from 8.5 per cent to 28.3 per cent. Nevertheless, while the share in GNP had declined, agriculture sector still possessed higher labour absorption, suggesting that Indonesia is still predominantly an agricultural-based country with emerging manufacturing and service sectors. In 1970s, the number of workers in the agriculture sector represented 67 per cent while manufacturing contributed only 7 per cent. Since 2006, the share of agriculture workers had declined to 44.5 per cent while manufacturing labour had risen to 12.16 per cent. This tendency illustrates that Indonesia is still an agricultural-based country with an emerging manufacturing and service sector.

The manufacturing industry deregulation in the 1980s forced the growth of foreign investment and export-orientation industries. To protect a few sensitive local industries, the government announced negative lists that limit certain investment and ownership in Indonesia. For example, observing the districts of Jakarta, industry intensification in the coastal and suburban zones with the establishment of industrial zone by the domestic private firms in the boundaries of Jakarta and industrial parks by foreign firms in the neighbouring districts of Tangerang. Presidential Decree No. 41/1996 introduced more organized industrial parks as a centre for industrial activities with integrated infrastructure and supporting facilities, developed and operated by licensed park developers. In 2011, BKPM granted 317 new FDI licences in the Jababeka area comprising of 75 domestic with 30 countries and 1,500 MNCs.

In Batam, an intergovernmental cooperation, developed by a Singaporean industry park developer, Sembawang, established the first industrial park named Batamindo. It hosted Singaporean and foreign manufacturing plants that had initially located in Singapore to the new industrial park. Thus, policies on industrial park provided a significant framework for the development of industries in Jakarta, its surrounding districts and Batam.

Creative Economy in Indonesia

The creative economy in Indonesia was initiated in 2005 when President Susilo Bambang Yudhoyono (SBY) inaugurated the year as a year of creative economy. In 2008, the Ministry of Trade published Indonesian creative economy development roadmap 2009–15[2] along with the role of agencies and actors in the new economy. In 2009, following his second term of administration, President SBY further marked the government's attempt to develop a creative economy with the establishment of the Ministry of Tourism and Creative Economy, appointing the former Minister of Trade, Mari Elka Pangestu, as its first minister.

In brief, the roadmap of Indonesian creative economy comprised six elements: the people, industries, technology, resources, institutions, and financing intermediaries. Although the creative economy has been touted as a new economy with a participatory approach (MoT, 2009), the national policy on the sector remains bureaucratic and top-down, both in programmes and organization. First, the aims and strategies of the programme were decided at the elite national level and then translated through programmes and activities implemented by certain bureaucratic units as executors. Second, the strategy for the enhancement of a creative mindset, for example, was designed through education curriculum that supports creativity and entrepreneurship programmes coordinated by the Ministry of National Education (MNE). Third, the government organization structure to implement creative economy consisted of coordinating and supporting teams, whose members come from representatives of ministries, including the ministries of trade, industry, and tourism and creative economy. This bureaucracy-style governance neglects the involvement of local stakeholders including the creative communities, academics, and local government in each region.

The roadmap of the Indonesian creative economy 2009–15 stated the annual target as follows: data gathering and mapping the economy for its first year; targeted development for the second year; creation of domestic market and improvement on efficiency and productivity of the creative industry for the third year; innovation acceleration for the fourth year, and brand excellence for the fifth year. The roadmap also shows that the creative economy has yet to achieve any significant and high contribution to the national economy. The data showed that the creative economy share was only 5.67 per cent of national GDP and 9.13 per cent of the total export in 2006. The sector also only absorbed 5.14 per cent of new employment, or about 4.9 million workers. The GNP contribution share of the fashion sub-sector was the highest (43.71 per cent) and the lowest was the performance and visual art (movie, video, and photography) sub-sector (0.12 per cent).

This chapter examines the impact of this bureaucratic and top-down policy on creative economy development in the districts. Using Bandung as a case study, the chapter provides an empirical analysis the policy effectiveness and role of agents in the creative city development.

Nonetheless, the campaign and policy implementation for creative economy had spread to provinces and districts between 2009 and 2014. The British Council programmes contribute to gather creative community that initiate the creative city movement in the city. The British Council had cooperated with local governments and communities in Bandung, Solo, and Jogjakarta on the initial development of creative cities. They had introduced and applied a "mapping toolkit" — based on a simple matrix that groups creative industries into four domains based on the final product output: (1) the book and press; (2) audio visual; (3) performance art and visual arts; and (4) design[3] — to identify, collect, and map the data on creative industries and their distribution in these cities. Another more complicated and comprehensive, mapping toolkit developed by the Nesta (2006) analysed the supply chain networks of an industry, drawing similarities and networks among practitioners. Both these models had provided analytical tools for national and local policymakers to generate appropriate creative economy development concept that supports place-based economy development, national innovation policies or cultural policies. For example, an animation firm in Batam had successfully hired

300 animators from across Indonesia.[4] Another example is the infamous distribution outlets (*distro*) area in Bandung that promotes the growth and share locations with other type of small-medium industries such as small restaurants, cafes, and street vendors. These instances illustrated some small-scale economic spillovers of the creative economy.

However, the importance of the creative economy lies not only in its capacities to absorb new employment or salary, but also in how the sector inspires and encourages the emergence of new entrepreneurship in both creative and related sectors. This is crucial considering Indonesia has a very high number of unemployment of people with diploma and bachelor degrees (409,890 people in 2006, and 740,206 in 2009).

Thus far, Bandung had garnered the most publicity as the leading creative city in Indonesia, with 205 news and features in its local newspaper, *Pikiran Rakyat*, in 2010, compared to only 62 mentions in Surabaya, 31 in Bali and 28 in Solo during the same year. Some local governments had launched and promoted their local creative symbols and activities to boost the creative economy. Examples included the Old Town (KotaTua) festival and Jakarta Jazz (JakJazz) concert in Jakarta; Helarfest, Braga Festival, and art market (Pasar Seni) in Bandung; Solo Batik Carnival and Pasar Minda Jenar in Solo; Bali Fashion Week and Bali Art Festival in Bali.

In the next section, I will illustrate by drawing on case studies of Batam as a manufacturing city and Bandung as a creative city. In both studies I elaborate how institutional change at the state level induced institutional rearrangements and actor networks at local level.

THE MANUFACTURING CITY: BATAM

The first case is Batam City, where the relationships between agents and institutional changes also reflect the accumulation of knowledge and behaviour inherited from the previous regime. The institutional changes had forced agents to adapt but this capacity was bound by previous knowledge and behaviour. Two development engines of Batam were infrastructure development and institutional arrangement under the "technological state" (Amir 2013).

Lineage of Regional Institutions and Disparities

Batam Island has been exposed to international development strategies since early development. For instance, German and Singaporean consultants were involved in the Batam master plan with an earlier plan that Batam was to host wood manufacturing in Tanjung Uncang and Batu Ampar and as a oil refinery hub with investment from Kuwait in 1972. Industrial activities in Batam began with the establishment of a logistic base for Indonesia Oil and Gas Company (PERTAMINA) as the company utilized the region as a strategic location for oil mining warehouses and distribution routes.

Considering Batam's prime and strategic location, in 1973 the Indonesia government developed the region as an industrial zone, with the Batam Industrial Development Agency (BIDA) responsible as administrator of the region. The strong institutions of Batam as a manufacturing hub started in 1978 when Dr B.J. Habibie took over the island's development and the Batam Industrial Development Authority (BIDA) from Ibnu Sutowo, the chairman of the state-owned oil company, PERTAMINA. Under his leadership, the development orientation shifted from oil and gas hub to manufacturing industry development. The shift implemented Habibie's concept on Batam development that was based on the "balloon theory", where he argued that Singapore needed Batam to receive the industry production spillover and prevented it from bursting like a balloon (Kumar and Siddique 2013).

This was supported by the government-to-government (G2G) cooperation with the establishment of Batamindo, the first and largest industrial park developed by Sembawang, a prominent industrial park developer from Singapore. The formal agreement signed by the two countries was conducted by then Brigadier-General (Res) Lee Hsien Loong, Singapore's Deputy Prime Minister and Minister for Trade and Industry and the late Drs Radius Prawiro, Indonesia's Coordinating Minister for Economy, Finance, Industry and Development. Following this, Singapore government-linked and private companies cooperate with local firms in Batamindo to form joint ventures. The government also granted bonded zone status and special regulations (including the ease of obtaining land permits, along with low land-lease fees) to Batam to support the manufacturing industries. As a result, Batam was extensively developed to support its new role as an extension of Singapore's manufacturing base.

Consequently, multinational companies (MNCs) particularly from the United States and Singapore exerted dominant influence over the social order in the city. For example, Phelps (2004) found that their presence compelled the establishment of a development-oriented and efficient bureaucratic system, as opposed to the proliferation of Indonesian common institutional shortcomings including corruption (Phelps 2004).

As a result, Batam has been long known for its breakthrough and innovative policies. During this period, Batam became the central government's pilot project on e-government, e-business, and e-public infrastructure services (G2G, G2B, G2C), which further established and boosted its status as Batam Intelligent Island (BII) (Putra 2003). For instance, to improve the city's competitive strengths, five areas were enhanced: (1) stable legal framework; (2) human resources; (3) intense network between business and labour; (4) economic incentives; and (5) improvements on infrastructure. While stable legal framework is under the state control, the local authorities have established a straightforward task division between the Customs, BIDA and the local investment coordinating board through a single window investment procedure.[5] In mid-1980s to the 1990s, policy innovations such as cooperation between the BIDA and BKPM on investment promotion and coordination of investment approval allows the national investment board to promote Batam as a part of the ASEAN FTA that provides free movement of ASEAN products within the member countries.

> For example, Batam's progress is promoted as a part of ASEAN FTA and also exclusive FTA with Singapore, which both have benefited from each other on the investment and business. (Director of Sectors Promotion at the BKPM, 23 November 2009.)

The period also acknowledged the importance of education and training to support the manufacturing industry in the city. This was visible with the establishment of the higher education to support the manufacturing industry in the island. First, the Batam Skills Development Centre (BSDC). Initially, the centre was established as a vocational higher education institution for skill and practical training during the Indonesia-Malaysia-Singapore growth triangle (IMS-GT) cooperation in 1992. After decentralization, the administration overseeing the centre's inter-organizational relations was transferred from a central government body (Directorate of Technical Education) to the municipal government. However, the municipal government was reluctant to maintain continued funding for the centre as they viewed the BSDC as a potential failure when it comes came to financial self-sufficiency (Phelps 2004). In addition, as the students came from the middle-income group, the lack of revenue from student fees contributed to this failure. Presently, the struggling BDSC focuses to support vocational high schools qualities and its graduates to improve technical competencies.[6]

Another crucial element of Batam development was that Habibie had included BIDA into his technological web networks — the "technological state" where the New Order regime leader, President Suharto attempted to develop Indonesia through technological capacities with Habibie as the front man.[7] In his technological networks, Habibie emphasized interactions among employers across organizations. He recruited a large number of new employers for BIFZA from BPPT (Badan Pengkajian dan Penerapan Teknologi or Agency for Assessment and Application of Technology) and employed several engineers from BPPT in the design and construction of the six Barelang (Batam, Rempang and Galang) bridges that connect Batam with seven other smaller islands. At the time of writing, many of these BPPT employees remain working in Batam and holding important positions.

Decentralization: Critical Juncture of Batam Institutions

This section analyses the organizational decisions during the transition period that defines institutional arrangements in the following period. First, the establishment of the ICT master plan, which was known as Batam Intelligence Island (BII), which had been initiated in the early 2000s whilst other regions focused on administrative and political arrangements.

> The leaders by that time were very visionary on Batam future development ... they see that Batam should compete with other FTZs and a strong ICT will support both Batam investment and industry development. (Head of Centre of Data and Information System BIFZA, 18 June 2013.)

It is unfortunate that most books on Batam — including a recently published monograph by Kumar and Siddique (2013) — had neglected this crucial initiative, which had laid the foundation of Batam's current strength on ICT. The master plan showed the grand strategies of ICT development in Batam empowered by broadband internet and local telecommunication infrastructures to enhance competitive advantages. Combining both hard infrastructure of ICT and soft infrastructure of human capital, currently Batam is the leading and frontrunner of local ICT and electronics government (E-Gov) in Indonesia, that in 2012 the Ministry of Home Affairs (MoHA) appointed Batam to host the mirror servers of Indonesia electronic identity card (*elektronik kartu tanda penduduk*/E-KTP).[8] This had also provided incentive for BIFZA to improve its capabilities and services in ICT.

The ICT roadmap was consequential in monitoring and reviewing the specific stages of ICT development, including human development, infrastructure and policy issuance. The human resources, for example, recruited abundant graduates from universities in Java such as Bandung Institute of Technology (ITB), Sepuluh November Institute of Technology (ITS), and University of Indonesia (UI) at the early period. Presently the IT officers comprise graduates from local universities such as Batam International University (Universitas Internasional Batam/UIB) and Batam Polytechnic.

This highlights breakthrough on education learning with the establishment of Batam polytechnic,[9] which is a leading vocational higher education focusing on manufacturing and management training in Batam. The polytechnic's curriculum is designed to produce ready-to-work graduates suitable for the real industry environment, with 50 per cent of the curriculum devoted to theory and the rest to practical courses and industry working hours in subjects on industry, electronics, IT, hospitality and management. Laboratories and up-to-date technological tools are available to keep pace with industries. The polytechnic curriculum facilitates communication with industries through technical workshops and job placements. The majority of rapid growth stems from the manufacturing and shipyard industries, however, prospective student interested in electronics and machinery have been very low, causing a shortage in skilled operators in manufacturing and shipyard industries.

> The polytechnic's existence is certainly relevant and significant for the region … foreign and domestic firms prefer skilled local people rather than migrating people … but this means that the polytechnic should be supported by the government and firms financially to overcome limitation as it could only accepts 300 students annually. (Director of Batam Polytechnic, 19 November 2009.)

Another example of higher education institution is the Batam International University that focuses on international academic curriculum and cooperation with international universities. Thus, it is expected that their graduates would be employed as engineers and managers by international manufacturing industries. As one lecturer puts it, their students "have been recruited even before graduation, with some already working since the second year."[10]

Regional Institutional Reproduction and Learning

This section explores the regional institutional reproduction and learning as a consequence of organizational and institutional decisions during the critical juncture.

Local Government and Regulation Shifts

The issuance of Law 44/2007, Government Regulation 46/2007 and 5/2011 that regulated Batam Island as a Free Trade and Port Zone, and Presidential Decree 9/2008 that regulated the role of Regional Council (Dewan Kawasan), led to a new responsibility and functions of Batam Authority. In the new organization, the BIDA was renamed as Batam Indonesia Free Zone Authority (BIFZA) that curtailed the policy authority of BIDA, which is transferred to the Dewan Kawasan.

After decentralization, institutional changes induced by decentralization have introduced (1) institutional layering in the dynamic relationship between the BIFZA and the municipal government, as well as (2) the delineation of the Batam FTZ as enclaves,[11] which required institutional adaptation and learning. The above discussion shows that both FTZ status and AFTA have accelerated Batam to compete with similar special economic regions, especially in the decentralization period. The FTZ status provides special regulations for investors in Batam and this has become the region's competitive value.

The new organization structure under the BP Batam Law 44/2009, which delegates the central government authorities to the BIFZA, had arguably assisted the adjustment to the current global condition and decentralization in Indonesia. Presently BIFZA is a company and the Dewan Kawasan as its supervisor that consisted of a group of appointed people led by the Governor of Riau Islands Province with the Mayor of Batam as its chairman, acts as a commissioner that sets policy and directions. With its function limited to investment and industry policy, there will be no overlap of responsibility and biased decision-making between the Governor's decision and as head of the Regional Council (Dewan Kawasan).[12] Dewan Kawasan reports the Batam development to the President through the Dewan FTZ which consists of various ministries such as Ministry of Trade, Ministry of Transportation, Ministry of Industry, and Ministry of Research and Technology.

The secretariat of the Dewan Kawasan holds the crucial responsibility that requires an in-depth analytical knowledge on central government policy and global manufacturing and trade conditions to translate and adopt central government policies to appropriate policies that BIFZA should implement. For instance, the Dewan Kawasan has introduced the Central Government's policy on *angka pengenal industy* (API) which divide the items as industry and trade products. Industry products are raw and capital, while trade product is categorized as an importer in one section. BIFZA has developed an Information Technology (IT) internal system, available to all divisions in BIFZA, that allows input and retrieve information on the products to improve the implementation and effectiveness of this policy.

Despite continuing tensions, the current arrangement — with BIFZA focusing on investment and an industrial issue on one hand and the local government concentrating on urban social and political issues — has provided a convenient structure for Batam allowing BIFZA to develop experiences and networks globally from past institutions. Nevertheless, after the state restructuring, there is a need for institutional learning and feedbacks that allow reproduction of institutions. Several cases can illustrate how actors develop communication and institutional improvement in the local development.

First, the annual Development Planning Meeting (Musyawarah Perencanaan Pembangunan or Musrenbang) provides a forum between local government and BIFZA to coordinate and synchronize municipality and industrial development in the city. The public and NGOs gained information only through attending discussion and coordination forums. The forum provides opportunities for local trade chambers (Kamar Dagang Industry or KADIN), academia and central government to understand and identify their roles in coordinating development strategies. The Riau province also held development forums to coordinate local development and international cooperation. For instance, a meeting in June 2013 involving BIFZA, local government, Dewan Kawasan, KADIN and Singapore's Economic Development Board (EDB), provided business and investment meeting for potential economic collaboration for private and public opportunities in Batam.

Second, an internal organization unit such as the one-stop service allows internal feedback and learning through continuous meeting and coordination on investment strategies and regulations between BIFZA, BKPM, customs and coordinating economy ministry. For instance a discussion with a prospective investor is attended by BIFZA as coordinator and investment and tax holiday, BKPM for invest permit, Customs for custom procedures and the permit from Ministry of Industry to ensure the cohesion with national manufacturing industry master plan. This allows rapid and effective investor assessment.

After decentralization, BIFZA believes that it is important to have clear investment procedures. Thus, BIFZA not only provides early stage of investment advices and permit, but also a task force called a "marketing team"[13] that accompanies the investor through each level of investment line including investment lockets, land permit application and construction sites. This reflects the shift of BIFZA marketing strategies, which was "outward" and external oriented such as participation in business exhibitions and forums, has been replaced by comprehensive and individual services. This "marketing team" programme was established mainly due to the feedback gained from: (1) studying other FTZs, particularly after realizing the importance of continuous information and guideline for prospective investors; and (2) previous experiences and institutional arrangement suggesting that the marketing and promotion process were frequently terminated during the investment deal. There is also lack of clear procedure and guidance for the investors on business and investment permits.[14]

Third, Batam has adapted to the new system of municipality master plan (*rencana tata ruang wilayah* or RTRW). In the past, the BIFZA has the authority to manage land use and industry in Batam without the parliament and master plans are mostly based on physical and academic assessment. After decentralization, all district governments, including Batam city, has to develop RTRW that should be legalized by local parliament, which is more complicated to change once a development requires adjustment and adaption to the current condition. On the other hand, the issuance of President Regulation No. 87/2011 on Batam, Bintan and Karimun RTRW regulates spatial development for the land use and industrial activities in the islands as part of the national Free Trade Zones (FTZs).

This one-size-fits-all policy could affect Batam's capacity and attractiveness on global competition. For instance, in the master plan, the Tanjung Uncang area was planned as a wood manufacturing industry. When it was ready to be launched with divided parcels and investors, the issuance of law No. 5/1990[15] forbids woods to be transported outside its province and island. BIFZA had to abandon the plan and instead manoeuvre to attract a new manufacturing sector, the shipyard industry. Currently the Tanjung Uncang area is the largest and concentrated shipyard industry on the island and in Indonesia. It is with this flexibility and adaptive capacities, together with its strategic location that Batam survives and accelerates in the post-decentralization period. The issuance of law 44/2007 declares Batam as an FTZ and strengthens the pre-existing institutions. Thus, in decentralization period, it maintains very limited linkages to its surrounding regions. Batam has a limited regional cooperation and understanding of neighbouring regions' planning documents, leading to a lack of spatial and economic integration in decentralization, as confirmed below:

> There are communication regarding FTZ's but there has been no cooperation between Batam Island and neighbouring areas that might improve regional competitiveness. (Head of Division at Centre of Data and Information System BIFZA, 21 November 2009.)

Fourth, the extra layer of institutions added in the reorganization of Batam, including the municipality government, the Dewan Kawasan and provincial government, means that Batam development is integrated into the provincial development for two reasons. First, BIFZA investment and industry master plan should be submitted and integrated with the municipality master plan, and second, BIFZA is merely a company that follows instruction and policies issuance by the Dewan Kawasan. Previously BIFZA was directly under the president and coordinated by the Ministry of Research and Technology. Within the new institution, BIFZA focuses on investment and industry development of Batam. Despite a solid and clear organization structure, it will be difficult to analyse how BIFZA could continue its international competitive incentives and policies under such inward organization and political institutions. The vital role and capacity of Dewan Kawasan to translate the central government's policy to the BIFZA has further complicated the Batam development as an FTZ, particularly since Dewan Kawasan itself is a non-structural organization without any fixed organizational structure or permanent staff to support its function.

The development of new manufacturing regulations on the free trade zone was processed through two schemes: first the visits that BIFZA conducted to various free trade zones (FTZs) across the world such as Tanjung Pelepas (Malaysia), Subic (the Philippines), Shenzhen (People's Republic of China), and Aden (Yemen); second, the electronic government (E-gov) and information, technology and communication (ICT) development in Batam that benefited from the long period of ICT development.

Industrial Development

The extensive policies on business-based administration and policy innovation include one-stop services (OSS), E-gov infrastructures, and cargo tracking systems. The BIFZA had installed wi-fi across the offices and other facilities maintained by BIFZA including airport, ports and investment offices. The establishment of the ICT and E-Gov infrastructures enhanced government public services by increasing service reliability and the tools for the prevention of corruption.[16] With these technologies, business actors can complete business permits online, while shipping officers can inform port administrators regarding their arrival times and other detailed information. The authorities argue that Batam require these technologies to improve its competitive values in attracting foreign investments and manufacturing, especially those that spill over from Singapore. AFTA has pushed Batam to optimize institutional authority in implementing innovative regulations and the ICT to compete with other FTZs such as Bayan Lepas and Subic. A high number of FDI projects require workers with qualified higher education, a requirement that within the region can be fulfilled through education from Batam Polytechnic, which specializes in information technology, manufacturing, and machinery courses.

The industry agglomeration is the region's competitive value as a special region with intensive policies on manufacturing and machinery industries. Through the state-granted status as a free trade zone (FTZ), Batam benefits from the central government's special funding and policies. In the labour sector, after three decades of special policies, the region has acquired competitive edge in labour pooling, technical management, and industry-related trainings. In 2003, Batam had a capacity to absorb industry labours with an annual labour growth rate of 14 per cent (Sanyoto 2003), and it continues to enhance labour skills with various competency training and educational programmes to meet the high demand for professional engineers — who currently only comprise 3.64 per cent of the total labour — within the semi-high technology export-oriented industries. In addition, more than twelve industrial zones had been established and had provided more than 172,000 jobs. Both domestic and foreign investments were worth US$7.3 billion with more than 8,000 companies.

In addition to the continuation of manufacturing industry, the BIFZA has also attempted to adapt to current global and regional economy. Following a recent finding by an international consultant Frost & Sullivan that as Singapore industry has shifted to hi-technology and financial sector, the need for cheap labour has declined rapidly. Currently 60 per cent of Batam revenue comes from manufacturing industry and 70–80 per cent of its output is exported to Singapore. For instance, the establishment of Kinema, a newly established Animation Company with a 30,000 square feet studio in Batam has employed 300 Indonesian animator designers and gain market benefit from its proximity to Singapore. This suggested that the strategic location benefits Batam to diversify its industry into green technology, tourism, and ICT, and to ensure sustainable local economic development.[17]

Socio-economic Changes

As an inherited state-controlled region, connections in central positions remain important, as evident in the heads of BIFZA. Until recently, the governor of the Riau Islands was the former BIFZA chairman, enabling him to build political coalitions and societal support through his former officers and bureaucrats, who then replaced him as the BIFZA chairman. For instance, two of his officers became the mayor of Batam and head of BIFZA which allows him strategic network to design and implement his provincial policies and development plans, which include Batam.

Here, we can reflect on the few conditions that have shaped the development of the region. First, agents' knowledge and understanding play crucial roles in determining the continuity of previous policies. Given that the governor is an institutional agent whose practices are bound by antecedent institutions, the knowledge and policies that he transferred to provincial bureaucrats and political actors are bound to Batam's institutions. Thus, these policies remain visible and significant for the island's development. For instance, the development of electronic government (E-gov), an emerging ICT-based government service, is supported by the strong ties with Ipteknet, a strong prominent centre of Internet development and system network research in the BPPT.

Second, current policies are limited by past institutions through institutional experience and agents. For example, because the former colleagues of the governor became leaders of local agencies in Batam, provincial policies are more likely accepted and supported by district leaders. As a former head of the BIFZA, the governor has a strong relationship with the BIFZA as reflected in Batam being the province's growth centre and its being home to the provincial representative office. The office is also the location of OSS facilities for investment and business services, and government-business routine meetings for the provincial government.

Third, a political-bureaucrat prominent leadership in development became an alternative to the lack of political and ideological philosophy within political parties, as argued by von Luebke (2009). The FTZ status has motivated Batam authorities to develop policies for regional development with a competitive edge; economic agglomeration drives Batam's economic policies. At the same time, they are supported by previous or existing institutional agents. Path dependence is clearly reflected in this example because current policies were determined by the industrial paths that had been established in Batam since the 1980s.

THE CREATIVE CITY: BANDUNG

The second illustration in Bandung provides three cases of institutional changes and adaptations by looking at the emergence of creative industry and its discourses. Specifically, I explored the role of the Bandung Creative City Forum (BCCF), a creative industry-related community. The forum continued to hold an important role in developing Bandung as a creative city in the following years. Their activities work in tandem with the provincial government's strategy of developing creative industry policy between 2008 and 2013, which is expected to accelerate the growth of creative industries in Bandung.[18] These actors actively promote the Cultural and Creative Industries (CCI) that relies on the emergence of technology and highly skilled creative graduates, establishing the notion of "Bandung Creative City". This shift has laid the future path for Bandung as the creative city in Indonesia.

Lineage of the Creative City: Hub of Creativity, Science, and Technology

Bandung is a relatively small city with viable infrastructure that has reputedly attracted those working in cultural and creative industries to live and exchange ideas. Urban forms and policies play great roles in shaping it as a creative city. Many popular artists that have enhanced cultural and creative industries in Indonesia live in Bandung. Unlike in other countries, art galleries with regular programmes are still rare in Indonesia. However, privately owned and maintained art galleries such as Sunaryo and Nyoman Nuarta galleries host scheduled activities including art exhibitions, poetry and theatre performances, creating public spaces and interactions.[19] The Sunaryo gallery, for instance, has multifunctional facilities for arts and cultural exhibitions where public could appreciate art exhibitions and creative products free of charge.

The city has also benefited from its proximate distance with Jakarta. Since the Dutch colonial period, Bandung has developed strong links and economic dependence with Jakarta, and with its cosy and cool weather, the city has long been an attractive destination for tourists, particularly from Jakarta. In 1888, the first railroad between Bandung and Jakarta (then called Batavia) was built to link both cities. The city hosted various entertainment events and places for Dutch tourists from Jakarta and plantation landlords from West Java. One of the most famous streets was Braga Street where all sorts of shops — food, confectionery, cinemas, jewellery and watch stores, and festivals (*feestterrein*) that held opera, drama, and *silat* performances — could be found (Dienaputra 2005). This first wave of cultural industries with European lifestyle cafes, restaurants, shops, art-deco hotels, large ballrooms and theatres propelled Bandung's fame as "Paris van Java" (Soemardi and Radjawali 2004).

The city is also known as the centre of science and technology since the central government allocated Bandung to host strategic industries including the National Institute of Electronics (Lembaga Elektronika Nasional or LEN), Indonesian Aerospace (PT. Dirgantara Indonesia or PTDI), National Nuclear Energy Agency (Batan Tenaga Nuklir Negara or BATAN), and the Centre for Geological Survey (Pusat Survei Geologi).

Between the 1980s and 1990s, another wave of cultural industries flourished in Bandung, attracting consumers from Jakarta to flock to famous area boasting unique local brands such as homemade yogurt at

Cisangkuy Street and Kartika Sari, and fashion shops such as jeans clusters at Cihampelas Street. This was supported by the establishment of textile, garment, and machinery sectors following the deregulation on investment permits, known as the October Package (Paket Oktober or Pakto) in 1993 that established the city as a manufacturing industry centre. In the 1990s these cultural and creative activities stagnated, however following the Asian Financial Crisis (AFC), a new fashion trend emerges.

Furthermore, despite being regarded as one of the most urbanized cities with one of Indonesia's highest economic growth in Indonesia, social interactions within Bandung remain rooted in traditional Sundanese traditions,[20] and *silaturahmi*[21] is still embedded in local expressions and interactions. The Sundanese tradition is regarded as an important factor for the growing creative economy in Bandung.

> Sundanese people are open to new things ... yet they are also reluctant to confront [if there is any issue] and choose to *pundung* [hold anger within] ... these two factors are crucial to provide a conducive place to nurture creative activities as one need inspirations and peace in mind to work. (Creative Education Activist, 13 August 2013.)

The open culture was also the main reason of the large impact of creative economy and cities notion in Bandung. Unlike other cultural cities in Central Java such as Surakarta and Jogjakarta, Bandung is not historically related to strong traditional cultures and customs. The city was specifically built by the Dutch colonial government to host the entertainment and performances for plantation owners and tourists from Jakarta.[22] This historical role plays a crucial role in shaping the relatively open and Western-oriented designs that are commonly found in Bandung. For instance, famous local clothing brands from Bandung such as C 59, UNKL347 and Airplane are Western-style design clothing *distro*, compared to its counterpart from Yogyakarta such as Dagadu.

Bandung has long been known for its high public engagement and open society. During the authoritarian regime of the New Order, despite its strong control on censorship, many Internet café (*warung Internet* or *warnet*) flourished across the city, attracting youths not only for Internet surfing and gaming, but also in intense political discussions and movement during the end of New Order regime and early decentralization.[23]

During the authoritarian regime in the 1990s, NGOs emerged despite severe surveillance and the number increased rapidly after the fall of this regime. The transition period under Habibie (1998–99) saw a relaxation of socio-political activities and the number of NGOs reached its peak (Latief 2013). This growth of NGOs in Indonesia coincided with the rise of NGOs all over the world and the increasing number of highly educated people who chose NGO as a career path. For instance, Pijar successfully developed nodes of information through a server in Germany that distributes online information by pro-democracy contributors (Lim 2006, p. 11). Another case is related to the Partai Rakyat Demokratik (PRD), a small, pro-labour, student-based party. Despite the arrest of the leaders in 1996, it continued to post online through an ISP outside Indonesia (Sen and Hill 2007, pp. 202–203). The PRD also used the Internet to communicate and coordinate at the national level, which links members through Internet cafes (Lim 2006).

Critical Juncture of Creative Industry and Products

After a decade of institutional frenzy following the manufacturing industry boom in the 1990s that has aggravated the sunk cost of past infrastructure development, there was a decline of infrastructure and barriers to new economic activities. The weakening of state power led to the creation of new institutions to organize the spaces of identity to develop the creative economy and embrace local endowments. There were three events that accelerate the development of the creative city in Bandung.

First, the financial crisis and the fall of the regime brought fundamental changes, not only to the economic and political institutions, but also to social and institutional arrangement that have dictated and organized the communities in Bandung. This suggested some of the social, economy, and political dimensions led to the emergence of a creative class and economy in Indonesia. The society that was once oppressed by the authoritarian regime channelled their voice and identity independently from mainstream culture empowered by the culturally and knowledgeable society of Bandung.

Second, the birth of the clothing industry was a hallmark creative economy in Bandung. The industry began to grow with the needs of specific communities, such as the skateboard community and surfers, for specific clothing and accessories (Luvaas 2013). The supply was initially imported, but following the AFC, the escalating exchange rate led to higher prices beyond the reach of most individuals, but demand for these products remained strong. As a result, the industry began designing and producing it own clothing labels. Initially, the production was to satisfy their own needs, and the design styles were adaptations of established brands, such as Nike, but with additional elements, such as punk (Luvaas 2013), to reflect their sporty and independent spirit.

To meet external demand, these products were sold through *distro* across the city and exported to other cities. The design and product scope have also extended beyond the skateboard community to surfers, indie music bands, and bikers community. For instance, the UNKL/347 represents these communities.[24] Presently, there are 400 clothing companies with 30 being members of Kreative Independent Clothing Kommunity (KICK). The local clothing labels gained interests from other communities and outside the city.

Third, Jakarta's economy and social spillovers continue to greatly affect Bandung, especially since the development of a new highway connecting Jakarta and Bandung in 2004. The highway has reduced travelling time to only two hours, which in the past had required four hours of drive through mountainous regions. The "Jakarta effect" is seen clearly from the following quote:

> Bandung's proximity with Jakarta certainly has its perks ... Jakarta is the market for my products; however Bandung is a small city that allows point-to-point access easily ... that is the reason I base my business here in Bandung. (New Media Artist, 10 April 2013.)

Regional Reproduction and Learning

Shift in Local Government Regulation

The Bandung master plan in 1999 acknowledged the emergence of a creative economy and was designed to accelerate Bandung as a service city with focus on art and cultural economy, significantly influencing policies and land use system in the next decade. For instance, the master plan has allowed the shift in land use in Dago area along H. Juanda Street and the housing area behind the street to accommodate the growing number of factory outlets in the early 2000s, and thus geographically bring the booming fashion industry into a prominent visible location, particularly for tourism. Along the street, other vibrant activities and small-medium enterprises from café, bakeries, confectioneries, music performances, retail banks, and 24-hour convenience stores have also developed. The large colonial architecture, surrounded by public amenities such as parks and wide streets, creates a relaxing atmosphere and provides convenience for consumers to relax, dine and shop in restaurants, coffee shops, boutiques and book stores found in this housing area behind H. Djuanda Street.[25] Thus, inherited infrastructure and facilities contribute to the intimacy of the city where people tend to be more relaxed and have the time to hang out. Combined with the many higher education institutions (about 149 universities and colleges), the city attracts both young entrepreneurs and consumers.

Following decentralization, Bandung has committed itself to both top-down and bottom-up decision-making processes as indicated by its 2009 local regulations. The processes have included active participation from NGOs, universities, professional associations, and creative communities, along with the municipal government. To attract investments into the city, the municipal government established the One-Stop Service Agency (Badan Pelayanan Perizinan Terpadu or BPPT), with learning avenues from other regions such as the Sragen and Jembrana regencies.

The Internalization of Creative Economy

Continuing with the open society trend, the decentralization period witnessed the integration of cooperation and network with the collaboration of creative communities, local government and international agencies. For example, the British Council (BC) introduced the creative economy and city in Bandung in 2006 through programmes focused on the development of human resources of the creative community with design skill training, technology, business workshops and network development. At the initial stage, the BC conducted the creative industry mapping by identifying creative actors, networks and products.

The BC has also organized the Indonesian Young Creative Entrepreneurs (IYCE) award to acknowledge and nurture creative artists and entrepreneurs. It was through this conference where three frontrunners of the city's creative communities — Ridwan Kamil (architect), Fiki Satari (clothing apparel entrepreneur) and Gustaff (writer) — met and established the Bandung Creative City Forum (BCCF). BCCF is a specific forum for communication and network among artisans formed by a group of creative communities.

The creative economy and creative city concepts, along with the policies brought about by the BC, were thus easier to be accepted and developed widely by the cultural and creative communities in Bandung. However, initially some communities had displayed reluctance to join the BCCF network. More importantly, it should be highlighted that their reluctance have little to do with the creative city concept and the BC per se. Rather their reluctance is based on their principle to remain independent. They pointed out their discomfort that BCCF might claim any projects and activities, especially as the BCCF received programme supports and funding from the central and local governments, and international agencies such as British Council. These reluctance and doubt were further compounded when Ridwan Kamil, the former chairman of BCCF, became a mayoral candidate supported by certain political parties. Thus, the communities avoided joining as they were concerned about their independence and reputation since they might be associated with the government, the forum's donor or the political parties.

Despite various misgivings from several communities, the BC programmes are arguably successful in two factors; first, the workshop they initiated has helped to identify and map the presence of creative industries in Bandung. The result of this mapping allowed local and national level policymakers to develop a road map for the creative industry and economy. Second, competitions such as the IYCE and workshops have identified, launched and provided a hub to identify potential artists and networks.

There is also a strong link between the forum and the local government and academic community: first, the local government has exhibited fresh approaches with their policies by giving opportunities to street vendors and informal business to reallocate pedestrian shopping locations. The new locations provide new shopping experience to leisure and relaxing environment through architectural design buildings and social engagement. The place-making of public space replaces mall whilst empowering informal business as part of the community. As a result, it enhanced social interaction and a sense of place that place-making is not merely a space but also different time expressing different meaning and interaction of place (Haman 2010, p. 452). For example the public space activities at Gasibu, which for years has been transformed into a temporary market with vibrant activities and products ranging from sport, culinary tourism, clothing, and pets. This market operates from early morning to noon on Saturdays and Sundays. The temporary markets Gasibu and Gedung Sate, located at the heart of the city, have been designated as public space to accommodate social interaction and engagement in the city. This also illustrates the mixing of the cultural and creative industry with tourism, leisure and social interaction.

Second, the government has also positively responded to the bottom-up initiatives of creative community by providing a space called Simpul for community hub and creating a special task force. The team cooperated with BCCF to design policies on investment permit, public place creation and infrastructure development to support the Bandung creative city. For instance, there is in-depth communication between the BCCF advisors and consultants with the local government on issues such as the creation of theme parks, a car-free day, and the urban forest activities. Another case is the establishment of bike rental location across the city centre initiated by a graduate of ITB in collaboration with BCCF and the local government to provide an alternative urban mobility. This project mirrors the bike rental projects found in London and Paris.

Several activities have also been collaborated between the government and communities from creative industries such as Helarfest, Kreative Independent Clothing Kommunity Festival (KICKfest), and as well as launching creative awards and the creation of more public spaces. The Helar Festival, a creative industry festival, initiated by the BCCF, attempted to integrate fifteen creative industry actors and businesses within the West Java province.

Third, the ITB and its faculty of Arts and Design have been known as the initiator of the Creative Industries and Innovation movement in Bandung with the four-yearly art market events (Pasar Seni). Another role of ITB is the establishment of Artepolis, a bi-annual international conference on creative city and urban design organized by the Architecture department. The conference was held the first time in 2006, and each of the conference has different topics on creative city and urban design, inviting numerous leading international scholars such as Charles Landry (creative cities, U.K.), Masayuki Sasaki (creative cities, Japan), and Lily Kong (cultural and creative cities, Singapore). As the conference has been sponsored by various institutions including governments, state-owned enterprises, real estate developers, creative companies, and donor agencies, the conference participants also range from government officers, developers, artists, business people, scholars, students, and international agency representatives. Thus, the conference facilitates both formal academic and practical knowledge exchanges as well as networking among creative city professionals and scholars.

Regional Institutional Learning

The learning and feedback processes of community institutional changes can be seen at several levels.

First, at the community level, there are differences on the recent progress between communities. For example, the development of the Common Room, an open platform for art, culture, and media based in Bandung, initially started by facilitating various activities such as film screening, workshops, small music concerts and discussions. The space becomes a hub for interaction and networks of people and community from different backgrounds. Despite a lack of financial support and certainty of the continuity of the programme, the space has become a dynamic place for the creative community to engage in social and political expression leading to the emergence of urban discussions, visual arts, fashion and multimedia. This is different from BCCF, which has more stable sources of funding, and thus more regular, continuous programming such as *ngaduide* forum that matches business ideas with professionals, and the creative entrepreneur network (CEN) that promotes networks among creative entrepreneurs. These BCCF events are well publicized, promoted through radio, and led by a professional marketing company in Indonesia, Mark Plus.

Second, the Ministry of Tourism and Creative Economy have allocated several programmes in Bandung, in cooperation with the BCCF. One leading programme is the establishment of creative centres, designed to gain benefit from the abundant ICT and multimedia research and researchers across Bandung. Similarly, the Ministry of Research and Technology has provided research and development (R&D) marketing grants to individual projects such as Batik Fractal[26] and sponsorship in for the BCCF magazine, *Magz.bdg*.

Third, the increasing network and popularity of actors are becoming more visible as they grow along with the increasing number of activities by the communities. For example, BCCF members currently range from artists, architects, urban planners, lawyers, journalists, and students.

> The communities and individual that come here and join us is voluntarily and self-motivated ... this drives the communication and networks among us. (Chairman of BCCF, 10 April 2013.)

There was a presentation by a committee member on the creative village cluster project on a Wednesday night, which was initiated by BCCF. The initial project chose five creative villages — Taman Sari (urban farming, bamboo), Leuwianyar (tourism, eyeglass and snacks), Cicadas (craft and music), Cicukang Ciroyom (recycled water for handcrafts) and Dago Pojok — where representatives of BCCF have to work together with local communities and attempt to develop sustainable urban and neighbourhood regeneration through shifts in lifestyle behaviour and environmentally-friendly activities. There was also a presentation by the Bandung Hobbies community, where they presented their case study on a hobby fair organized in August 2013. The presentation was interesting as it was argued that even though the hobby groups in Bandung are productive, they are overshadowed by the more famous, more media-exposed counterparts in Jakarta. Another interesting activity is an urban forest activity, Regia, in Babakan Siliwangi where the programmes are collaborations between communities. For instance, there is a dining-in-the-forest event in collaboration with a café-restaurant, Café Halaman; a jazz music concert in cooperation with the Bandung Jazz Community; and B.U.L.B. (Barudak Urban Light Bandung) with a light graffiti community.

Fourth, Bandung politics has become more vibrant as a result of the creative city and economic movement as will be seen below. A number of prominent figures have emerged from BCCF and rose to the challenge to lead the city as a mayor. The current chairman of BCCF, Fiki Satari, was a former independent mayoral candidate for Bandung. During his mayoral campaign, he realized that engaging and communicating with local communities do not need to be conducted through a government office. Instead, he prefers to stimulate policies through creative activities and networks with the local government. Based on his experiences, he led the BCCF as a communication forum for various communities and individuals from creative industry communities including traditional arts, clothing and fashion, music and visual arts, urban enthusiasts, and urban heritage society.[27]

The election of Ridwan Kamil, a former chairman of BCCF, as Bandung Mayor marks a new leadership; it shows that a local government leader can be an established scholar and a public figure who is not a member of any political party. He envisioned that the future of Bandung is defined by the happiness of its people that can be achieved through hard work based on creativity, solidarity, and awareness.[28] Using his image as an established architect and a creative community leader, he gained support from the Justice and Prosperous Party (Partai Keadilan Sejahtera/PKS) and the Great

Indonesia Movement Party (Gerakan Indonesia Raya/Gerindra) to run as a Mayor candidate. He argued that political parties were his political vehicles and that they have no connection with him individually.[29] His campaign emphasized on his expertise and his engagement with youths and creativity. For instance, during his campaign, his team launched a cell phone online application[30] called "ngaBandungan" that allows anyone in the community to report any urban infrastructure problems such as traffic jam, damaged roads and potholes. Immediately after he was elected as Mayor, he organized the "ngaBandungan" users and general public into a forum where he met and discussed his programmes with them.

Lastly, the strong notion and rebranding of creative city in Bandung attracts the Governor of West Java province to develop a creative economy for the province. The governor established a special team to develop the creative economy in West Java to oversee and design the sector's master plan, coordinating the development of networks and cooperation between local governments and creative communities in the province.[31] A study by the West Java province government and ITB found that the industry absorbs 2.54 per cent labour and contributed 7.82 per cent of the province's GRDP. Focusing on young creative professionals and the promotion of the textile and crafts sectors, the West Java province postulated Bandung, its capital, as a creative city by combining historical institutions with proximity to Jakarta, leading art colleges, and aspiring young artists.

Despite having two laws — the President Instruction 6/2009 and Provincial Regulation 500/2012 2012 — and supporting programmes such as marketing and financial mentoring, and ICT training, the effort to advance creative industries and the economy, including institutional promotion and knowledge-creation, are limited by human capital qualities, business environment, and regulations such as intellectual property and patents.[32] Similarly, at the national level, two national activities such as the establishment of a creative centre and Taman Bandung in 2012 by the Ministry of Tourism and Creative Economy, has been a lack of evaluation over its impact of creative economy development in Indonesia. This is in contrast to in-depth annual economic and cultural effects reports from the European Cultural City programme.

Above, I have examined the institutional changes under the creative city discourses. The historical institutionalism provides a framework to analyse the lineage of creative city process in Bandung. The need to accelerate stakeholder networks to strengthen institutional building is important factor to develop the creative city. The strong ties between the faculty of Fine Arts and architecture from ITB with BCCF also play an important role in the Bandung creative industry development. BCCF can be seen as an institutional arrangement that bind diverse actors to cooperate and collaborate in shaping local policies and creative expressions. Thus, as actors are bounded in certain institutions, knowledge exchanges and trust among actors are enhanced. In this case, the understanding of local government about the needs of the creative community and industries has led to local policies supporting the industry. Innovations and learning are greatly enhanced in regions where diverse actors are able to learn from each other and communicate these feedback to the (local) government for further actions and development.

Again, the need for community engagement and networks remains important in the process of creative city development. This discussion emphasizes the uniqueness of individual region, its production system and community networks in developing a creative city. Thus this confirms that it should not simply copy elements of creative class and technology as argued by the growing literature on creative economy and city in the economic geography such as Scott (2011), Pratt (2009) and Peck (2005).

THE EFFECTS OF AFTA IN REGIONAL DEVELOPMENT

In both case studies, however, the role of AFTA is noticeably limited. In Batam, the effect of AFTA on manufacturing industry is limited for the following reasons. First, there is a limited awareness amongst the business people about the presence of Form D due to its inefficient distribution. Second, the small tariff differences between the AFTA CEPT and the MFN rates have further discouraged the usage of AFTA. In Bandung, as the creative industry firms are normally considered as SMEs, the export value is relatively small; hence the AFTA CEPT tariff hardly attracts the industry. Although there is a noteworthy amount of inter-provincial and inter-island trade and exports, it remains within specific communities and interests.

INSTITUTIONAL IMPACT OF DECENTRALIZATION AND AFTA IN REGIONAL DEVELOPMENT

The discussions above explained the effects of decentralization and AFTA from institutional perspectives. After decentralization, formal rules have substantially altered intergovernmental relationships and arguably empowered some local authorities. Several conclusions can be drawn. First, decentralization on administration, political, and fiscal arrangement cause differences in the local economic development. For instance, there is variation of development policies initiatives such as Batam and Bandung with the development of manufacturing and creative city, respectively. One possible explanation of this variation is the limited fiscal resources causing unfunded development and potentially leading to bankruptcy. Another explanation is that the laws do not explicitly state that it is the local government's responsibility to promote local development (Brodjonegoro 2003). At the same time, decentralization has also significantly increased previously existing regional divergences. The regional disparities and divergences had been inherited from the policies of the New Order regime before decentralization, but they strongly shaped the degree of state restructuring on individual districts.

Second, regional institutions that were established in the previous period determined regional response to state restructuring policies. Two case studies, Bandung and Batam, showed how these cities influenced the discourse raised during the 1998 critical juncture, as well as at different institutional reproductions and learning trajectories. Bandung showed strong capacity for community and society-led development, whereas stronger government-led development was observed in Batam.

Third, the study shows the inefficiency of devolution and the central government's weakening power, for mainly three reasons. First, the empowerment of the regional government tend to add an additional layer (or more) of bureaucracy that can constrain economic growth by possible overlapping responsibilities, increasing administration costs and inefficiency of bureaucratic processes and devolution (Rodríguez-Pose and Bwire 2004). Second, inter-regional competition can lead to inefficient development, as shown by the case of the local district regulations that emphasize attracting investments as an attempt to increase higher local revenue (Seymour and Turner 2002). Third, local resources in physical endowment and networks affect the non-financial gains of the fiscal decentralization (Rodríguez-Pose and Gill, 2005). This study shows that historical institutions and personal networks strongly determine political and policy support from the central government.

Fourth, previous institutions remain influential to future development, as shown in the importance of existing political linkages that the state provides (for examples, the IMS-GT and FTZ status of Batam, and the regional hub and manufacturing park of Bandung).

Fifth, at the supranational level, the AFTA implementation is based on the ASEAN Way, but it lacks supranational authority over the individual member country's policies in implementing the agreements. In Indonesia, the AFTA implementation of governance is dominated by the state and only a limited number of actors are involved in the AFTA trade modules. Hence, the AFTA implementation has imposed no significant effects on the sectors or local development in terms of trade agreement benefits. Thus, this discussion discloses that member countries are exempt from trade agreements if there are sectors that are viewed as threats to the domestic economy.

Overall, decentralization has not improved public services at the district level despite the shifts in business and investment procedures. The report by KPPOD (2007) points out that although the municipality of Batam is supported by the national act of FTZ status designation, the municipality of Dumai is the second worst local government in terms of problematic local laws (235 laws). On the other hand, business costs in West Java are higher than those in Riau and East Java, with the municipality of Cimahi ranking first, followed by Indramayu Regency and Bandung City at the fifth and seventh positions.

Notes

1. For details of methodology, see Chapter 2 and Appendix G.
2. See Ministry of Trade (2008).
3. See the British Council promotion on the mapping toolkit (British Council, 2010).
4. *Tabloid Diplomasi*, 18 October 2012.
5. Interview with senior officer at BIFZA.
6. The BSDC profile webpage <http://www.bsdc.or.id/?Profil_BSDC>.
7. For the technological state reading, see Amir (2013).
8. BIFZA Public Relations website <http://humasotoritabatam.blogspot.com>.
9. The Batam Polytechnic was established by BIFZA with cooperation with Municipality of Batam, Riau University and ITB in 2000 <http://www.polibatam.ac.id/06_overview_us.php?lang=ind>.
10. Interview with B.B., Dean at the UIB, 19 June 2013.
11. Government Regulation (Peraturan Pemerintah) No. 46 Tahun 2007.

12. An interview with the Secretary of Dewan Kawasan, he added that the position of Dewan Kawasan is as a representative to the central government, while as a Governor he overlooks the whole province.
13. Each year a group of staff from the local government, BIFZA, BKPM, and Customs are recruited and trained as a marketing team member. Since 2012, there are thirty-two members of the marketing team distributed throughout the municipality government (in the labour and transmigration, and tax agencies) and in BIFZA (the logistics, one stop service, land, and marketing directorates).
14. Interview with the Director for Marketing, BIFZA, 2013.
15. Law No. 5/1990 on Conservation of Natural Resources and Ecosystem, article 21(1).
16. Interview with Head of ICT BIFZA, 2013.
17. The report suggests eight industries that Batam should consider; ICT, oil refinery, outsourcing service, computer, electronics, optical products, tourism, and transportation equipment including transshipment.
18. Interview with the Head of Agency for Industrial and Trade, Province of West Java.
19. Information on schedules and galleries in these galleries can be found at its respective website, <www.selasarsunaryo.com> and <www.nuarta.com>.
20. The Sundanese are known to love their culture and heritage, have strong family ties, open minded but sensitive heart (Harsojo 1971).
21. *Silaturahmi* refers to family ties, not only blood family, but also extended networks such as ethnicity, race, school friends, and work colleagues.
22. For a history of Bandung economic history, see Soemardi and Radjawali (2004) and Dienaputra (2005).
23. See Lim and Padawangi (2008) for urban socio-political movement in Bandung.
24. See Irawati (2011) for an in-depth discussion on music and clothing communities in Bandung.
25. See Anderson et al. (2008).
26. See <http://www.ristek.go.id/?module=News%20News&id=3339> and <http://www.ristek.go.id/?module=News%20News&id=2700>.
27. Website and information regarding the actors of Bandung Creative City is available at http://www.bccf-bdg.com/ and http://commonroom.info.
28. Pikiran Rakyat, 10 March 2013.
29. Detik.com 22 May 2013.
30. The application is based on Android platform and was launched by Ridwan Kamil's campaign team on 10 June 2013. Up to September 2013, it has been downloaded 78 times. The application is available at <https://play.google.com/store/apps/details?id=com.metric.ngabandungan&hl=en>.

31. Provincial Regulation 500/2012.
32 P. Rufaidah, "Prospek Ekonomi Kreatif Jawa Barat 2012", *Harian Pikiran Rakyat*, 30 December 2011.

7

STATE RESTRUCTURING IN INDONESIA
Towards a Balanced Regional Economic Development

This study investigates the effects of the decentralization and AFTA on regional convergence between 1993 and 2005, by applying quantitative statistical analysis and historical institutionalism to explore the effects. This chapter summarizes the research findings and analysis results by discussing the current impact of state restructuring on persistent regional disparities and the growing economic convergence, the politico-economy complications of the AFTA beyond trade liberalization per se, and how local governments and actors develop various opportunities and development trajectories depending on their institutional history. The chapter ends by providing some suggestions on policy implications and limitations.

CURRENT IMPACT OF STATE RESTRUCTURING

This research on the effect of state restructuring on Indonesian regional development focuses on two events: decentralization and AFTA implementation. From the study, we can draw several research conclusions. First, despite evidence of convergence process, persistent and severe regional disparities continued throughout the state-restructuring period. The statistical analysis showed that regional disparities fluctuated and peaked during the financial crisis between 1998 and 2001, while the geographical analysis demonstrated significant regional disparities between Java and non-Java districts. Outside of natural resource industries, the western part of Indonesia reported higher economic levels and growth than the central and eastern regions. The sectoral analysis accordingly revealed that manufacturing industries were concentrated and agglomerated in the western part of Indonesia. Additionally, the case study on high-technology manufacturing industries showed a high index of spatial concentration in Java and Sumatra districts. Consequently, these areas have higher economic levels and growth than other regions.

Second, the econometric analysis revealed evidence of regional economic convergence over the observation period, and indicating regional endowments and capacities that determine variations in development. The state restructuring of decentralization and AFTA have different effects on regional economic development. The economic analysis showed that decentralization was associated with lower regional economic growth, whilst AFTA impact was insignificant. This finding was found both in the OLS and panel data analysis. The study also revealed that the control variables — the road accessibility and labour productivity — corresponded proportionally with higher economic growth. A higher share of manufacturing industries on GRDP is associated with economic growth, implying that this sector contribute significantly on local development.

In addition, the lobbying variable implies the importance of political and economic lobbying to secure additional development budget through DAK (Dana Alokasi Khusus or Special Allocation Fund). This finding is elaborated in Chapter 6 that showed how personal capacity and network are crucial for this lobbying process, causing regional leaders to spend a significant amount of time in Jakarta rather than in their respective regions. Decentralization has weakened and disintegrated multi-level administration between provincial and district governments, while at the same time generated regional competition amongst districts. As the role of governors in regional development had diminished, mayors or regents often disregarded regional meetings with the governor. Districts were growing oblivious to the larger development scheme related to their surrounding areas, leading to poorly integrated provincial development, economic policy and spatial equality. The lack of coordination by provincial governments was also another obstacle to development. The large number of district regulations that the Ministry of Home Affairs (MoHA) rejected indicates high competition amongst districts during the decentralization.

If we revisit Musgrave's theory of public sectors (1959), the Indonesian decentralization has not met the ideal core objectives of efficiency in allocation of resources, income distribution, and macroeconomic stability. After almost a decade, the Indonesian decentralization has only achieved the first objective, whilst the second and the third remain in question. The first objective was realized with citizen participation in fiscal budgeting, implementation, and evaluation. This participation has also promoted economic efficiency (Calamai 2009) and improvement in regional administration (Rondinelli and Nellis 1986). On the other hand, regional income remained unequally distributed as Chapter 5 concluded. The highest regional income persisted to be concentrated in Java districts, especially in districts with advanced manufacturing activities during the periods under observation. More equitable regional incomes were expected with the enactment of the new decentralization Law No. 34/2004 concerning State Treasury, but this had only benefited industrial districts such as Jakarta, Bandung, Surabaya and Batam.

On the other hand, the converging effect of AFTA rejects the notion that trade liberalization promote core peripheral conditions, where core regions exploit peripheral economies through "race to the bottom" competition, as argued by the neo-Marxist perspective (Jessop 2002). The negative sign provides evidence that concentration of value-added and trade volume causes a cyclical process of extensive development of infrastructure and centripetal forces for further economic development (Armstrong and Taylor 2000; Florida 2008).

A comprehensive perspective should be applied to examine the impact of AFTA as trade liberalization depends on the size of the free trade area, market, and policy commitments. The economic scale of AFTA is limited to ten countries, and AFTA has not confirmed a form of governance and regulation that can impose authority and decision-making among state members. For example, without any regulation of custom union agreements each member state in ASEAN has no limitation with its preferred trade partners, unlike the EU or NAFTA, where *de jure* sovereignty of nation-state at a certain level has been transferred to a supranational level. The politico-economy reasoning should also be considered in studying the impact of AFTA since the initial purpose of the trade integration was as a building block towards the ASEAN Economic Community (AEC) (Tongzon 2005, p. 145). As the main goal is not only for economic reasons but also for political and social integration, intra-trade performance has become an additional target. AFTA thus should not be measured only in terms of trade, but also in the amounts of FDI it generates, as a confirmation of ASEAN's political and economic power (Soesastro 1991). This limited effect of AFTA can be explained by the study of Bowles and MacLean (1996), which explored the reason for trade bloc formations and showed that AFTA should not be treated as trade liberalization per se.

Finally, using historical institutionalism, I explored the above-mentioned econometric results and explained the variations in regional development. The study demonstrated that institutional history and path development strongly influenced current development progress. Past institutions determined how local institutions responded to institutional changes and adapted to new regional paths. The study also demonstrated that state restructuring afforded opportunities and path creation for local economic development. Decentralization and trade liberalization provided network access for local governments and actors, as well as opportunities to develop local endowments.

In the case studies, for instance, the path development of Bandung as a creative city was predetermined by its previous institutional experiences and capacities as a hub for cultural and creative industries. The recent rise of young and highly skilled creative professionals has further elevated its status as a creative city. Chapter 6 shows that Bandung Creative City represents the integration of past institutional capacities in cultural industries with creativity and knowledge agglomeration. On the other hand, the case study in Batam showed that, despite decentralization causing rapid institutional change in the regions, institutional layering of conversion[1] only appeared in regions with exceptional history on politico-economy condition. Whilst other regions struggled with new economic and political institutions, Batam development agency, BIFZA, persistently focused on social and economic development throughout the institutional transition.

THE FUTURE POLICY FOR STATE RESTRUCTURING

The research findings suggest policy implications for Indonesian development policies in the decentralization and trade liberalization era. First, this study argues that institutional changes at the national level influence regional disparities. National political and economic policies determine the level and dynamic of spatial economic convergence, as argued by Rodríguez-Pose and Bwire (2004). This study showed that institutional changes in the AFTA and decentralization had influenced regional disparities in Indonesia across the periods under observation between 1993 and 2010. The institutional shift of decentralization and the AFTA had different impacts on the dynamics of regional convergence. In both pre- and post-state restructuring, fiscal authority had contracted regional convergence by increasing fiscal disparities among districts. However, the negative effects had been markedly reduced in the state restructuring period.

Trade liberalization in the AFTA variable appeared to be significant before the state restructuring period, indicating that trade liberalization had more effects to increase regional disparities when there are more policy intervention from the central government. During the state restructuring period, AFTA did not significantly impact regional economic growth, implying that shifts in Indonesia political system and local institutional changes have minimized negative effects. The institutional characteristics and trade policies of the ASEAN Way had limited the trade integration in the post-financial crisis period. Hence, although the econometric analysis showed that decentralization variable promoted regional growth and AFTA was insignificant, regional convergence was maintained during the periods under observation. Econometric analysis, however, revealed that there were other significant variables that contributed to economic performance.

Second, spatial development should be a priority of policymaking. The convergence of growth development remained very limited with growth still focusing on core regions. Macroeconomic stability had not been fully achieved due to constant conflicts between different levels of governments and persistent disparities between the western region on one hand and the central and eastern regions of Indonesia on the other. This research also found that rich and border regions had gained the most from FTA, as determined by Juan-Ramón and Rivera-Batiz (1996). Abundant local endowments and infrastructures had attracted investments and economic activities, which led to growth divergence among regions, with selected regions experiencing higher growth rate.

Third, given that path dependence and untraded industries are embedded within a specific location, policies should embrace local knowledge and institutions. The adaptation of policies, such as cluster industries and innovation systems, is crucial to developed specialization and competitive advantage. Furthermore, because trade liberalization effects depend on market size, gains also depend on economic structure and flexibility for supranational economic integration. The study suggests that regions with a strong capacity for innovative policymaking, and a dynamic form of governance capable of mobilizing local actors, have more opportunities to gain from state restructuring (Uyarra 2011). Policies such as pro-cyclical dimension of economic growth (Petrakos, Rodríguez-Pose and Rovolis 2005, p. 1853) and place-based policies (Barca, McCann and Rodríguez-Pose 2011) emphasized the differences between local endowments, infrastructure, cultural, and institutional. By isolating individual regions, the above studies highlight the important role of manufacturing industries and labour productivity as argued by endogenous growth theory (Lucas 1986; Romer 1988, 1994).

Thus, integrating pro-cycle dimension and place-based policies are expected to control regional disparities level based on local endowments and institutions in both expansions and poor economic periods. This is possible in a country where the nation-state policies determine national economic growth and regional spatial disparities level policies (Pike et al. 2012). For example, throughout the periods of observation, the Indonesian manufacturing industry was highly concentrated in Java districts and Batam due to manufacturing policies and free trade zone development in these districts. Hence, balanced development with emphasis on locational and geographical policies should take advantage of the implementation of the decentralization and trade liberalization through precise local economic policies, local tax collections, and inter-governmental transfer funds.

Fourth, the study found poor technological level in Indonesian manufacturing industries, indicating the neglected state of research and development (R&D) activities in Indonesia and the limited capacity technology had contributed on economic growth. Technological innovation policies such as the regional innovation system (RIS) and the National Research Council (Dewan Riset Nasional or DRN) are crucial to formulate science and technology (S & T) strategic development policies. The S & T law requires provinces to establish Regional Research Council (Dewan Riset Daerah or DRD) to advise and assist regional government in S & T and innovation system.[2] However, over a decade of the law issuance, technology R&D remains poor in Indonesia. A report by Santoso et al. (2012) shows that the current level of technology R&D on six provinces in the Java Island[3] is at level 3, suggesting that technology R&D remains as an analytical experiment and yet to be validated in the laboratory environment. The study further argues the lack of political and economic support such as research collaboration and market creation are persistently neglected in Indonesia.

Fifth, the qualitative chapter argued that institutional arrangements determined local economic growth. The place-specific policy recognized past institutions and knowledge that had shaped and influenced current regional regulations to respond to institutional changes at the national level. According to Bertrand (2004), the fall of the New Order regime in 1998, exogenously triggered by the Asian financial crisis, can be considered as the critical juncture — a massive rupture whereby the institutionalized national project crumbled as it was questioned and modified, and a variety of institutional discourses and changes developed and jostled their way into the (re)negotiation of power.

Trade liberalization and decentralization, however, have introduced state (re)scaling and multi-level governances as a result of institutional transformation to accommodate state reconfiguration, both at upwards (supranational cooperation) and downwards (sub-national authorities) (Coe, Kelly and Yeung 2007, p. 137). This research findings support literatures on state rescaling (Jessop 1996; Brenner 2004), in contrast to the arguments that nation-states have lost their power and become victims of globalization (Gill 1993; Ohmae 1995). In this sense, the nation-state is reorganized — functionally, institutionally, and geographically — to achieve its new role in promoting and mediating socio-spatial transformations as states are being rescaled upwards and downwards. This suggest the making of a state space that is "qualitatively new, polymorphic, plurilateral institutional geographies that no longer overlap evenly converge into a single, dominant, geographical scale or nested organizational hierarchy" (ibid, p. 67).

The administrative and fiscal decentralization, such as monitoring of local regulations and limitation on local tax collection, remain under the control of the central government. The absence of supranational authorities replaced by the nation-state's powerful authority such as the Ministry of Trade (MoT) determines the degree of sectoral industry participation in the AFTA trade liberalization. Thus, the central government's role remains important in determining regional development. Specifically, the central government-driven policies in decentralization and AFTA reflect the continuity of nation-state in formulating, implementing, coordinating and supervising urban polices. The role of local governments may have increased with autonomy on local governance and unrestricted DAU (Dana Alokasi Umum or General Allocation Fund) spending, confirming the existence of local development rescaling as found by Swyngedouw (1997). However, the central policies of the nation-state remain crucial for ensuring balanced development through the creation of development opportunities in decentralization and welfare distribution from trade liberalization. For instance, the introduction of Law No. 28/2009 concerning local taxation and charges, that removes provincial and districts discretionary to create new taxes and levies under the closed-list system.

The research also showed conflicts amongst government agencies, confirming the reluctance to accept decentralization and trade liberalization, as argued by Sonn (2008). Conflicts and power asymmetries between state departments and agencies imply evidence of reluctance within the government. The empirical studies revealed evidence of limited experiences and capacities in providing public services. This confirms Prudhomme's (1995) findings that the assumption "supply is always perfect" does not apply to public service, especially for governments in developing countries.

Overall, this study provides a preliminary look into the state (re)scaling and multi-level governance in developing countries to fill the gaps in this field since existing researches have mainly focused on developed countries, especially those belonging to the European Union (Brenner 1999, 2004; Hooghe and Marks 2001; Jessop 2002; MacLeod 2001). These perspectives may thus be used as a starting point for studies on political economy and nation-state roles, and how they influence development.

Lastly, a strong central government that can develop more dynamic, efficient and equitable competitive strategies is needed in the decentralization period to manage territorial competition and to minimize negative effects from rivalries of fiscal and resources capacity. The legislations of new laws related to decentralization have been passed, indicating the potential versatility and ability of the central government to adjust to current political and economic demand. For example, the legislation of Government Regulation (Peraturan Pemerintah) No. 19/2010 showed that the central government responded to the demand to overcome institutional obstacles. As the representative of the central government at the local level, the law empowered the provincial government through coordination authority to ensure integrated local policies and to prevent inter-district disputes. Under the notion of state restructuring on decentralization and trade liberalization, this study investigates the interplay of the state in balancing regional development and global trade. Although the issue of governance rescaling is emerging, this study shows that in the era of decentralization and trade liberalization, nation-states continue to play crucial roles in directing regional development through national policies.

Notes

1. See Mahoney and Thelen (2010).
2. Law No. 18/2002 on National System of Research, Development, and Application of Science and Technology.
3. The report adopts NASA's Technology Readiness Level (TRL) techniques, which ranges from 1 (Basic principles observed and reported) to 9 (Actual system is proven through successful mission operations) (Mankins 1995).

Appendices

APPENDIX A
Regional Inequality Measurements

GRAPHICAL DISTRIBUTION

First, the systematic inequality measurement comprises the graphical index to observe regional economic distribution using the Lorenz curve analysis uses the initial GDP per capita level and its growth. This method calculates the area between the Lorenz curve and the 45° line. The further the Lorentz curve is from the line, the higher the disparities (Canaleta, Arzoz and Garate 2004). However, the systematic inequality approach is disadvantageous in that it explains only overall inequality and does not reveal sub-regional inequality dynamics. Inequality variations explore the expansion of the above-mentioned measurements.

DISTRIBUTION INDEX

Second, the distribution index is a generalization of three indices that relate distribution and disparities across regions. The indices are Coefficient Variations (CV), Gini coefficient and the entropy index with deployment of the Theil index. The first index is the coefficient of variation (CV) following Williamson (1965) as the dispersion index to describe the variation in the income of a region. The higher the CV index the larger the disparity among regions. The formula is written as follows:

$$CV = \frac{\sqrt{\frac{1}{n}\sum_{i=1}^{n}\left(x_i - \frac{1}{n}\sum_{i}^{n}x_i\right)^2}}{\frac{1}{n}\sum_{i}^{n}x_i}$$

(1)

Where x_i is the x variable of the ith region (province or municipalities/regency), n is the number of regions, pi is the population of the ith region, and P is the total population. Since this research studies the disparities among regions, CV is constructed from regional income or gross regional domestic product (GRDP) per capita (Fujita and Hu 2001). The weakness of this method is that it considered only initial and end points of the period that do not take into account fluctuations within the period. Thus, any coefficient measured should be seen as an indicator the dynamic between periods (Azzoni 2001).

An alternative measurement for regional inequalities is the Gini Coefficient. The range and interpretation of this coefficient is similar as to the CV. The equation of Gini coefficient is as follows:

$$G = \frac{1}{\bar{x}} \sum_i p_i \sum_j p_j |x_i - x_j| \qquad (2)$$

The Theil index is an entropy calculation that decomposed inequality index analysis from a higher spatial scale to lower level regions, as well as between and within groups of regions. In some literature, the group could be regions of a country while others are groups of provinces. Many studies have used this method to analyse factors determining income inequality (Canaleta, Arzoz and Garate 2004). Following Akira and Alisjahbana (2002), this study considers hierarchical structure of inequality in Indonesia: region, province, and district. With district as the underlying regional unit, the inequality measures province as the sum of district inequality, and region as the sum of all provinces. This is measured by Theil inequality index as below:

$$T = \sum_{i=1}^{n} \left(\frac{P_i}{Pid} \right) \ln \left[\frac{P_i}{P_{id}} \Big/ \frac{Y_i}{Y_{id}} \right] = \sum_{i=1}^{n} p_i \ln t_i \qquad (3)$$

Where: P is the total population
          Y is GRDP per capita
          Subscript i is provinces
          Subscript d is districts
          n = 26 for the number of provinces in this empirical analysis.

This index exhibit and compare inequality at three spatial levels of administration (region, province, and district), and to allow analysis of a certain district contribution to provincial inequality. With these analyses, the research can reveal convergence progress among regions within a particular country across time. The offset of using this index is that it requires large data at various spatial levels over a long time-period with complex mathematical methods.

The last index in the distribution indices is to view presence of income convergence among regions. There are two types of convergence analysis, the σ convergence and β convergence. The σ Convergence is measured as the standard deviation of GDP per capita within province and district, and β convergence is a regression analysis to study the convergence rate (Barro and Sala-i-Martin 1991). The β convergence analysis is discussed and applied further in the following quantitative chapter.

The σ Convergence analysed dispersion of GDP per capita in each administration level. While β Convergence explains that the faster the poor regions grow relative to the rich regions, the sooner they catch up, therefore, convergence will be faster. The cross sectional dispersion of per capita income or product is measured with its sample variance of log given by:

$$\sigma^2 = \frac{1}{N} \sum_{i \to 1}^{N} [\ln(y_{i,t}) - \mu_t]^2 \tag{4}$$

Where μ is the sample mean of $\ln(y_{i,t})$. If N is large, the sample variance will be close to the population variance. From equation (1) we can write the equation for the evolution of σ^2:

$$\sigma^2 = (1 - \beta)^2 \sigma_{t-1}^2 + \sigma_t^2 \tag{5}$$

However, this is not a satisfactory condition as new disturbances may arise whether the value of σ is above or below the steady state (Petrakos, Rodríguez-Pose and Rovolis 2005; Barro and Sala-i-Martin 2004).

GEOGRAPHICAL DISTRIBUTION INDICES

Third, the geographical distribution index involves mapping of the distribution of wealth amongst regions using the individual region's inequality values. This method adopts technical calculation from the Markov transition matrix, in which a square matrix describing the probabilities of a particular value moves from one state to another in a dynamic system.

By substituting the transition matrix with a stochastic kernel, we can show the probabilities of transition between a hypothetically. The stochastic kernel is obtained by estimating the density function of the distribution in a given period, t+K, conditioned on the values corresponding to the previous period. Hence, the joint function at moments of t and t+K are estimated and divided by the implicit marginal distribution to obtain the current conditional probabilities (Ezcurra, Pascual and Rapún 2006, p. 406).

In the matrix, each row represents the probabilities of moving from a respective row to the other states. The first column explains the number of provinces in a particular GDRP per capita state in the initial year. This method measures income, Ft, at a given time t+1, Ft+1. This study is important to analyse the dynamic position of a particular region within the regional system. Over time, the analysis of cross section dynamics could show the presence of convergence or divergence of regional economic development. Using this method, Quah (1996) concludes that there is divergence among regions, with a limited number of regions having higher growth rate than other regions. This evidence leads to bi-polarization of coalition of the club convergence and the divergence convergence dynamic rate. The ability to demonstrate the dynamic position of each region across time while integrating neo-classical B convergence analysis is the strength of this measurement. The weak point is that the measurement category depends on the knowledge level of the researcher. The more experience researcher has with this calculation, the more accurate the calculation and analysis findings. The evolution is described by the following motion:

$$F_{t+1} = M \cdot F_t \tag{6}$$

The regions under observation for this approach can be applied at the regional (west, central, and eastern parts of Indonesia), provincial, and district levels.

SECTORAL DISTRIBUTION INDICES

Last, the sectoral distribution index calculates the Herfindahl index (H-index) in order to measure industrial localization within a region. In this research, the H-index analysis covers the industry establishment and employment data. A small index indicates a competitive industry with no dominant players. If all firms have an equal share, the reciprocal of the index shows the number of firms in the industry. When firms have unequal shares, the reciprocal of the index indicates the 'equivalent' number of firms in the industry.

The H-index has the highest value of one; this explains that activity in sector i is concentrated in one region. The lowest value of zero shows that the activity of sector i is perfectly dispersed. The measurement calculates P_{ij}, which represent the proportion of industry sector i in region j (equation 7). The symbol P_{ij} is defined as X_{ij}/X_i, where X_{ij} is the activity of sector I in region j and Xi is the total amount of activities sector i in a region (Rhoades 1993). An economic spillover from region A to region B will be considered as a decline of economic growth in region; hence a close observation is needed to accompany this index. Furthermore, the index neglects to draw an absolute conclusion based on the comparison between industries within a region (Sjöberg and Sjöholm 2004).

$$H = \sum_{i=1}^{n} P^2_i \qquad\qquad (7)$$

APPENDIX B
The β Convergence Research Model

This section shows the model of the state restructuring impact on regional economic growth. The model is derived from a simple Cobb-Douglas production function using several variables related with decentralization and AFTA trade liberalization. The model in this research follows a basic estimation model suggested by Rivas (2007) with slight adjustments to Indonesian districts. The model begins with a Cobb-Douglas production function:

$$Y_{it} = A_{it} K^{\alpha}_{it} L^{\beta}_{it} \varepsilon_{it} \qquad (9)$$

With the i and t represent region and time period. Y is the real income, A is the level of technology, K represents the physical capital stock, and L is the number of workers.

If function (1) is expressed in per worker terms and factors in natural logarithms, the function becomes:

$$\ln y_{it} = \ln A_{it} + \alpha \ln k_{it} + (\beta + \alpha - 1) \ln L_{it} + \ln \varepsilon_{it} \qquad (10)$$

Where all the variables are the same as in function (1), but the lowercase are expressions in per worker terms.

Following Rivas (2007), I modified the function (2) to calculate income growth per capita and take natural log differences for each period as follows:

$$\ln y_{it} - \ln y_{it-1} = (\ln A_{it} - \ln A_{it-1}) + \alpha (\ln k_{it} - \ln k_{it-1}) +$$
$$(\beta + \alpha - 1) (\ln L_{it} - \ln L_{it-1}) + (\ln \varepsilon_{it} - \ln \varepsilon_{it}) \qquad (11)$$

The equation expanded as the capital is divided into two terms, C and I. Term C is used to represent capital spending such as government expenditure for development and private investments that is used in the production function that determines economic growth directly. Meanwhile the I term reflects physical capital that effects the production process indirectly, for example, public infrastructure and change of political order. Thus, the function becomes:

$$\ln k_{it} - \ln k_{it-1} = f(\ln C_{it} - \ln C_{it-1}) + w(\ln I_{it} - \ln I_{it-1}) \tag{12}$$

Where f and w are linear functions

In order to capture the economic growth from state-restructuring, the physical capital is shown as a function of two terms. The first term is private investments in each district. The second term is the level of GRDP per capita as the initial income variable, and used to capture the convergence level, as seen in the convergence literature. The function is:

$$f(\ln C_{it} - \ln C_{it-1}) = d(\ln C_{it-1}) + z(\ln y_{it-1}) \tag{13}$$

Where d and z are linear functions.

To capture indirect effects variables, this research uses state restructuring on decentralization and trade liberalization. Two other variables that support the economic development are the public infrastructure and government politico-bureaucracy condition, which is represented by the lobbying capacity by local governments. These variables are explained in the empirical analysis chapter. The last variable is the bordering effects which is the interaction between AFTA CEPT tariff with dummy variable of regions in the border. The function becomes:

$$w(\ln I_{it} - \ln I_{it-1}) = p(\ln I_{it}) + q1(D_{it}) + q2(T_{it}) + \\ 1\,(\ln N_{it}) + s\,(\ln C_{it}{}^{*}S) \tag{14}$$

Where $p, q1, q2, 1$ and s are linear function.

Combining function (5) and (6) into (4), the overall function for capital function is:

$$\ln k_{it} - \ln k_{it-1} = d(\ln C_{it-1})\,) + z(\ln y_{it-1})\,(7) + \\ p(\ln I_{it-1}) + q1(D_{it}) + q2(T_{it}) + 1\,(\ln N_{it}) \tag{15}$$

In addition, to measure the growth in technology, $(\ln A_{it} - \ln A_{it-1})$, the following equation is conducted:

$$(\ln A_{it} - \ln A_{it-1}) = g(\ln h_{it}) + m(A_{it}) + u(\ln U) \tag{16}$$

Where g, m, and u are linear functions. The first term expresses the direct and independent effect of human capital to the technology level. The second term represents technological levels of each district. The last term indicates the effect of the share of people living in urban areas on economic growth.

The full econometrics equation for the impact of state restructuring on regional economic growth is as follows:

$$
\begin{aligned}
\ln y_{it} - \ln y_{it-1} = \ & g(\ln h_{it}) + m(A_{it}) + u(\ln U) + d(\ln C_{it-1}) + \\
& z(\ln y_{it-1}) + p(\ln I_{it-1}) + q1(D_{it}) + q2(T_{it}) + \\
& l(\ln N_{it}) + s(\ln C_{it}*S) + (\beta + \alpha - 1)(\ln L_{it} - \ln L_{it-1}) + \\
& (\ln \varepsilon_{it} - \ln \varepsilon_{it})
\end{aligned}
$$

$$(17)$$

The model in equation (9) is estimated with simple OLS and panel data fixed-effects to address unobservable factors related to economic growth in each district. To investigate the spatial relationship between districts, the analysis also includes a spatial lag variable, $\rho(Wy)$, with ρ is the spatial lag coefficient, W is the spatial weight matrix based on population of neighbouring districts, and y is a vector of district's per capita GDP.

APPENDIX C
Convergence Model:
Traditional and Spatial Econometrics

Absolute β Convergence Regression. The β Convergence is tested with regression analysis and it is calculated to encompass the absolute convergence (poorer regions grow faster than rich regions) that exists. The equation includes the variable of natural logarithm of an end year (y_t) and initial year of GDP per capita (y_0). It is important to note that β convergence can occur without σ convergence, but it is not sufficient enough (Barro and Sala-i-Martin 1991). The regression equation for Absolute β Convergence is as follows:

$$\frac{\ln(y_t / y_0)}{t} = \gamma + \beta \ln(y_0) \qquad (18)$$

Where the dependent variable is the logarithm of per capita income or product, γ and β are constants, with $0 < \beta < 1$, and ε_i as the random disturbance term. At $\beta > 0$ implies a divergence since the annual rate of growth is negatively related with $\ln(y_{i,t})$, with the higher value of β showing convergence.

CONDITIONAL AND SPATIAL β CONVERGENCE REGRESSION

Conditional convergence occurs (poorer regions grow faster than rich regions if other variables are taken into accounts besides initial income level). For conditional β convergence, the empirical model is suggested by Resosudarmo and Vidyatamma (2006) as:

$$\frac{(y_{it} - y_{it-1})}{y_{it-1}} = \gamma_1 + \beta \ln y_{it-1} + X'_{it}\gamma_x + Z'_{it}\gamma_z + C'_{it}\gamma_d + \eta_i + u_{it} \qquad (19)$$

$$\frac{(y_{it} - y_{it-1})}{y_{it-1}} = \gamma_1 + X'_{it}\gamma_x + Z'_{it}\gamma_z + C'_{it}\gamma_d + \rho Wy + \eta_i + u_{it} \qquad (20)$$

$$\frac{(y_{it} - y_{it-1})}{y_{it-1}} = \gamma_1 + X'_{it}\gamma_x + Z'_{it}\gamma_z + C'_{it}\gamma_d + \lambda W\xi + \varepsilon_i + u_{it} \qquad (21)$$

This regression equation (11) is for convergence analysis as included in the conditional variables and regression specification for the trade impact spatial lag model equation (12) and spatial error model (13).

The i represent the district administration, t is the index of time, y_{it} is GDP per capita, the X'_{it} are the vector of variables that are used to understand growth regression. Z'_{it} are the main variables that this research are interested, which are the free trade and devolution variables, and C'_{it} is a group of control variables. The model needs the individual effect, η_i, to capture all the determinants of growth for various regions in panel data analysis. The u_{it} is the random disturbance not to be correlated when the time or region is not the same. It assumes u_{it} is constant.

The ρ refers to spatial lag coefficient, while λ is the spatial error model coefficient. To show whether spatial convergence is present, this research follows Rey and Montouri (1999) that employ robust Moran's I and robust Lagrange multiplier (LM). The significant of ρ-value of robust Moran's I provides strong evidence of spatial dependence; the strategy from Anselin and Rey (1991) elaborates to determine whether it's a partial error and spatial lag type of spatial dependence.

Besides OLS methods with fixed-effect, this research employs maximum likelihood (ML) for the spatial lag and spatial error models. Technical methods in spatial econometric convergence include spatial autocorrelation and spatial growth convergence. Spatial convergence is calculated in the form of speed of convergence β and half-life (equations 14 and 15). Speed of convergence confirms the presence of convergence across time annually and half-life explains the amount of years to reduce disparities among regions (Arbia and Piras 2005). The β refers to the coefficient of convergence and the T is the number of years under observation.

$$b = -\frac{\ln(1 + \beta)}{T} \qquad (22)$$

$$thalf - life = \frac{\ln(2)}{b} \qquad (23)$$

Spatial autocorrelation analysis is divided to global and local autocorrelation. While spatial convergence methods using autocorrelation, known as I-Moran's, relates with autocorrelation of spatial areas for regional income over a period of time, also found in the non-spatial autocorrelation as σ convergence of per capita income dispersion among regions. The methods used are CV of log real income per capita and local I-Moran's that plots standardized income of regions against its spatial lag (also standardized).

Meanwhile spatial convergence studies the spatial convergence growth with OLS and LM techniques in term of spatial lag and spatial error modelling. Spatial lag is concerned with the expected value of growth rate of each region's per capita income, depending not only on its initial value, but also compared with other regions. This method answers how the growth in a region could relate to its neighbours and to what extent it influences (Rey and Montouri 1999). Another method is the spatial error dependence convergence analysis that occurs when the dependence works through an error process, in that, the errors from different regions might result in spatial covariance. Hence, this approach focuses on estimating parameters for the independent variables of interest, and disregards the possibility that the observed correlation may reflect some information about the data generation process. In other words, instead y_j directly affecting y_i, the spatial error model assumes that the errors of the model are correlated (Ward and Gleditsch 2008).

Estimation of spatial lag and spatial error using OLS will cause unbiased estimates when non-spherical errors are present, but biased estimates of the parameters variance lead to a misleading estimation by OLS. This leads to a conclusion that spatial error models should be based on ML or GMM. The spatial structure change could also be seen in the SUR models with ML in the spatial method. The model can describe structural changes occurrences between sub period times of study.

To consider which regression model is the best fit, it is common to use the Akaike information criterion (AIC) and Bayesian information criterion (BIC). The AIC is used to compare the values of estimation between OLS and the spatial dependence model with the lowest AIC value is chosen as the preferable estimation. In addition, the criterion may also use the BIC to solve over-fitting in maximum likelihood estimations, due to adding additional parameters, by introducing a penalty term for the number of parameters in the model. This penalty for additional parameters is stronger than that of the AIC. The BIC was developed by Gideon E. Schwarz who gave a Bayesian argument for adopting it (Schwarz 1978).

APPENDIX D
Tariff Data Construction

First, we construct a five-digit output tariff by taking a simple average of the HS nine-digit codes within each five-digit industry code, by using unpublished concordance between HS nine-digit and five digits ISIC available by Amiti and Konings (2007). Second, for each five-digit industry, we compute an input tariff as a weighted average of the output tariffs (equations 18 and 19).

$$input\ tariff_t^k = \sum w_{jk}^{1998} \times output\ tariff_t^j \qquad (26)$$

$$w_{jk}^{1998} = \frac{\sum_i input_{ijk}^{1998}}{\sum_{ij} input_{ijk}^{1998}} \qquad (27)$$

The weights, w_{jk}^{1998}, are the cost shares of industry j in the production of goods in industry k, based on data in 1998. If industry k uses 60 per cent of sacks of paper and 40 per cent of cement, I calculated a 60 per cent weight to the sacks of paper tariff and 40 per cent weight to the cement tariff.

Third, a similar calculation is performed to obtain the tariff impact on individual districts (equations 20 and 21). I computed an input and output tariff impact as a weighted average the industry's share within the district.

$$district\ tariff_t^l = \sum w_l^{1998} \times output(input)\ tariff_t^k \qquad (28)$$

$$w_l^{1998} = \frac{\sum_i input(output)_{kl}^{1998}}{\sum_{ij} input(output)_{kl}^{1998}} \qquad (29)$$

The weights, w_t^{1998}, are the cost shares of industry k in district l, based on data in 1998. In addition, to address concerns about trade structure post-decentralization, I also constructed the input/output table for the 2002. The data needed to be cleaned due to missing variables for some observations and for large output and input growth distribution numbers.

APPENDIX E
Tariff Impact

The impact of AFTA on regions based on the number of industries in 1993 and 2005 is not significantly different. The figures show that the number of firms that gained from tariff elimination and reduction to less than 5 per cent has declined between the years. However, there is a significant increase in the number of firms that gained from tariff reduction where the tariff is higher than 5 per cent. This indicates that AFTA significantly reduces the tariff rate for the tariff group that is higher than 5 per cent. Specifically, the sub-sectors that benefit the most are food industries (International Standard Industrial Classification/ISIC 31) and other industries, including light equipment (ISIC 39). The table indicates that the CEPT tariffs are significantly lower than the MFN tariffs — the tariff for metal products (ISIC 37) have even been eliminated since 2005 in Indonesia. The tariff on paper products (ISIC 34) had the most reduction with an average of 35 per cent in each period. Table E.4 also notes the changes in average tariff rates and growth for each sector in the manufacturing industry. From the table, it can be argued that the liberalization in Indonesian industries have started since the early 1990s, and reached its peak during the second half of the decade.

TABLE E.1
AFTA CEPT Tariff Impact Based on Total Firms in 1993 and 2005

	Impact	Total firm	
		1993	2005
1	0%	3893	3918
2	<5%	10204	7225
3	5%+	4066	9586

TABLE E.2
AFTA CEPT Tariff Impact Based on Industry ISIC 1993

Impact	ISIC									
	31	32	33	34	35	36	37	38	39	
0%			2,256				139			3,893
<5%		4,258		779					344	10,204
5%+	4,823				2,154	1,498		1,912		4,066
	4,823	4,258	2,256	779	2,154	1,498	139	1,912	344	

TABLE E.3
AFTA CEPT Tariff Impact Based on Industry ISIC 2005

Impact	ISIC									
	31	32	33	34	35	36	37	38	39	
0%			1,325			1,523	1,070			3,918
<5%		4,347		958					1,920	7,225
5%+	5,580				2,540			1,466		9,586
	5,580	4,347	1,325	958	2,540	1,523	1,070	1,466	1,920	

TABLE E.4
Effects of Trade Tariff

ISIC Industry	Tariff Rate CEPT-AFTA	Tariff Rate (MFN)				Change in Tariff		
		1991	1995	2001	2005	1991–1995	1995–2001	2001–2005
31 Food	5	21	20.99	16.21	6.9	−0.1	−22.8	−57.4
32 Textile Clothing	5	27.8	20.1	9.39	7.5	−27.7	−53.3	−20.1
33 Wood	5	24.2	17.95	6.91	5	−25.8	−61.5	−27.6
34 Paper	5	21.21	10.09	4.03	2.5	−52.4	−60.1	−38.0
35 Chemicals	2.5	15.6	12.05	6.92	5	−22.8	−42.6	−27.7
36 Metals	0	23.04	10.62	5.65	5	−53.9	−46.8	−11.5
37 Machinery	5	11.5	8.08	5.77	5	−29.7	−28.6	−13.3
38 Equipment and Electrical	5	18.9	14.75	6.72	5	−22.0	−54.4	−25.6
39 Other	5	32.48	22.11	10.97	10	−31.9	−50.4	−8.8
All	5	20.88	15.6	8.44	5.8	−25.3	−45.9	−31.3

APPENDIX F
Decentralization and AFTA Indices

This appendix elaborates the procedure on the construction of the decentralization and AFTA indices. The aim of these indices is to show the comprehensive impact of an event or variable on regional economic growth and as an alternative variable if multicollinearity is found between the proxies. Index variable construction formula is as follows:

$$DI_{kt} = D_1 \, {}^*D_2 \tag{24}$$

Where DI_{kt} is the decentralization variable index, D_1 is the normalization of local revenue and D_2 is the normalization of central allocation fund.

The normalization of each variable is constructed with the following formula. Normalization formula:

$$D_{kt} = \frac{x - \overline{X}}{SD} \tag{25}$$

Where D is normalization of an individual variable, x is the district's share of an individual variable, $\overline{X}$ is the mean of share of an individual variable, SD is the standard deviation of an individual variable, k is the district, t is the time variant (year)

APPENDIX G
Historical Institutionalism
Research Methodology

Using historical institutionalism theory, the qualitative analysis proposes the argument that the regional economic variation in Indonesia is related to past institutional capacity. Following historical institutionalism, the analysis was concerned with the components of the framework, including critical antecedents, critical junctures, and reproduction of institutions, as adapted from political science (Hall and Taylor 1996; Skocpol 1979; Thelen 1999; Pierson 1996).

RESEARCH PROCEDURE

The analysis of historical institutionalism and economic growth was illustrated with a context-based strategy and decision-making, as well as with networks and conflicts between actors. This illustration was directed towards the specific place of the Batam and Bandung municipalities in post-trade liberalization and decentralization. Furthermore, the case study was contextualized by connecting the analysis at this level of institutional evolution and policy innovation with key issues that occurred at higher governance levels and external processes that determined economic growth. This includes the supranational, national, and regional levels that were influenced through formal, informal, and cultural rules.

In institutional analysis, narratives are essential to contextualizing and constructing empirical situations (Healey, 2007). In this sense, narratives are sequences of connected events and the relationships between events and their consequences. After constructing such narratives, interpretation and conclusion are generated with coding techniques. This approach, as with other qualitative methods, is expected provide insights that combine the effects of several factors and 'multiple conjectural causation' (Silverman, 2005).

To gather such narratives, semi-structured interviews were conducted with experts including government officers at all levels, NGO officials, and international consultants such as the APCO Worldwide and ASIA Foundation. All categories of interviewees represent agents at different stages of the institutional process. Thus, each category of interviewees shows the roles, influence, path dependence, and path breaker that contributed to the regional economic growth differences. The interviews normally lasted for approximately 60 minutes.

The interviews aimed to acquire historical data and reveal the individual subjective experiences of the respondents who were involved in institutional building. Emphasis was placed on institutional building, network, and discourses that prompted the actors to innovate economic policies. Furthermore, the interviews explored how the respondents constructed policies, networks, and innovation that determined innovation in policies. The information from the interviews was analysed using the standard coding technique and compared with other sources such as field observations, official documents, and newspapers.

The interviewees were selected based on their core competence and experience with the research topic. If possible, the chairman or highest rank bureaucrats were interviewed, as it is assume that institution leaders have comprehensive knowledge on its organization institutional issues.

The interview structure refers to institutional theories, and additional questions are aimed to confirm findings from the quantitative chapter analysis. First, the interview explores the experts' views on state restructuring issues and the role of economic variables on regional development. This is performed to support and justify the quantitative chapter analysis. Second, the interviewees explain about impact of state restructuring on their institution and institutional adjustment efforts to respond state restructuring.

The respondents were contacted through the personal networks provided by the research supervisor, the author's professional networks, and other colleagues. The snowballing technique was also employed to identify potential interviewees through suggestions provided by previous respondents; these potential respondents were also selected based on professional knowledge and job position. An informal relationship with gatekeepers is crucial for gaining access to key experts and ensuring effective interviews. The snowballing and gatekeeper methods are regarded as the best approaches to distributing semi-structured questionnaires to senior government officers and other socio-economic stakeholders. The survey consisted of 15 questions grouped into three main parts: political and economic background, state and local policy discourses, and past and current effects on economic development. The interviews were conducted to select government agencies at three levels, NGOs, and higher education actors for a total of 32 interviewees.

The empirical study does not represent overall regional institutional building and economic growth. The case studies were used to illustrate how institutional building, action, and innovation determined economic growth within a specific location. Thus, the narratives presented in the analyses were limited to a certain regional institutional capacity and to the external conditions that were considered. This study does not comprehensively describe the complexity and extent of regional institutional capacity and economic growth. However, it provides insight into the relationship between institutional building and economic growth in a developing country, which can be applied to conceptual frameworks and replicated in other cases.

REFERENCES

Akita, T. and R. Lukman. "InterInequalities in Indonesia: A Sectoral Decomposition Analysis for 1975–92". *Bulletin of Indonesian Economic Studies* 31, no. 2 (1995): 61–81.

———— and A. Alisjahbana. "Income Inequality in Indonesia and the Initial Impact of the Economic Crisis". *Bulletin of Indonesian Economic Studies* 38, no. 2 (2002): 201–22.

————, P.A. Kurniawan and S. Miyata. "Structural Changes and Regional Income Inequality in Indonesia: A Bidimensional Decomposition Analysis". *Asian Economic Journal* 25 (2011): 55–77.

Amir, S. *The Technological State in Indonesia: The Co-constitution of High Technology and Authoritarian Politics.* London and New York: Routledge, 2013.

Amiti, M. and L.A. Cameron. *Economic Geography and Wages: The Case of Indonesia.* SSRN eLibrary, 2004.

———— and J. Konings. "Trade Liberalisation, Intermediate Inputs and Productivity: Evidence from Indonesia". C.E.P.R. Discussion Papers, 2005.

Anderson, K., D. Cohen, A. Kane-Speer, M. Noble and M. Skowronsk. "The Bandung Creative City Movement: An Exploration of the Social and Spatial Implications of Policy Transfer". Proceedings of Artepolis 2 Conference Bandung, Institute Teknologi Bandung, 2008.

Angeles, L. "Institutions, Property Rights, and Economic Development in Historical Perspective". *Kyklos* 64, no. 2 (2011): 157–77.

Anselin, L. "Spatial Externalities, Spatial Multipliers, and Spatial Econometrics". *International Science Review* 26, no. 2 (2003): 153–66.

———— and S. Rey. "Properties of Tests for Spatial Dependence in Linear Regression Models". *Geographical Analysis* 23, no. 2 (1991): 112–31.

Arbia, G. and G. Piras. "Convergence in per-capita GDP across European regions using panel data models extended to spatial autocorrelation effects". ISAE (Institute for Studies and Economic Analyses), Rome, Italy, 2005.

Aritenang, A.F. "The Impact of State Restructuring on Indonesia's Regional Economic Convergence". Unpublished PhD Thesis, Bartlett School of Planning, University College London, UK, 2012.

————. "The Role of Technology In Regional Development: TFP And Econometrics Analysis". *Journal of Indonesian Economy and Business* 28, no. 1 (2013): 149–58.

————. "The Impact of the AFTA Tariff Reduction on Districts Economic Growth in Indonesia". *Jurnal Perencanaan Wilayah dan Kota*. Bandung: Institut Teknologi Bandung, forthcoming.

Armstrong, J.S. *Principles of Forecasting*. Springer, 2001.

Asia Foundation. *Decentralisation and Local Governance in Indonesia*. Jakarta: The Asia Foundation, 2002.

Asian Development Bank. *Asia Economic Monitor*, 2008.

Aswicahyono, H.H., K. Bird and H. Hill. "What happens to industrial structure when countries liberalise? Indonesia since the mid-1980s". *Journal of Development Studies* 32 (1996): 340–63.

Azzoni, C.R. "Economic growth and income inequality in Brazil". *Annals of Science* 35, no. 1 (2001): 133–52.

Baldwin, R. and C. Wyplosz. *The Economics of European Integration*. 2nd ed. McGraw-Hill Higher Education, 2006.

Balisacan, A. and N. Fuwa. *Changes in Spatial Income Inequality in the Philippines: An Exploratory Analysis*. UNU-WIDER, 2004.

Bappenas. "Pengurangan Ketimpangan Pembangunan Wilayah". *Rencana Pembagunan Jangka Menengah* (RPJM), 2006.

Barca, F., P. McCann and A. Rodríguez-Pose. "The Case for Regional Development Intervention: Place-Based Versus Place-Neutral Approaches". *Journal of Regional Science* 52, Issue 1 (2012): 134–52.

Barnes, T.J. "Retheorizing Economic Geography: From the Quantitative Revolution to the 'Cultural Turn'". *Annals of the Association of American Geographers* 91, no. 3 (2001): 546–65.

Barro, R.J. "Inequality and Growth in a Panel of Countries". *Journal of Economic Growth* 5, no. 1 (2000): 5–32.

———— and X. Sala-i-Martin. "Convergence across States and Regions". *Brookings Papers on Economic Activity* 22 (1991): 107–82.

———— and X. Sala-i-Martin. *Economic Growth*. 2nd ed. Cambridge, MA: MIT Press, 2004.

Berry, A., E. Rodriguez and H. Sandee. "Small and Medium Enterprise Dynamics in Indonesia". *Bulletin of Indonesian Economic Studies* 37, no. 3 (2001): 363–84.

Bertrand, J. *Nationalism and Ethnic Conflict in Indonesia*. Cambridge: Cambridge University Press, 2004.

Booth, A. "Decentralisation and poverty alleviation in Indonesia". *Environment and Planning C: Government and Policy* 21, no. 2 (2003): 181–202.

————. "The evolving role of the central government in economic planning and policy making in Indonesia". *Bulletin of Indonesian Economic Studies* 41 (2005): 197–219.

———. "Splitting, splitting and splitting again: A brief history of the development of government in Indonesia since independence". *Bijdragen tot de Taal-, Land-en Volkenkunde* 167, no. 1 (2011): 31–59.

Boudeville, J.R. *Problems of Economic Planning*. Edinburgh University Press, 1966.

Bowles, P. and B. MacLean. "Understanding trade bloc formation: The case of the ASEAN free trade area". *Review of International Political Economy* 3, no. 2 (1996): 319.

BPS. "Realisasi Penerimaan Pemerintah Provinsi Seluruh Indonesia Menurut Jenis Penerimaan 2005–2013". 2012 <http://www.bps.go.id/tab_sub/view. php?kat=2andtabel=1anddaftar=1andid_subyek=13andnotab=3> (accessed 10 December 2013).

Braczyk, H.-J., P. Cooke, and M. Heidenreich. *Innovation Systems: The Role of Governances in a Globalized World*. 2nd ed. Routledge, 2004.

Brenner, N. "Beyond state-centrism? Space, territoriality and geographical scale in globalization studies". *Theory and Society* 28, no. 2 (1999): 39–78.

———. *New State Spaces: Urban Governance and the Rescaling of Statehood*. OUP Oxford, 2004.

British Council. *Mapping the Creative industries: A toolkit*, 2010.

Brodjonegoro, B. "The Indonesian Decentralisation after law revision: Toward a better future?". Department of Economics, University of Indonesia, 2003.

Bruell, N. "Exporting Software from Indonesia". *Electronic Journal on Information Systems in Developing Countries* 13 (2003): 1–9.

Calamai, L. "The link between devolution and disparities: evidence from the Italian regions". *Environment and Planning A* 41, no. 5 (2009): 1129–51.

Canaleta, Gil C., P. Pascual Arzoz and M. Rapun Garate. "Economic Disparities and Decentralisation". *Urban Studies* 41, no. 1 (2004): 71–94.

Canonica-Walangitang, R. *The End of Suharto's New Order in Indonesia*. Peter Lang Pub Inc., 2004.

Capello, R. "Spatial Transfer of Knowledge in High Technology Milieux: Learning Versus Collective Learning Processes". *Studies* 33, no. 4 (1999): 353–65.

Capone, F. "Mapping and analysing creative systems in Italy (1991–2001)". In *Creative cities, cultural clusters and local economic development*, 2007.

Chandra, A.C. *Indonesia and the ASEAN Free Trade Agreement: Nationalists and Integration Strategy*. Lexington Books, 2008.

Chang, H.-J. "Institutional Change and Economic Development: An Introduction". In *Institutional Change and Economic Development*, edited by H.-J. Chang. United Nations University Press, 2007.

Chapain, C. and R. Comunian. "Enabling and Inhibiting the Creative Economy: The Role of the Local and Regional Dimensions in England". *Regional Studies* 44, no. 6 (2010): 717–34.

Christaller, W. *Central Places in Southern Germany*. Translated by Charlisle W. Baskin. Prentice Hall, 1966.

Clark, G.L., M.S. Gertler and J.E.M. Whiteman. *Dynamics: Studies in Adjustment Theory*. Unwin Hyman, 1986.

Coe, N.M., P.F. Kelly and H.W.-C. Yeung. *Economic Geography*. Wiley-Blackwell, 2007.

Cooke, P.N. and K. Morgan. *The associational economy: Firms, regions, and innovation*. Oxford University Press, 1998.

Darise, N. *Pengelolaan Keuangan Daerah: Pedoman untuk Eksekutif dan Legislatif*. Jakarta: Indeks Jakarta, 2009.

De Hoyos, R.E. and L. Iacovone. *Economic performance under NAFTA: A firm-level analysis of the trade-productivity linkages*. World Bank, 2011.

de Wit, Y.B. "The Kabupaten Program". *Bulletin of Indonesian Economic Studies* 9 (1973): 65–85.

Di Fabbio, M. "Taranto and its steel production". *Regional Insight* 2 (2011): 21–23.

Dicken, P. *Global Shift, Fifth Edition: Mapping the Changing Contours of the World Economy*. 5th ed. The Guilford Press, 2007.

Dienaputra, R.D. "Bandung 1906–1970: Studi tentang Perkembangan Ekonomi Kota". In *Kota Lama Kota Baru*, edited by F. Colombijn, M. Barwegen, P. Basundoro and J.A. Khusyairi, pp. 188–208. Jogjakarta: Ombak, 2005.

Doak J. and N. Karadimitriou. "(Re) Development, Complexity and Networks: A Framework for Research". *Urban Studies* 44, no. 2 (2007): 209–29.

Eaton, K. "Designing Sub-national Institutions". *Comparative Political Studies* 37, no. 2 (2004): 218–44.

Eilenberg, M. *At the edges of states: Dynamics of state formation in the Indonesian borderlands*. Leiden: KITLV Press, 2012.

Elliott, R.J.R. and K. Ikemoto. "AFTA and the Asian Crisis: Help or Hindrance to ASEAN Intra-Trade?". *Asian Economic Journal* 18, no. 1 (2004): 1–35.

Eng, P. van der. "Indonesia's new national accounts". *Bulletin of Indonesian Economic Studies* 41 (2005): 243–52.

Ertur, C. and W. Koch. "Disparities in the European Union and the enlargement process: An exploratory spatial data analysis, 1995–2000". *Annals of Science* 40, no. 4 (2006): 723–65.

Evans, G. "Creative Cities, Creative Spaces and Urban Policy". *Urban Studies* 46, nos. 5 and 6 (2009): 1003–40.

Ezcurra, R., P. Pascual and M. Rapún. "Spatial disparities in the European Union: An analysis of polarization". *Annals of Science* 41 (2006): 401–29.

Fan, C.C. and E. Casetti. "The Spatial and Temporal Dynamics of U.S. Income Inequality, 1950–1989". *Annals of Science* 28, no. 2 (1994): 177–96.

———— and A.J. Scott. "Industrial Agglomeration and Development: A Survey of Spatial Economic Issues in East Asia and a Statistical Analysis of Chinese Regions". *Economic Geography* 79, no. 3 (2003): 295–319.

———— and M. Sun. "Inequality in China, 1978–2006". *Eurasian Geography and Economics* 49, no. 1 (2008): 1–20.

Feridhanusetyawan, T. and M. Pangestu. "Indonesian Trade Liberalisation: Estimating the Gains". *Bulletin of Indonesian Economic Studies* 39 (2003): 51–74.

Fitrani, F., B. Hofman and K. Kaiser. "Unity in diversity? The creation of new local governments in a decentralising Indonesia". *Bulletin of Indonesian Economic Studies* 41 (2005): 57–79.

Florida, R. *Who's Your City? How the Creative Economy Is Making Where to Live the Most Important Decision of Your Life.* Basic Books, 2008.

Frankel, J.A., E. Stein, and S.-J. Wei. *Trading Arrangements.* Center for International and Development Economics Research, Institute for Business and Economic Research, UC Berkeley, 1996.

Friedmann, J. *Development policy: A case study of Venezuela.* MIT Press, 1966.

Fromhold-Eisebith, M. and G. Eisebith. "The Indonesian Technology region of Bandung: High Potential, low profile". *IDPR* 24, no. 1 (2002): 41–57.

Fujita, M. and D. Hu. "Disparity in China 1985–1994: The effects of globalization and economic liberalisation". *Annals of Science* 35, no. 1 (2001): 3–37.

———— and P. Krugman. "The new economic geography: Past, present and the future". *Papers in Science* 83, no. 1 (2004): 139–64.

————, P.R. Krugman, and A.J. Venables. *The spatial economy.* MIT Press, 2001.

Garcia, J.G. and L. Soelistianingsih. "Why Do Differences in Provincial Incomes Persist in Indonesia?". *Bulletin of Indonesian Economic Studies* 34, no. 1 (1998): 95.

Gill, G.J. *The Nature and Development of the Modern State.* Palgrave Macmillan, 2003.

Hall, P.A. and R.C.R. Taylor. "Political Science and the Three New Institutionalisms". *Political Studies* 44, no. 5 (1996): 936–57.

Harvey, D. *Spaces of Global Capitalism: A Theory of Uneven Geographical Development.* London: Verso, 2006.

————. *The Limits to Capital Updated.* London: Verso, 2007.

Harsojo. "Kebudajaan Soenda". In *Manusia dan Kebudayaan di Indonesia*, edited by Koentjaraningrat, pp. 305–26. Jakarta: Djambatan, 1971.

Healey, P. *Collaborative Planning: Shaping Places in Fragmented Societies.* 2nd ed. Palgrave Macmillan, 2005*a*.

————. "The New Institutionalism and the Transformative Goals of Planning". In *Institutions and Planning (Current Research in Urban and Studies)*, edited by N. Verma. 2005*b*.

Heinelt, H. and K. Zimmermann. "How Can We Explain Diversity in Metropolitan Governance within a Country? Some Reflections on Recent Developments in Germany". *International Journal of Urban and Research* (2010).

Hew, D., ed. *Brick by Brick: The Building of an ASEAN Economic Community.* Singapore: Institute of Southeast Asian Studies, 2007.

Hill, H. *The Indonesian Economy*. 2nd ed. Cambridge: Cambridge University Press, 2000.

———, B.P. Resosudarmo and Y. Vidyattama. "Indonesia's Changing Economic Geography". *Bulletin of Indonesian Economic Studies* 44, no. 3 (2008): 407–35.

Hirschman, A.O. *The strategy of economic development*. Yale University Press, 1958.

Hooghe, L. and G. Marks. *Multi-Level Governance and European Integration*. Illustrated edition. Rowman and Littlefield Publishers, 2001.

Hoover, E.M. *The location of economic activity*. McGraw-Hill, 1948.

Hudalah, D., D. Viantari, T. Firman and J. Woltjer. "Industrial Land Development and Manufacturing Deconcentration in Greater Jakarta". *Urban Geography* 34, no. 7 (2013): 950–71.

Islam, N. "What have We Learnt from the Convergence Debate?". *Journal of Economic Surveys* 17, no. 3 (2003): 309–62.

Jessop, B. "Capitalism and its future: remarks on regulation, government and governance". *Review of International Political Economy* 4, no. 3 (1997): 561.

———. "Liberalism, Neoliberalism, and Urban Governance: A State-Theoretical Perspective". *Antipode* 34, no. 3 (2002): 452–72.

Juan-Ramón, V.H. and L.A. Rivera-Batiz. "Growth in Mexico: 1970–93". *MF Working Paper* (1996): 92.

Kaldor, N. "The Case for Policies". *Scottish Journal of Political Economy* 17, no. 3 (1970): 337–48.

———. "The Role of Increasing Returns, Technical Progress and Cumulative Causation in the Theory of International Trade". *Economie Appliquée* 24, no. 4 (1981): 593–617.

Keputusan Presiden (Keppres)/President Regulation (1978): No. 41.

Kessler, Anke and Christian Lessmann. "Interregional Redistribution and Regional Disparities: How Equalization Does (Not) Work". *CEPR Discussion Papers* 8133, C.E.P.R. Discussion Papers, 2010.

Kingsbury, D. "Diversity in unity". In *Autonomy and disintegration in Indonesia*, edited by H. Aveling and D. Kingsbury. Routledge (2002): 99–114.

KPPOD. Tata Kelola Ekonomi Daerah: Survei Pengusaha dari 243 Kabupaten/Kota di Indonesia, KPPOD: Jakarta, 2007.

Krätke, S. "A regulationist approach to studies". *Environment and Planning A* 31, no. 4 (1999): 683–704.

Krueger, A.B. and M. Lindahl. *Education for Growth: Why and For Whom?*. National Bureau of Economic Research, Inc., 2000.

Krugman, P.R. *Geography and trade*. MIT Press, 1991.

Kumar, Sree and Sharon Siddique. *Batam: Whose Hinterland?* Singapore: Select Books, 2013.

Kuncoro, A. "Bribery in Indonesia: some evidence from micro-level data". *Bulletin of Indonesian Economic Studies* 40, no. 3 (2004a): 329–54.

————. *Otonomi dan Pembangunan Daerah: Reformasi, Perencanaan, Strategi, dan Peluang*. Jakarta: Penerbit Erlangga, 2004*b*.

————. *Decentralization and Corruption in Indonesia: Manufacturing Firms Survival under Decentralization*. Kitakyushu: International Centre for the study of East Asian Development, 2006.

————. *Ekonomika Indonesia: Dinamika Lingkungan Bisnis di Tengah Krisis Global*, 2009.

Kuoni. *Far East: A World of Difference*. Kuoni Travel and JPM Publications, 1999.

Lagendijk, A. "Learning from conceptual flow in studies: Framing present debates, unbracketing past debates". *Studies* 40 (2006): 385–99.

Levinsohn, James and Amil Petrin. "Estimating Production Functions Using Inputs to Control for Unobservables". *Review of Economic Studies* 70, no. 243 (2003): 317–41.

Lewis, B.D. "The New Indonesian Equalisation Transfer". *Bulletin of Indonesian Economic Studies* 37 (2001): 325–43.

————. "Indonesian Local Government Spending, Taxing and Saving: An Explanation of Pre- and Post-decentralisation Fiscal Outcomes". *Asian Economic Journal* 19, no. 3 (2005): 291–317.

————. "Local Government Capital Spending in Indonesia: Impact of Inter-governmental Fiscal Transfers". *Public Budgeting and Finance* 33, no. 1 (2013): 76–94.

Lewis, M.P. *Ethnologue: Languages of the World*. 16th ed. 2009.

Lim, M. "Cyber-Urban Activism and Political Change in Indonesia". *Eastbound Journal* 2006/1 (2006): 1–19.

———— and R. Padawangi. "Contesting alun-alun: Power relations, identities and the production of urban". *International Development and Planning Review* 30, no. 3 (2008): 307–26.

Logan, J. "Belted by NAFTA? A Look at Trade's Effect on the US Manufacturing Belt". *Studies: The Journal of the Studies Association* 42 (2008): 675–87.

Lösch, A. *The Economics of Location*. New Haven: New Haven, 1954.

Lowndes, V. "Rescuing Aunt Sally: Taking Institutional Theory Seriously in Urban Politics". *Urban Studies* 38, no. 11 (2001): 1953–71.

Lucas, R.E. "On the mechanics of Economic Development". *Journal of Monetary Economics* 22 (1988): 3–42.

Luvaas, B. "Material Interventions: Indonesian DIY Fashion and the Regime of the Global Brand". *Cultural Anthropology* 28 (2013): 127–43.

MacLeod, G. "New Regionalism Reconsidered: Globalization and the Remaking of Political Economic Space". *International Journal of Urban and Research* 25 (2001): 804–29.

Madariaga, N., S. Montout and P. Ollivaud. *Convergence, trade liberalisation and agglomeration of activities: An analysis of NAFTA and MERCOSUR cases*. Cahiers de la Maison des Sciences Economiques, 2004.

Marshall, A. *Principles of Economics*. Revised ed. London: Macmillan; reprinted by Prometheus Book, 1920.

Martin, R. "Roepke Lecture in Economic Geography — Rethinking Path Dependence: Beyond Lock-in to Evolution". *Economic Geography* 86, no. 1 (2010): 1–27.

——. "The Political Economy of Britain's North-South Divide". *Transactions of the Institute of British Geographers* 13, no. 4 (1988): 389–418.

—— and P. Sunley. "Slow Convergence? The New Endogenous Growth Theory and Development". *Economic Geography* 74, no. 3 (1998): 201–27.

—— and P. Sunley. "Path dependence and economic evolution". *Journal of Economic Geography* 6, no. 4 (2006): 395–437.

Matsui, K. "Post-Decentralization Regional Economies and Actors: Putting the Capacity of Local Governments to the Test". *The Developing Economies* 43 (2005): 171–89.

Mccann, P. and S. Sheppard. "The Rise, Fall and Rise Again of Industrial Location Theory". *Studies* 37, nos 6–7 (2003): 649–63.

McCulloch, N. and B.S. Sjahrir. *Endowments, location or luck? Evaluating the determinants of sub-national growth in decentralised Indonesia*. The World Bank, 2008.

—— and E. Malesky. *Does Better Local Governance Improve District Growth Performance in Indonesia*. London: IDS, 2011.

McLeod, R.H. "The struggle to regain effective government under democracy in Indonesia". *Bulletin of Indonesian Economic Studies* 41, no. 3 (2005): 367–86.

Miranti, R. "Poverty in Indonesia 1984–2002: The impact of growth and changes in inequality". *Bulletin of Indonesian Economic Studies* 46 (2010): 79–97.

Moulaert, F. and F. Sekia. "Territorial Innovation Models: A Critical Survey". *Studies* 37 (2003): 289–302.

Musgrave, R.A. *The theory of public finance: A study in public economy*. McGraw-Hill, 1959.

Myrdal, G. *Economic theory and under-developed regions*. G. Duckworth, 1957.

Narjoko, D.A. and P.D. Amri. "The Developmental Gap between the ASEAN Member Countries: The Perspective of Indonesia". *ASEAN Economic Bulletin* 24, no. 1 (2007): 45–71.

Nasution, A. "Fiscal Distress in Indonesia Following The 1997–98 Economic Crisis". Paper presented at the 14 General Meeting of Pacific Economic Cooperation Council (PECC XIV), Hong Kong, 28–30 November 2001 <https://www.pecc.org/resources/1658-fiscal-distress-in-indonesia-following-the-1997-98-economic-crisis?path> (accessed 10 October 2013).

Negara, S.D. and L. Adam. "Foreign Direct Investment and Firms' Productivity Level: Lesson Learned from Indonesia". *ASEAN Economic Bulletin* 29, no. 2 (2012): 16–127.

Nesadurai, H.E.S. "Attempting developmental regionalism through AFTA: The domestic sources of governance". *Third World Quarterly* 24, no. 2 (2003): 235.

North, D.C. *Institutions, Institutional Change and Economic Performance*. Cambridge: Cambridge University Press, 1990.

———. "Economic Performance through Time". *American Economic Review* 84, no. 3 (1994*a*): 359–68.

———. *Institutional Change: A Framework of Analysis*. EconWPA, 1994*b*.

———. *Understanding the Process of Economic Change Revised*. Princeton University Press, 2005.

——— and B.R. Weingast. "Constitutions and Commitment: The Evolution of Institutional Governing Public Choice in Seventeenth-Century England". *Journal of Economic History* 49, no. 4 (1989): 803–32.

Oates, W.E. "Fiscal Decentralisation and Economic Development". *National Tax Journal* 46, no. 2 (1993): 237–43.

Ocampo, E.B.J.A. and M.A. Parra. *Explaining the Dual Divergence: The Role of External Shocks and Specialisation Patterns, in Growth Divergences: Explaining Differences in Economic Performance*, edited by E.B.J.A. Ocampo and J.K.S.A.R. Vos. Zed Books, 2007.

Oktaviani, R., A. Rifin, and H. Reinhardt. "A Review of Tariffs and Trade in the ASEAN Priority Goods Sectors". In *Brick by Brick: The Building of an ASEAN Economic Community*, edited by Denis Hew, pp. 59–85. Singapore: Institute of Southeast Asian Studies, 2007.

Paelinck, J.H.P. and M. Polèse. "Modelling the Impact of Continental Economic Integration: Lessons from the European Union for NAFTA". *Regional Studies* 33, no. 8 (2000): 727.

Peck, J. "Struggling with the Creative Class". *International Journal of Urban and Regional Research* 29, no. 4 (2005): 740–70.

Pepinsky, T.B. and M.M. Wihardja. "Decentralization and Economic Performance in Indonesia". *Journal of East Asian Studies* 11, no. 3 (2011): 337–71.

Peraturan Pemerintah Republik Indonesia Nomor 38 Tahun 2007 tentang "Pembagian urusan Pemerintahan antara Pemerintah Pusat, Propinsi dan Kabuapten/Kota" [Republic of Indonesia Government Regulation Number 38, 2007 regarding the Government affairs division between central, provincial and regency/municipal authority].

Peraturan Pemerintah Republik Indonesia Nomor 46 Tahun 2007 tentang "Kawasan Perdangan Bebas dan Pelabuha Bebas Batam" [Republic of Indonesia Government Regulation Number 46, 2007 regarding the Batam Free Trade Zone and Free Port].

Peraturan Pemerintah Republik Indonesia Nomor 26 Tahun 2008 tentang "Rencana Tata Ruang Nasional " [Republic of Indonesia Government Regulation Number 26, 2008 regarding National Spatial Planning].

Peraturan Pemerintah Republik Indonesia Nomor 108 Tahun 2008 tentang "Tata Cara Pertanggungjawaban Kepala Daerah" [Republic of Indonesia Government Regulation Number 108, 2000 regarding the Head of Regions Accountability].

Peraturan Pemerintah Republik Indonesia Nomor 19 Tahun 2010 tentang "Tata Cara Pelaksanaan Tugas dan Wewenang serta Kedudukan Keuangan Gubernur sebagai wakil Pemerintah di Wilayah Propinsi" [Republic of Indonesia Government Regulation Number 19, 2010 regarding Governor position as the Central Government's representative in the Province].

Perrons, D. *Globalization and Social Change: People and Places in a Divided World*. Routledge, 2004.

Perroux, F. "Economic Space: Theory and Applications". *Quarterly Journal of Economics* 64, no. 1 (1950): 89–104.

Petrakos, G., A. Rodríguez-Pose and A. Rovolis. "Growth, integration, and disparities in the European Union". *Environment and Planning A* 37, no. 10 (2005): 1837–55.

Phelps, Nicholas A. and M. Tewdwr-Jones. "Scratching the surface of collaborative and associative governance: Identifying the diversity of social action in institutional capacity building". *Environment and Planning A* 32, no. 1 (2000): 111–30.

Phelps, N.A. "Archetype for an archipelago? Batam as anti-model and model of industrialization in reformasi Indonesia". *Progress in Development Studies* 4 (2004): 206–29.

Pierson, P. "The Path to European Integration". *Comparative Political Studies* 29, no. 2 (1996): 123–63.

———. *Politics in time: History, institutions, and social analysis*. Princeton University Press, 2004.

Pike, A., A. Rodríguez-Pose and J. Tomaney. *Local and Development*. Routledge, 2006.

———, A. Rodríguez-Pose, J. Tomaney, G. Torrisi and V. Tselios. "In search of the 'economic dividend' of devolution: Spatial disparities, spatial economic policy and decentralisation in the UK". *Environment and Planning C: Government and Policy* 30, no. 1 (2012): 10–28.

Piore, M. and C. Sabel. *The Second Industrial Divide: Possibilities for Prosperity*. Basic Books, 1986.

Pratt, A. "Policy transfer and the field of the cultural and creative industries: Learning from Europe?". In *Creative Economies, Creative Cities: Asian-European Perspectives*, edited by L. Kong and J. O'Connor, pp. 9–23. Heidelberg: 2009.

Prihawantoro, Socia, Ramos Hutapea and Irawan Suryawijaya. *Peranan Teknologi dalam Pertumbuhan Ekonomi Indonesia: Pendekatan Total Factor Productivity*. Badan Pengkajian dan Penerapan Teknologi, Jakarta. 2012.

Prud'homme, R. "The Dangers of Decentralisation". *World Bank Research Observer* 10, no. 2 (1995): 201–20.

Quah, D. "Empirical cross-section dynamics in economic growth". *European Economic Review* 37, nos. 2–3 (1993): 426–34.

———. "Empirics for economic growth and convergence". *European Economic Review* 40, no. 6 (1996): 1353–75.

Ramasamy, B. "The ASEAN Free Trade Area: Implications for Indonesia's Imports". *Bulletin of Indonesian Economic Studies* 30 (1994): 149–57.

Ray, D. and G. Goodpaster. "Indonesian Decentralisation". In *Autonomy and disintegration in Indonesia*, edited by D. Kingsbury and H. Aveling, pp. 75–96. Routledge, 2002.

Read, M. and D. Marsh. "Combining Qualitative and Quantitative Methods". In *Theory and Methods in Political Science*, edited by D. Marsh and G. Stoker. New York: Palgrave Macmillan, 2002.

Resosudarmo, B.P. and Y. Vidyattama. "Income Disparity in Indonesia: A Panel Data Analysis". *ASEAN Economic Bulletin* 23, no. 1 (2006): 31–44.

Rey, S. "Spatial Empirics for Economic Growth and Convergence". *Geo-graphical Analysis* 33, no. 3 (2001): 195–214.

——— and B. Montouri. "US Income Convergence: A Spatial Econometric Perspective". *Regional Studies* 33, no. 2 (1999): 143–56.

Rhoades, S.A. "The Herfindahl-Hirschman index". *Federal Reserve Bulletin* (Mar 1993): 188–89.

Richardson, H.W. *Economics*. University of Illinois Press, 1979.

Rivas, M.G. "The effects of trade openness on inequality in Mexico". *Annals of Science* 41 (2007): 545–61.

Rodriguez, F. "Growth Empirics in a Complex World: A Guide for Applied Economists and Policymakers". In *Growth Divergences: Explaining Differences in Economic Performance*, edited by E.B.J.A. Ocampo and J.K.S.A.R. Vos. Zed Books, 2007a.

———. "Openness and Growth: What we have learned?". In *Growth Divergences: Explaining Differences in Economic Performance*, edited by E.B.J.A. Ocampo, and J.K.S.A.R Vos. Zed Books, 2007b.

Rodríguez-Pose, A. and A. Bwire. "The economic (in)efficiency of devolution". *Environment and Planning A* 36, no. 11 (2004): 1907–28.

——— and N. Gill. "On the 'economic dividend' of devolution". *Regional Studies* 39, no. 4 (2005): 405–20.

——— and J. Sánchez-Reaza. "Economic polarization through trade: trade liberalization and regional growth in Mexico". In *Spatial inequality and development*, edited by Ravi Kanbur and Anthony J. Venables, pp. 237–59. Oxford: Oxford University Press, 2005.

——— and N. Gill. "How does trade affect regional disparities?". *World Development Elsevier* 34, no. 7 (2006): 1201–22.

——— and M. Storper. "Better rules or stronger communities? On the social foundations of institutional change and its economic effects". *Economic geography* 82, no. 1 (2006): 1–25.

———, S.A.R. Tijmstra and A. Bwire. "Fiscal decentralisation, efficiency, and growth". *Environment and Planning A* 41, no. 9 (2009): 2041–62.

——— and R. Ezcurra. "Does decentralization matter for regional disparities? A cross-country analysis". *Journal of Economic Geography* 10, no. 5 (2010): 619–44.

——— and R. Ezcurra. "Is fiscal decentralization harmful for economic growth? Evidence from OECD countries". *Journal of Economic Geography* 11, no. 4 (2011): 619–43.

Romer, Paul M. "Increasing Returns and Long Run Growth". *Journal of Political Economy* 94 (1986): 1002–37.

———. "Endogenous Technological Change". *Journal of Political Economy* 98, no. 5, Pt 2 (1990): S71–S102.

———. "The Origins of Endogenous Growth". *Journal of Economic Perspectives* 8, no. 1 (1994): 3–22.

Rondinelli, D.A. "Decentralization, Territorial Power and the State: A Critical Response". *Development and Change* 21, no. 3 (1990): 491–500.

——— and J.R. Nellis. "Assessing Decentralisation Policies in Developing Countries: The Case for Cautious Optimism". *Development Policy Review* 4, no. 1 (1986): 3–23.

Rosser, A. *The Politics of Economic Liberalization in Indonesia: State, Market and Power*. Annotated edition. Routledge, 2001.

Rothstein, B. *Just Institutions Matter: The Moral and Political Logic of the Universal Welfare State*. Cambridge: Cambridge University Press, 1998.

Santoso, S., S. Wibowo, N.A. Fuad, A.F. Aritenang and Suripto. *Informasi Indikator dan Statistik IPTEK: Pengukuran Technology Readiness Level (TRL) Hasil Inovasi*. Jakarta: Kementerian Riset dan Teknologi, 2012.

Sarundajang S.H. *Pilkada Langsung: Problematika dan Prospek*. Jakarta: Kata Hasta Pustaka, 2011.

Sánchez-Reaza, J. and Andrés Rodríguez-Pose. "The Impact of Trade Liberalisation on Disparities in Mexico". *Growth and Change* 33, no. 1 (2002): 72–90.

Saxenian, A. *Advantage: Culture and Competition in Silicon Valley and Route 128*. New ed. Harvard University Press, 1996.

Schiff, M.W. and L.A. Winters. *Integration and development*. World Bank Publications, 2003.

Schoenberger, E. "The Corporate Interview as a Research Method in Economic Geography". *The Professional Geographer* 43, no. 2 (1991): 180.

Schumpeter, J.A. "Economic Theory and Entrepreneurial History". In *Essays on Economic Topics of Joseph Schumpeter*, edited by R.V. Clemence. Port Washington, NY: Kennikat Press, 1951.

Scott, A.J. *Regions and the World Economy: The Coming Shape of Global Production, Competition, and Political Order*. New Ed. Oxford: Oxford University Press, 1999.

———. "Economic geography: the great half-century". *Cambridge Journal of Economics* 24, no. 4 (2000): 483–504.

———. "Creative Cities: Conceptual Issues and Policy Questions". *Journal of Urban Affairs* 28, no. 1 (2006): 1–17.

———. "Cultural Economy and The Creative Field of the City". *Geografiska Annaler: Series B, Human Geography* 92, no. 2 (2010): 115–30.

——— and M. Storper. "High technology industry and development: a theoretical critique and reconstruction". *International social science journal* 39, no. 2 (1987): 215–32.

——— and M. Storper. "Regions, Globalization, Development". *Regional Studies* 41 (2007): S191–S205.

Sen, K. and D.T. Hill. *Media, Culture and Politics in Indonesia*. Jakarta: Equinox, 2007.

Seymour, R. and S. Turner. "Otonomi Daerah: Indonesia's Decentralisation Experiment". *New Zealand Journal of Asian Studies* 4, no. 2 (2002): 33–51.

Shankar, R. and A. Shah. "Bridging the Economic Divide Within Countries: A Scorecard on the Performance of Policies in Reducing Income Disparities". *World Development* 31 (2003): 1421–41.

Silva, J.A. "Devolution and disparities in the Philippines: is there a connection?". *Environment and Planning C: Government and Policy* 23, no. 3 (2005): 399–417.

Silver C, I.J. Azis and L. Schoeder. "Intergovernmental transfers and decentralization in Indonesia". *Bulletin of Indonesian Economic Studies* 37 (2001): 345–62.

Silverman, D. *Doing qualitative research: A practical handbook*. Sage Publications, 2005.

Sinha, A. "The Changing Political Economy of Federalism in India: A Historical Institutionalist Approach". *India Review* 3 (2004): 25–63.

Sjöberg, Ö. and F. Sjöholm. "Trade Liberalisation and the Geography of Production: Agglomeration, Concentration, and Dispersal in Indonesia's Manufacturing Industry". *Economic Geography* 80, no. 3 (2004): 287–310.

Skocpol, T. *States and social revolutions: A comparative analysis of France, Russia, and China*. Cambridge: Cambridge University Press, 1979.

Slater, D. and E. Simmons. "Informative Regress: Critical Antecedents in Comparative Politics". *Comparative Political Studies* 43, no. 7 (2010): 886–917.

Soedarsono, W.K. *Creative Communities and the Making of Place: Sharing Bandung Experiences*. 2009.

Soemardi, A. and I. Radjawali. *Creative Culture and Urban Planning: The Bandung Experience*. Barcelona, International Society of Planning History, 2004.

Soesastro, H. *The ASEAN free trade area (AFTA) and the future of Asian dynamism*. 1991.

Soja, E.W. "The Socio-Spatial Dialectic". *Annals of the Association of American Geographers* 70, no. 2 (1980): 207–25.

Sonn, J.W. "Synonimisation for Annihilation: A Discourse Strategy for State (Non) Rescaling in South Korea". Unpublished paper, 2008.

Sorensen, A. "Uneven Processes of Institutional Change: Path Dependence, Scale and the Contested Regulation of Urban Development in Japan". *International Journal of Urban and Research* (2010).

Steinmo, S. and K.A. Thelen. *Structuring politics: Historical institutionalism in comparative analysis*. Cambridge: Cambridge University Press, 1992.

Storper, M. and R. Salais. *Worlds of production: The action frameworks of the economy*. Harvard University Press, 1997.

———— and A.J. Venables. "Buzz: face-to-face contact and the urban economy". *Journal of Economic Geography* 4, no. 4 (2004): 351–70.

———— and R. Walker. *The capitalist imperative: Territory, technology, and industrial growth*. Basil Blackwell, 1989.

Streeck, W. and K.A. Thelen. *Beyond continuity: Institutional change in advanced political economies*. Oxford University Press, 2005.

Stubbs R. "Signing on to liberalisation: AFTA and the politics of economic cooperation". *Pacific Review* 13, no. 2 (2000): 297–318.

Sunley, P. "Urban and Growth". In *A Companion to Economic Geography*, edited by E. Sheppard and T. J. Barnes, pp. 187–201 (2000).

Swyngedouw, E. "Excluding the Other: The Contested Production of a New 'Gestalt of Scale' and the Politics of Marginalisation (Manchester eScholar — The University of Manchester)". In *Society, Place, Economy: States of the Art in Economic Geography*, edited by R. Lee and J. Willis, pp. 167–76. London: Edward Arnold, 1997.

Tambunan, T. *Perekonomian Indonesia Sejak Orde Lama hingga Pasca Krisis*. Jakarta: Pustaka Quantum, 2006.

Tan, K.G., M. Amri, L. Low, and K.Y. Tan. *Competitiveness Analysis and Development Strategies for 33 Indonesian Provinces*. Singapore: World Scientific, 2013.

Taylor, M.Z. "Empirical Evidence Against Varieties of Capitalism's Theory of Technological Innovation". In *Debating Varieties of Capitalism: A Reader*, edited by Bob Hancké. Oxford: Oxford University Press, 2009.

Tewdwr-Jones, M. and Nicholas A. Phelps. "Levelling the Uneven Playing Field: Inward Investment, Interregional Rivalry and the Planning System". *Regional Studies* 34, no. 5 (2000): 429–40.

Thelen, K. "Historical Institutionalism in Comparative Politics". *Annual Review of Political Science* 2 (1999): 369–404.

————. *How Institutions Evolve: The Political Economy of Skills in Germany, Britain, the United States, and Japan*. Cambridge: Cambridge University Press, 2004.

Tiebout, C.M. "A Pure Theory of Local Expenditures". *Journal of Political Economy* 64, no. 5 (1956): 416–24.

Timmer, M.P. "Indonesia's Ascent on the Technology Ladder: Capital Stock and

Total Factor Productivity in Indonesian Manufacturing, 1975–95". *Bulletin of Indonesian Economic Studies* 35, no. 1 (1999): 75–97.

Tongzon, J.L. "Role of AFTA in an ASEAN Economic Community". In *Roadmap to an ASEAN Economic Community*, edited by Denis Hew, pp. 127–47. Singapore: Institute of Southeast Asian Studies, 2005.

Topalova, Petia and Amit Khandelwal. "Trade Liberalization and Firm Productivity: The Case of India". *Review of Economics and Statistics* 93, no. 3 (2011): 995–1009.

Triana, R.W. "Capacity Building in Local Government". *Jurnal Studi Pemerintahan* 4, no. 1 (2013): 1–18.

Undang Undang Republik Indonesia Nomor 22 Tahun 1999 tentang "Pemerintahan Daerah." [Republic of Indonesia Law Number 22, 1999 regarding 'Governance'].

Undang Undang Republik Indonesia Nomor 25 Tahun 1999 tentang "Perimbangan Keuangan Antara Pemerintah Pusat dan Daerah." [Republic of Indonesia Law Number 25, 1999 regarding the Fiscal Balance Between the Central Government and the Regions].

Undang Undang Republik Indonesia Nomor 32 Tahun 2004 tentang "Pemerintahan Daerah." [Republic of Indonesia Law Number 32, 2004 regarding 'Governance'].

Undang Undang Republik Indonesia Nomor 33 Tahun 2004 tentang "Perimbangan Keuangan Antara Pemerintah Pusat dan Daerah." [Republic of Indonesia Law Number 33, 2004 regarding the Fiscal Balance Between the Central Government and the Regions].

Undang Undang Republik Indonesia Nomor 43 Tahun 2008 tentang "Wilayah Negara." [Republic of Indonesia Law Number 43, 2008 regarding the State Territory].

Uyarra, E. "Innovation Systems Revisited: Networks, Institutions, Policy, and Complexity". In *The Role of Regions? Networks, Scale, Territory*, edited by T. Herrschel and P. Tallberg. Sweden, 2011.

van der Heijden, J. "Institutional Layering: A Review of the Use of the Concept". *Politics* 31, no. 1 (2011): 9–18.

Venables, A.J. "Equilibrium Locations of Vertically Linked Industries". *International Economic Review* 37, no. 2 (1996): 341–59.

Verbeek, M. *A Guide to Modern Econometrics*. 3rd ed. Wiley, 2008.

Vial, V. "New Estimates of Total Factor Productivity Growth in Indonesian Manufacturing". *Bulletin of Indonesian Economic Studies* 42, no. 3 (2006): 357–69.

Vidyattama, Y. "A Search for Indonesia's Regional Growth Determinants". *ASEAN Economic Bulletin* 27, no. 3 (2010): 281–94.

———. "Regional convergence and the role of the neighbourhood effect in decentralised Indonesia". *Bulletin of Indonesian Economic Studies* 49, no. 2 (2013): 193–211.

von Luebke, C. "The political economy of local governance: findings from an

Indonesian field study". *Bulletin of Indonesian Economic Studies* 45, no. 2 (2009): 201–30.

von Thünen, J.H. *Von Thünen's isolated state* (an English translation of *Der Isolierte Staat*), translated by C.M. Wartenberg; edited and with an introduction by P. Hall. Oxford: Pergamon Press (originally published 1826), 1966.

Ward, M.D. and K.S. Gleditsch. *Spatial Regression Models*. Sage Publications, 2008.

Weber, A. *Theory of the Location of Industries*, translated by Carl J. Friedrich. Chicago: University of Chicago Press, 1929.

Williamson, J.G. "Inequality and the Process of National Development: A Description of the Patterns". *Economic Development and Cultural Change* 13, no. 4 (1965): 1.

Winters, J. *Power in Motion: Capital Mobility and the Indonesian State*. Cornell University Press, 1996.

Wooldridge, J. *Introductory Econometrics: A Modern Approach*. 2nd ed. South-Western College, 2002.

World Bank. *The rationale for decentralisation*, 2001.

———. *Doing Business: Indonesia*. 2008.

Yeung H, W.-chung. "Practising New Economic Geographies: A Methodological Examination". *Annals of the Association of American Geographers* 93 (2003): 442–62.

Young, R.D. *State Reorganisation in South Carolina: Theories, History, Practices and further Implications*. Columbia: Institute for Public Service and Policy Research, University of South Carolina, 2002.

Zukowski, R. "Historical path dependence, institutional persistence, and transition to market economy: The case of Poland". *International Journal of Social Economics* 31, no. 10 (2004): 955–73.

INDEX

ABOUT THE AUTHOR

Adiwan Fahlan Aritenang is Assistant Professor at the Regional and City Planning Program at the School of Architecture, Planning and Policy Development, Bandung Institute of Technology (ITB). Previously he was a researcher at the Agency of Assessment and Application of Technology, Indonesia. He received his PhD in Urban and Regional Economics from University College London (UCL), United Kingdom. He was a Postdoctoral Fellow at the ISEAS – Yusof Ishak Institute during the completion of this book.

www.ingramcontent.com/pod-product-compliance
Lightning Source LLC
Chambersburg PA
CBHW060407220326
41598CB00023B/3043